THE RISE AND FALL OF THE MATINÉE IDOL.

THE RISE AND FALL OF THE MATINÉE IDOL

*Past deities of stage and screen, their roles,
their magic, and their worshippers*

EDITED BY ANTHONY CURTIS

Illustration consultants: Raymond Mander and Joe Mitchenson

ST. MARTINS PRESS NEW YORK

Contents

I

'Lovely Lily Elsie'   3
by Cecil Beaton

The Role of the Reasoner   20
(Charles Wyndham and George Alexander)
by George Rowell

Edwardian Idols of My Youth   31
by Ivor Brown

Father's Footsteps   39
(Gerald du Maurier)
by Daphne du Maurier

II

From Gladys Cooper to Gertrude   50
Lawrence
by Cecil Beaton

Twenty-Five Years of Leading Ladies
(and Gentlemen)   58
by Vivian Ellis

Jack, Bobby and Ivor   75
by Sandy Wilson

The Light of Many Lamps   85
by Micheál Mac Liammóir

The Master   89
(Noël Coward)
by Sheridan Morley

A Tea-tray in the Stalls   99
by Philip Hope-Wallace

The Great Days of Broadway   108
by George Oppenheimer

Life with Lillian   122
by O. Z. Whitehead

Sacred Monsters Off and On the
Boulevards   132
by Roland Gant

IV

The Mute Idols   142
by David Robinson

Time of the Talkies   153
by Dilys Powell

'A Pantheon of Gods'   163
a conversation between George Axelrod and
Anthony Curtis

V

Cutting My Teeth   170
by Anthony Curtis

The Last Idols?   180
by Ronald Hayman

The Loved Ones   188
by Anthony Storr

About the Contributors   197

Index   201

Foreword

This book had its origin in a conversation just over a year ago between the editor and Sir George Weidenfeld. The theme of our talk had ostensibly nothing to do with the theatre when the question was suddenly put to me: 'Why don't you edit a book for us on the matinée idol?' I knew immediately that this was something that I simply had to do. I must therefore thank my publisher for presenting me with so attractive a task and also those members of his staff who have helped me attempt to discharge it, especially John Curtis and Enid Gordon. I am also much indebted to Raymond Mander and Joe Mitchenson who, in addition to their official role as picture-consultants to the book, generously placed their vast knowledge of its subject at my disposal and went through the text with eagle eyes for errors of fact. For any such errors that may still be found therein I am myself, however, responsible. I wish also to thank my contributors for the enthusiasm with which they greeted the project and for the valuable help and advice which many of them have given me. Finally I would like to thank my wife for her encouragement; during the darker moments of editorial gestation she exercised a patience beyond that which anyone has a right to expect.

I feel it would be wrong for me to put a formal dedication at the head of a book that is in the main the work of other people but I hope I may be permitted nonetheless to offer it as a tribute to the memory of my former colleague and friend, A. V. Cookman (1894–1962) whose urbane writings about the theatre in *The Times* and the *Tatler* greatly enhanced enjoyment and understanding of much of the period we now put under review.

A. C.

*M*ATINÉE *idol is one of those theatrical expressions that become more and more nebulous each time they are used. In origin it meant an actor of outstanding presence and charm who commanded a huge and loyal following among leisured middle-class women who frequented the London theatre in the afternoon. There's a strong whiff of Chanel No. 5 in it combined with the rattle of teaspoons against chipped white crockery on little wooden trays. But once the term became current it began to be applied to many more people than that handful of handsome leading men who invariably received a round of delighted applause on their first entrance. If Lewis Waller was a matinée idol so was Marie Tempest; if Laurence Olivier is a matinée idol, so is Marlene Dietrich. It spread from the drama to the musical theatre and then from the stage to the cinema. Rudolph Valentino was a matinée idol, so was Greta Garbo. It eventually came to mean anyone who could ll a theatre by his mere presence, irrespective of the work in which he was appearing.*

Its value as a term lay in the fact that it brought into the light of day one essential feature of theatre experience, namely idolatry. The element in a performance to arouse such idolatry has shifted fascinatingly back and forth over the years between the actor, the author, the director, even in exceptional cases the impresario. But whatever his function the idol radiates a magic that sets him apart from us lesser mortals. It is this great gulf in status between performer and spectator that much of the liveliest contemporary theatre aims to eliminate. You can hardly idolise people who goad you into answering them back or who insist on showing you their private parts or who plop themselves down in your lap. It remains to be seen whether the deeply-rooted need to idolise which we all have will survive the powerful and talented forces in the contemporary theatre that are determined to engender a new kind of audience response.

In the meantime now seems a good moment to take stock of the whole matinée idol phenomenon in as wide a context as possible; we do so by inviting a spectrum of authors all of whom have been engaged in the theatre in various ways to focus upon the matinée idol at significant moments in his (and her) glorious history.

In this first section we look back to the emergence in England of the matinée itself in Edwardian times. We begin with a full-length portrait of a great female matinée idol of that time, Lily Elsie, the original English Merry Widow. Cecil Beaton describes her career both at its peaks of triumph and its aftermath of retirement and obscurity. Then George Rowell considers two formative idols of the straight theatre, Wyndham and Alexander. He shows how their appeal was not so much romantic as realistic in that they took upon themselves the role of the reasoner, speaking up for the values of a society of which their audiences formed a part. He discusses the special relationships that this involved with the playwrights whose work they interpreted, notably Henry Arthur Jones and Pinero. Not all the male idols of this first dawn of the matinée were reasoners in this sense. They were a diverse galaxy indeed, including such names as Charles Hawtrey, Henry Ainley, Forbes-Robertson, Owen Nares. They were all observed in his initiation to play-going – as now they are recollected in tranquillity – by a youthful galleryite named Ivor Brown. The section closes with perhaps the most influential of all idols in securing the adoration of his worshippers and in imposing upon the theatre that style of elegant unruffled naturalism which dominated the drawing-room interiors of the London stage for so long, Gerald du Maurier – as seen through the discerning eyes of his daughter.

A.C.

'Lovely Lily Elsie'

by Cecil Beaton

EARLY in this century when the West End was lit with gas lamps and motor vehicles were only starting to replace the hansom cabs, when Piccadilly was the centre of good-humoured old ladies selling wired button-holes and 'sweet lovely roses' to toffs on their way to a theatre and supper (stalls at ten and sixpence, supper at Romano's for about a guinea), London seemed to be an entity. It had its own very special flavour, and intimacy, and the scale and measure of life were comparatively small. And it seems to us today that it possessed a harmoniousness and a feeling of well-being that is not part of the contemporary scene. To a greater extent the young and the elderly, the poor, the bourgeoisie and the upper classes shared the same interests and tastes. Certainly in the world of the theatre (and there were some twenty theatres in the West End in comparison to more than forty today) audiences were more in the nature of one large family, and the leading players and the stars became universal favourites.

Of all the names that were 'household words' that of Lily Elsie was the most popular. But her fame went far beyond theatre audiences. Not only was she the personification of 'The Merry Widow' waltz, which was heard everywhere, but her face represented the fashionable concept of perfect beauty. It was seen on the popular picture postcards that arrived by almost every post, it appeared on chocolate and biscuit boxes, and newspaper and magazine advertisements proclaimed the sad wistfulness of her smile.

It was in 1907 that *The Merry Widow* came to Leicester Square. George Edwardes, 'The Guv'nor', as he was called, was a gentlemanly Irishman with piercing, blue, eagle eyes and white hair; by putting on a series of musical comedies he elevated the taste of this form of light entertainment just as C. B. Cochran was to do twenty years later. But the chain of successful George Edwardes productions was suddenly broken, and when, after several failures, *Les Merveilleuses* (or *The Lady Dandies*), a *Directoire* musical, also failed to please, The Guv'nor's empire was about to collapse. He had to find a successor – and quickly. Although he considered the popular Viennese operettas of a different genre from that in which he had worked, he conceived the idea of converting Franz Lehár's *Die Lustige Witwe* from not-so-light opera to a more effervescent musical comedy form of entertainment. In spite of the fact that this operetta was playing all over Europe, Edwardes really had little faith in what he considered to be a stopgap. He told the comedian, W. H. Berry, that he 'hoped to get a six week's run out of it'. But The Guv'nor decided he would have the best English comics to replace the heavy Austrian characters, and his leading singers must have, above all else, charm and allure. By choosing the American Joseph Coyne, with his slick modern charm, drooping eyelids and gangling grace, for Prince Danilo, Edwardes showed great audacity. Coyne was not the usual romantic hero of romantic operetta: he was a good actor, but a comedian, and could not sing a note. For the great role of the widow Sonia, The Guv'nor equally daringly picked a young actress who, though the theatre could be said to be in her blood, was comparatively unknown to the West End first-nighters.

Lily Elsie had been a sickly child living in Manchester under conditions of extreme poverty and suffering. Her mother, who kept a lodging house, did all she could to pamper her daughter, who went on the music halls at a very early age. By the time she was eight she had become known in the provinces as 'Little Elsie'. Before a front-cloth she gave impersonations of Harry Lauder, Vesta Tilley and other favourites of the time, and from the age of ten appeared in all forms of provincial entertainments from pantomime to a touring farce, *McKenna's Flirtation*. Unwillingly – for she found it a frightening city – she came to London and appeared in suburban pantomimes, but returned to Manchester, where George Graves spotted her as being full of promise; then George Dance brought her, again reluctantly, to London to take over a part in *A Chinese Honeymoon* and sing a new song called 'Egypt, My Cleopatra', for which she was the only member of the cast to have the taste to wear an oriental make-up. George Edwardes subsequently admired her, and gave her many small parts in London and in the provinces in *The Cingalee, Lady Madcap, The Little Michus, The Little Cherub, The New*

Aladdin and *See-See*. It was while she was playing *See-See* at the Queen's Theatre in Manchester that George Edwardes wired her to come immediately to London. Here he asked if she would accompany him to Vienna to see *The Merry Widow*, as he wished to offer her the leading part which, it is said, had been turned down by Marie Tempest, as she could not undertake the dancing.

This was Elsie's first trip to the Continent. The journey was exhausting. She and The Guv'nor had only time for a high tea of eggs and bacon before going to the theatre. To her dismay, Elsie found that the leading role of Hanna Glawari was sung by the operatic Frau Mizzi Gunther, whom she described as an enormously fat lady with voice to match. Elsie felt incompetent to be her London counterpart. Edwardes was confident, and by degrees he coaxed Elsie into unhappy submission.

Lucile and Pascaud were set to work on some of the more important dresses, but the Marsovian costumes, designed by Percy Anderson, were run up economically in the theatre wardrobe. For the second act Edwardes used a backcloth from *Les Merveilleuses*, but added the necessary summerhouse – a stage version of the Temple of the Sun at Stourhead.

The great Franz Lehár, former military band leader, solo violinist, director of Viennese operettas and disciple of Dvorák, agreed to come to London to conduct the first performance of his own work. When he arrived at Daly's the cast were already on the verge of nervous collapse, and the composer's presence only added to the general strain. Seeing Elsie, Lehár exclaimed: 'She's more like the widow's daughter!' When he heard Coyne recite his first song his astonishment grew. Edwardes pretended that Coyne had a bad cold, and at each subsequent rehearsal, whenever the actor was about to embark upon a song, The Guv'nor would shout from the stalls: 'Save your voice, Joe!' Finally, when Lehár discovered the ploy, he laid down his baton and left the theatre. At Lehár's hotel Edwardes frantically explained: 'Coyne is a remarkable actor and will be much more convincing as a dashing hero than any singer, and a fortune will go into your pocket! He has allure and is a very funny man!' 'I didn't write funny songs,' stormed Lehár – and then he upbraided the manager for employing only twenty-eight musicians in the orchestra pit. 'But there is no room for the six extra you need!' Lehár grudgingly returned to Daly's, which became a seething volcano of nervous hysteria with explosions heard in every part of the house.

The outwardly calm Guv'nor was more highly fraught than anyone, and his loyal assistants, fearing a collapse, managed successfully to steer him away for a quiet luncheon at Richmond. But they all knew there was much at stake and that they could not now afford to lose. Those who queued for the first-night seats in the pit and gallery were mostly foreigners from Soho who had heard of Lehár's success in their own countries.

However, the usual Edwardes 'first nighters' arrived in their flowing dresses, silk hats and tails, the rose-coloured carpet of the vestibule was banked with flowers, and the house manager graciously welcomed the well-known guests on the staircase. . . . The lights lowered.

Lehár conducted the introduction, which consisted, surprisingly, of only a few lively bars before the curtain rose, The audience reacted slowly and, at first, appeared a little baffled at so much that was unfamiliar and original. Gradually it came under the entrancement of the music, so full of harmony, lilt and variety. It did not notice that the lyrics were of a nursery-rhyme banality: it was carried along on the rise and fall, swaying grace of line and melody.

From his first entrance, the disdainful attraction of Joseph Coyne started to waft over the footlights. He was certainly not the usual comic opera hero, but how much more attractive! They loved his recitation of the delights of Maxim's delivered against the most infectious of refrains. Then in a great crescendo of drums, horns and violins, exciting yet ominous, the widow appeared. No heroine can ever have had a more musically dramatic arrival. A little flutter went through the house: an intake of breath, a whisper, conveyed the audience's admiration for the pearl-like apparition. She was tall and graceful, drenchingly lovely. And how beautifully she sang! Here was no vulgarian princess: she possessed a dreamlike quality, yet personified a perfect English rose. Everyone was completely fascinated by the way she and Danilo were looking at each other and dancing together. Lehár's music was compelling and sensuous. The two lovers quarrelled, their eyes telling only of their passion for each other, the excitement was intense.

The spell became even stronger. When Lily Elsie sang 'Vilia, Oh Vilia, The Witch Of The Woods', with a romantic yearning, the audience surrendered completely to her indefinable appeal, and insisted upon encore after encore. Danilo's recitation, 'There Once Were Two Prince's Children Who Loved When The World Was So Young', was even more effective than Edwardes had ever hoped for. The house was as if electrified. When Lily Elsie and her fascinating partner danced to the strains of the waltz, 'with an abandon which was as surprising as it was enchanting', the whole house was swept up and carried away in the emotion. Over and over the waltz was repeated – and still there were shouts for more. Lehár's music, the pathos, romance, fun and raucous gaiety and, above all, the brilliance of the two leading performers, had all conspired to create, from the stage, the impression that the audience was in the path of a typhoon. Everyone was ecstatically happy.

When the final curtain fell pandemonium broke loose. Such cheering can never before have been heard. It went on and on and seemed as if it would never stop. The relentless repetition of curtain calls acclaimed a new era of light musical entertainment, another milestone in theatrical history. *The Merry Widow* was to be the most popular operetta of the twentieth century.

Overnight the booking offices were besieged: Lily Elsie had 'the town at her feet'. Every woman wanted to look like her, and imitation 'Merry Widow' hats were sold in their thousands. Both she and Joseph Coyne were 'matinée idols *in excelsis*'.

Miss Cecily Howard, now Mrs Webster, one of the chorus girls and last survivor of the original cast, remembers watching Lily Elsie, on the first night, waiting backstage for her next entrance down a flight of stairs halfway through Act I. Slowly Elsie turned to her and, smiling, said: 'I think they like us.'

Cecily Howard did not consider Lily Elsie really beautiful, though she agreed she must have looked dazzling from the front. But Elsie, it seems, always had a rather bad complexion, thin skin, with spots around the mouth, and had I noticed that there was a quarter of an inch gap in the lashes over her right eye? Elsie's thumbs were not expressive, and had I noticed that the fingers were always curved even when the hands were thrown up in surprise or alarm?

The popular notion of a leading lady was someone with a flashing smile, dimples, a pointed index finger, an hour-glass figure and probably a naughty wink. Her voice would be lilting in the extreme with glissandos of heart-throb or ripples of laughter. Unlike those who had preceded her, Lily Elsie was never pert or coy. She had that quality, which today may sound somewhat ludicrous, that showed she was 'a lady', and by instinct could never be faulted. She had innate elegance, particularly in the way she moved. Her limbs were attenuated and slender, and she walked with the grace of a gazelle. She used her gestures sparingly and always as if in slow motion, and her dancing was a poem of easy fluidity. She appeared slightly remote, mysterious, lyrical, of an impeccable grace and dignity, but extremely vulnerable and poignant. She tugged at the strings of the heart.

When Messrs Foulsham & Banfield photographed her they retouched the line of her jaw to make it finer, but her somewhat round contours and wide expanse of cheek were the quintessential assets for the stage, where few faces look their best in the harsh overhead lighting. Not only had she the looks that are 'telling' even from the furthest reaches of the gallery, but she was blessed with the gentlest of smiles and with eyes like the sky reflected in pools. Before the days of glamour she was endowed richly with the equivalent of 'star quality'. Her voice had a choirboy purity and all the strength of youth, and it was expertly trained; in fact, her lengthy and varied stage experience stood her in good stead. At the age of twenty-one her beauty was at its height when this role of a lifetime was offered. How fortunate for George Edwardes, for Franz Lehár, for Lily Elsie and for all who saw her, that the time was ripe for this rare stage miracle. Lily Elsie gave a special fragrance to a whole epoch.

The young Winston Churchill said: 'It is inconceivable to me that anyone should wish to see *The Merry Widow* without Lily Elsie.' Desmond MacCarthy has written: '*The Merry Widow* was supreme—a cut above all others—and its sensational triumph was almost entirely due to its heroine.'

Nöel Coward first saw Lily Elsie when, as a boy of seven, he was taken to the theatre by his mother. 'She was so beautiful, and her voice true. She was such fun, too—a darling! One laughed with, and at her.'

Lady Diana Cooper also described Lily Elsie as being . . .

totally beautiful: one could not keep from admiring this Greek chiselled beauty with a profile like a cameo. Her voice was very good – at least we thought so. Perhaps she did not have vitality, but she had magnetism. She spoke with a slight suggestion of a foreign accent, may be to cover up traces of Leeds, and said 'Noh! Noh! Hoh!'. She wore exquisite Lucile clothes: a white Empire dress with a rose satin cape and her hair in a large bunch of curls at the back. Then she wore a black hat with the brim short in front, but wide over the curls at the back. We had not seen anything like it.

Harold Williamson, a delightful doctor with whom I stayed during the war in Delhi, described his pleasure, in his early youth, at switching on the electrophone (a couple of ear pads extending from a telephone which was connected to Daly's Theatre) to listen to Lily Elsie night after night. He knew every song, exactly when every song came on, and that 'Vilia' was sung at 9.15.

Cecily Howard recently said in retrospect the production was amateurish in comparison with today's musicals: that, for instance, the ensemble dancing was such that any schoolchild could pick it up in a few moments:

We in the chorus received 35/- per week salary, and it went a long way. We girls used to go mad when sour old Koski came up from the East End with his huge millinery bandboxes. There would be a scramble for the hats trimmed with feathers, flowers and ruching; the hats were 15/6d., but you could buy them on tick for 1/- a week. In those days shoes were 10/- and a good suit from Stag and Mantle cost £2, while at Swears and Wells you could find a long coat of Russian sable with ermine for £100.

When eventually, after a record-breaking run, George Edwardes had to find a replacement for *The Widow*, many feared that Lily Elsie would never again be seen at such an advantage. But these anxieties proved unnecessary, for in *The Dollar Princess* George Edwardes provided her with a musical that had lilting waltzes by Leo Fall. The Guv'nor boasted that the productions were 'all English' and capable of competing with any German, Austrian or French operettas. W. H. Berry was again in the cast. The story was a contemporary version of *The Taming of the Shrew*, with Joe Coyne again sparring with Lily Elsie. Now with much money to spare, Edwardes lavished sensationally elaborate sets on the stage, for which the three most acclaimed scenic designers were given credit. Although the fashions had changed to less voluminous lines the chorus girls wore dresses from Lucile that cost £40 apiece.

Lily Elsie was not considered difficult or temperamental behind the scenes. She never said anything unkind about anyone and would try to be helpful, but she knew she was to be the star of the show, that it would be difficult for her to be seen at such good advantage as before, and it was not to be wondered at that she became highly strung. When from the back of the stalls she watched Joe Coyne and Gabrielle Ray rehearsing an amusing 'Hansel and Gretel' duet she decided that she must have the number, and not 'Gabs' Ray. Before leaving the theatre she let her wishes be known to George Edwardes, and it was not until he had promised her the duet with Coyne that she reappeared for further rehearsal. Contrary to all expectations, *The Dollar Princess* was another triumph for George Edwardes. The King of Portugal, on a visit to Buckingham Palace, saw Lily Elsie perform twice in one week and rumours of a romance were circulated. Lloyd George a friend of Edwardes's, made a habit of watching Elsie's performance from the wings.

After another long run Edwardes decided, somewhat surprisingly, to revive *The Waltz Dream*, with music by Oscar Strauss, in which the bubbling Gertie Millar of the Gaiety had appeared only a few years earlier. Lily Elsie now played the part of a violinist, the directress of the women's orchestra in the garden restaurant of the Royal Castle of Flausenthum. When she fell in love with the tenor, who then announced his engagement to the plain Princess Helene, she was compelled to fall down a flight of stairs and throw her violin at her rival. Lily Elsie managed to be adorable in spite of the stupidities of the plot. The waltz music was irresistible, but the run was not a long one and Lehár's *The Count of Luxembourg* was chosen next. Although the composer considered this 'a mere trifle', again he arrived to conduct the first perform-ance, which was honoured by the presence of King George and Queen Mary in the royal box. Again Lily Elsie was acclaimed with salvos. The sensation of the evening was created when she, with her tall, broad and handsome new partner, Bertram Wallis, waltzed up a large staircase. Lehár had composed this waltz melody when walking on a summer day in the woods at Ischl, and he jotted down the notes on the back of his starched collar, which he had removed because he was hot.

Although none of her successive appearances topped the success of *The Widow*, none was less than remarkable, and the heroine's position in the field of musical comedy was never challenged. At a time just before the lights were to go dim all over the world, Lily Elsie was the serenely shining star. When she retired from the public scene four years after her first great London success, no one with her unique quality could be found to replace her in the night sky.

Lily Elsie always contrived to make her private life something of a mystery. Although there can have been no other woman in London with whom so many men were in love, and her admirers came from every walk of life—from schoolmasters to diamond magnates, from butcher-boys to marquesses—it was never certain to whom she gave her heart. Winifred Graham Hodgson, a friend to whom Elsie eventually bequeathed her important collection of jewellery, told me recently that on more than one occasion Lily Elsie had discovered, half hidden among a huge *jerbe* of florists' flowers, a large brooch or diamond rings from anonymous admirers. An elderly suitor named Tyser presented her with copies in real stones of all that she wore in *The Widow*. But she was known to show no interest in the young men who wished to take her out to supper, and on the few occasions when she appeared was extremely reticent and shy. It was rumoured that she had romantic feelings for the actor Seymour Hicks, who was married to Ellaline Terriss, but Elsie's friends knew that it was Willie Isaacs, a man-about-town, who most constantly intrigued her. For a long time her name was whispered in connection with this man, who was said to have worldly charm, a gay humour, bravura and vitality. When he died he left Elsie a considerable fortune.

It was, however, Ian Bullough, the twenty-six-year-old son of a millionaire textile manufacturer of Accrington, whom Elsie eventually married. Ian was the stepbrother of Sir George Bullough, who had built himself a castle with a ballroom to accommodate two thousand guests on the island of Rhum. Ian was a gay spark, popular in London, and a great landowner in Scotland where he owned the romantic picture-book Meggernie Castle in Perthshire. Extremely good-looking, with button eyes, dark wavy hair and a mouth that curved upwards at the ends, he was a dashing sportsman and great rider to hounds. He had previously married the musical comedy actress Maudi Darrell, who died at an early age, and he became devoted to Elsie when she gave so much time and tender care to her dying friend. When Maudi died, Ian realized that he was in love with Elsie.

They were married at All Saints, Ennismore Gardens, in November 1911. Elsie wore an Empire-style dress, made by Lucile, of palest pink embroidered with pearls and trimmed with ermine, which she later said was hideous. The bride was given away by the Hon. Charles Cussell. Her mother, Elsie Cotton, who, as Elsie Barrett, had kept a lodging-house in Salford, was a proud and portly figure with a large hat and musquash muff. Gertrude Glyn, her inseparable friend and understudy, was her one bridesmaid. In the register the bride was described as the daughter of the late William Thomas Cotton, theatrical manager from Wortley near Leeds. The honeymoon was spent in the largest suite in the Ritz in Paris, which was filled with flowers sent by Ian. When she and her husband arrived at Meggernie Castle, much traditional celebration of the new arrival ensued.

Although Lily Elsie had retired from the stage, 'at home' photographs of her with masses of dogs kept her alive in the public memory. When she visited London she posed for her old friend, Rita Martin, wearing a chinchilla cape, Grecian dress and three-tiered drop diamond necklace. The results were as popular as ever on picture postcard stands. Other photographs appeared regularly in the weekly magazines showing her leading a conventional sporting existence, shooting or fishing. 'Lovely Lily Elsie, gone but not forgotten' read the captions. When she was photographed in the hunting field her face seemed to have become a trifle more square of smile and jaw, but she was much admired for the traditional manner in which she wore her bowler and beautifully cut habit, for her straight grace of body, and for the expertise with which she jumped her fences.

Fashionable photographers no longer used the 'conservatory' daylight system of gentle lighting that had portrayed Lily Elsie to the world, but her beauty withstood the far more dramatic effects of the 'electric storm' lighting now employed by Bertram Park and Yevonde and Hugh Cecil. She even appeared restrained and beautiful in her Court presentation dress, in spite of the fashionable 'headache band' tiara worn low over the eyebrows.

The actress Zena Dare, also a great picture postcard favourite, and wife of Lord Esher's younger brother, Maurice Brett, periodically went to stay with her great friend from the world of the theatre. She was somewhat amused at the authoritativeness with which Elsie now spoke. On one occasion she forbade her guests to leave the 'grounds' as there were 'measles down in the village'. On another, when the guests were enjoying after-luncheon coffee on a terrace, a discussion arose as to the correct spelling of the plural of the word 'roof'. Zena suggested it was 'roofs', someone else 'rooves'. When a dictionary was produced to settle the matter and the pages were being turned, Elsie said, in a somewhat autocratic manner: 'If you can't find it under the "F"s, look under the "V"s.' But Elsie was the one to laugh most readily at herself.

For a time Elsie's marriage was blissfully happy. She was at heart a great lover of the country, and she had no regrets for the life of cities and the theatre. In replying to a questionnaire she said that she liked best to live in the Highlands, that her idea of happiness was to 'lead the simple life' and that her favourite amusements were fishing, hunting and dancing. Although she was easily tired, she was out with the hounds for hours on end. She even made entries in her 'hunting notebook'. Here are some extracts:

17th October, 1924.
First time I had jumped any fences or had a hunt for nearly two years. My second time out cubbing, and I have never enjoyed anything more for some time. First time I have taken any fences on Bubbles. She is the first hunter I have bought myself. I took the chair for the first time at the Women's Conservative meeting at Lowlands school during the evening which was most interesting. Altogether a thoroughly happy and interesting day. I must add that I had given up all hopes of hunting again, and it is wonderful to find I am able to do it and am more keen than I have ever been

before. Ian was on a new hunter called Luchan, and he bucked and bucked till we all thought he must come off. Ian was ragged because he hadn't christened him Buchan!*

7th November, 1924.

Ian's first day as Master. Our opening meet, and the thirteenth anniversary of our wedding day. We found in Collins (or Colins) Park. I was badly left owing to my having to jog along slowly, and I was miles behind everyone on the way to the covert; so I had to do about 3 miles on the road altho' he only ran about a mile towards Newent when he was given up.

Found again in Lumbury, ran several rings by Catesbury and Pheasantry, finally killing in Catesbury.

Bubbles was simply delighted. I love her, and she did everything perfectly. She went home as sound as a bell, and I am wretched to hear she is now dead lame. I only hope she will be sound again by next Friday. The Clives, 'Barbie' Wills and the Bulteels (Walter and Gertie) stayed with us, and we were a most cheery party. One of the happiest times I've ever spent. May all our anniversaries be just as happy. Ian gave me two lovely riding whips – one for each hand!!!

When, some years later and after much deliberation, Ian Bullough decided it would not be unwise for his wife to return to the stage, Lily Elsie appeared at the Palace in a musical love drama named *Pamela*. I was no longer of an age when this form of entertainment had much appeal for me, *Pamela* (with Owen Nares, another great matinée idol, as the hero) seemed strangely inept. But there was a moment when the lovelorn heroine sat staring at the audience from the side of the stage that created an unforgettable picture. I did not know such perfection was possible. Her eyes were the largest that can have ever been seen – of a heavenly blue that came across the footlights like a summer sky – and her mouth put to shame all the roses.

When Elsie again returned to the stage, her husband sat proudly in a box at the first night of *The Blue Train*. The enthusiasm of the audience ended in scenes of pandemonium with the leading lady too touched and tearful to say more than 'thank you'. The critics were unanimous in using the word 'magic'. But the Riviera express had a short run, and Lily Elsie's devoted adorers were agreed that she had been given scant opportunity.

Later, Ivor Novello, that most determined individual and kindest of friends, induced her to appear in a comedy of his, *The Truth Game*. Not only would she embellish his cast, but the activity would take her mind off the sadness resulting from her separation from her husband. Elsie's boyish grace and easy movement, and her plaintive, wistful mystery still cast its usual spell; but although untouched by the years, she was now almost disguised in the very

*No doubt Ian and Elsie both found added amusement in the fact that Elsie was whispered to be the illegitimate daughter of Lord Buchan.

different 'No, No, Nanette-ish' fashions of shingled hair and tubular, short-skirted dresses.

My enthusiasm for Lily Elsie started when, at the age of three, I discovered on my mother's bed a tinted picture postcard of this swan-like creature with her jewels dotted with sparkling tinsel. The perfection of her profile sent me into transports. For the first time I was on the track of the theatre, and a love was born in me that was to last a lifetime. My family were in no way theatrical but, as I have written elsewhere, my mother had a remarkable sister, Jessie, who had an extraordinary gift for giving treats to every child she encountered. One of my earliest excitements was being introduced – at an age when I could barely stand – to a smiling lady in furs at a children's party. She was the goddess of the postcard.

When I was perhaps four years old, my father intended to take me to see Lily Elsie at a matinée of *The Widow*, and he came back from the City for an early lunch before our expedition to the West End. But he brought bad news with him: Lily Elsie would not be playing the matinée. Would I prefer to wait and see her at a later evening performance? I had already suffered such pangs of anguished excitement at the prospect of this great revelation to come, and my fingernails were so painfully bitten to the quick, that I could brook no further delay. No matter: I was too young to remember anything of the afternoon of dazed delight except that in the last act a lady did a high-kicking dance on a supper table at Maxim's. Later, when my Aunt Jessie invited Lily Elsie and, inevitably, her friend Gertie Glyn to lunch, my brother and I burst into the dining-room, with the coffee and cigars, to perform *The Merry Widow* waltz.

Although my father was, in a somewhat subdued way, a lover of the theatre, family treats to the dress circle were rare. But as I began to grow to adolescence, the world of the musical comedy became my obsession. My passion was nurtured on the photographs I found in the weekly magazines and in *The Play Pictorial*. But far above all the other actresses in beauty and magnetism was my original love. From rapacious study I gleaned the fact that 'the lovely Lily Elsie' was on holiday at Stanmore, that there she played golf, climbed over a stile or posed among the Dorothy Perkins rambler roses in the well-tended garden of a country house of Pont Street architecture that had many white-painted loggias and balconies. I read with relish that 'in the Third Act, Miss Elsie wears *pervenche* blue charmeuse', that John Masefield was her favourite author, and Henry VIII her most loathed historical character. In fact, to me she personified the 'taste' of those pre-First World War years. Now, whenever I see the hanging baskets of geraniums and the white woodwork of the houses at Henley-on-Thames, my heart beats a little faster and I realize where this sudden state of inner exhilaration comes from.

The lure of Lily Elsie continued. When I had reached the age of eleven I was able to admire this lady, through a pair of binoculars, as she sat one late Sunday morning smoking cigarettes with laughing friends on a balcony at the Grand Hotel, Folkestone. During a vacation from Cambridge University, when she had long since left the stage, I spotted her walking with a friend towards Hanover Square in London and followed at a distance. I marvelled at her coltish, lilting, long-stepped walk, but was unable to summon up courage to speak to her before she and her companion disappeared to choose hats at Zyrot & Cie.

It was Olga Lynn, who had at one time given Lily Elsie singing lessons, who brought her into my life as a friend. The Second World War had started and Elsie was staying near Windsor. It was said that she was difficult and would seldom accept invitations, so this meeting was quite a rare event. A delightful Thames riverside lunch party developed into several other occasions when Elsie would readily, to everyone's surprise, agree to come for a meal. She was interesting and delightful as a guest. At one of these necessarily small and intimate gatherings, I suggested that I should like to photograph her in an original *Merry Widow* hat which I had discovered in the shop of a dear old hatmaker named Violet Round, whose heyday had been at the turn of the century. With alacrity Elsie agreed to pose. We took a taxi to a studio forthwith. Lily Elsie still looked beautiful in the fashions she had worn nearly forty years before.

Even when she had just 'come of age' Lily Elsie had found eight performances a week in the heavy singing role of the Widow, with much dancing as well, too physically taxing for her. She was said to have become 'difficult'. She would not 'go on' unless she were given new white kid gloves for every appearance. When Robert Michaelis succeeded Joseph Coyne as her Danilo, she fretted that he trod on her toes when they waltzed together. She would make excuses for not appearing at matinées; she hoped to take next week off; her complaints of fatigue became tiresome. The theatrical gossip pages of *The Pelican* referred to her as 'the occasional actress'. But it was a sad fact that Elsie was never strong. We have seen that 'Little Elsie' had been delicate as a small child; certainly during the brief years of her reign at Daly's she had to undergo several operations, and when she recovered from an appendicitis was extremely distressed to find that her surgeon had cut from her insides more than he had told her he might. It is quite probable that throughout her life her health was frail and that she suffered from anaemia.

It has been said that Elsie had the menopause at the early age of twenty-two.

Although this is rare, it is usually caused by general weakness. The result is lassitude – even frigidity – and a lack of interest in sexual matters. This may possibly have been the reason for Elsie's marriage being unsuccessful, for although she and Ian were always devoted and never quarrelled, her husband went through several bad phases as a serious alcoholic. Elsie tried her best – perhaps incompetently – to cope with the complications of such a situation, and in turn she became very nervous. She separated from Ian, then returned to him, but again found bottles secreted in the most unlikely places. Finally the marriage came to an end.

Elsie became a hypochondriac and spent much time in nursing homes. From a sanatorium in Switzerland she wrote that she was cured ('this sounds like bacon or ham'), and that she was now organizing a concert for the others in the *Kurhaus*, and could someone send her some songs 'in a rather low key as the old voice is not what it was'. But on returning to England her ill-health continued, taking the form of increasingly bad headaches, inertia and deep melancholy. She became fractious. She quarrelled not only with her friends and acquaintances, but, perhaps worse, with the servants upon whom she was utterly dependent. Her rather pathetic little niece, Elsie Wilkinson, looked after her devotedly, and so too did her older friend, Binkie Moss, who wrote to a friend that she was no longer free, that she had become a complete prisoner looking after Elsie.

Elsie wrote a long letter to herself – it was found after her death – of infinite sadness in which she described how the extreme poverty of her child-hood had ruined her physique for the rest of her life. She seldom felt well, and was always painfully shy and ill at ease. She admitted that she was difficult, and was desperately sad that she had quarrelled with friends and with those who loved her most.

Finally Elsie managed to have such severe quarrels with her niece and Binkie Moss that there was a permanent rift. Her headaches and melancholia increased to the extent that it was suggested that she should undergo a leucotomy – an operation in which a large needle is put through the brain to destroy certain tissues, thus alleviating tension and strain, but sometimes bringing about a lack of interest in life in general. Since Elsie had never had any particular interests apart from her own well-being after the break-up of her marriage, it was considered that no great damage would be done. So although she was desperately sad at having to have her hair shorn off, she finally agreed to the experiment. Since the more general use of hormone treatments this horrifying operation is nowadays seldom performed, but in fact much benefit was gained by Elsie. She became resigned to her quiet exile from life, and her health gradually improved. Yet it was said that she was too neurotic to live on her own. It was fortunate that she was well enough off to enjoy a high style of living, and to pay for being looked after in institutions where all adored her and where she was never anything but considerate and kind.

Some friends informed me that Elsie had started to have a few visitors at her nursing home, and that she enjoyed being taken out for an afternoon drive. I sent her a bunch of garden flowers, and she wrote that she would like to see me in the spring. The tulips were now out and we made a date for a short outing together. When I telephoned on the morning of our rendez-vous to confirm our arrangement, a nurse said: 'Oh, but Mrs Bullough is going to watch the Derby on television this afternoon.' However, since the race would be over before four o'clock I would call for her immediately after and bring her back to the hospital by 5.15. I did not have too much difficulty in finding the St Andrew's Hospital at Dollis Hill, and there, sitting in the sun with her pretty young nurse by her side, was a person I recognized to be Lily Elsie.

She had warned me that she had put on weight: 'I can't resist sweets and, of course, they are disaster.' It was nearly twenty years since I had last seen her. At that time she had appeared slightly worn, and had taken to wearing dark glasses, but she was still of an extraordinary elegance of line, and she held herself with the straight neck and back of a schoolgirl. Suddenly I saw that Lily Elsie was now wrapped in a cocoon of elderly fat. She exuded a serenity and calm that is a rare contrast to the haggard, *angst*-ridden faces of many today, but she had lost her romantic mystery. She looked, with her white curls and suburban clothes, like a well-preserved, handsome American grandmother. She acknowledged my greeting cheerfully and, wrapped in scarf and overcoat, with parasol, bag and gloves, made her way gamely to my car.

We drove off to the Mitre Hotel at Hampton Court, where we were to have tea on the terrace overlooking the river. There was no forced effort at conversation. She was, she said, wearing her first ready-made dress and it *would* ride up when she sat down. She talked about her nurse, Jenny, 'an Australian without a trace of accent', who was now on the Continent for her holiday. Jenny was a treasure: she missed her so much, but even so, she was well looked after at the hospital and her doctor came to see her twice a week. She often hired a car and came out to neighbouring towns for tea. Zena Dare and she had recently been to Harrow, and it was extraordinary what good patisseries there were at Finchley. By degrees I was able to scrutinize my companion as she sat enveloped in the anonymous disguise of old age. The beautiful cleft chin had now grown a full double chin, and there was a puffiness under the eyes, but her complexion was faultlessly white and singularly unlined and the large cheekbones stretched to the ears with healthy fullness. She admitted: 'It's because I've got big bones that my face has held up so well.' But I noticed through the dark glasses that the eyes had 'gone': they were half their usual size and the skin had sagged in a little swag by the bridge of the nose. But there were traits that were still recognizable; the little lump – the mole – by the left nostril, and the full, sweetly smiling lips still glistening and rounded with the slight declivity dividing the cushion of the lower lip. Her mouth was still so pretty in articulation, and the teeth the same rather receding, square-shaped ones that I had seen in the earliest photographs. But how tragic the respectable banality of old age! How I disliked the safe, drably coloured Jacqmar scarf, the gloves with the fancy edging and the glass beads round her neck! But the former beauty was chattering with great animation in a somewhat deeper, mellifluous voice. She did not speak as most people speak today. Her early training as an actress had stayed with her, and each syllable of every word was exquisitely enunciated: every sound could be heard by the people in the back seats of the gallery. Her manner of speech was certainly outdated, but it had authority, no apology, and it was unique to hear someone use the word 'patisserie' with such unction. In some ways she pronounced English words with a slightly French accent: 'lodging' became 'ludging'; and I noticed that there was a rise, an inflection on the last word of each sentence that carried on the narrative without interval: it sounded almost Welsh. She talked – a gloved hand jabbing the air for emphasis – about how unconscious she had always been of her effect on the public of her time. Even today she was sometimes remembered. When she had arrived at the hospital she had never told anyone who she was. One morning, six months later, her nurse ran into her room. 'Mrs Bullough, the old gentleman next door knows who you are: he's got a whole collection of postcards of you. I didn't know you were a film star!'

I asked her why she had not enjoyed her success at the time. 'I was so shy and nervous. Of course, I had to hide it, but even when on the stage I was terribly shy, and off stage I had an inferiority complex. I knew I had nothing to say, so I seldom went out. I used to receive all sorts of invitations to meet interesting people, but I never availed myself of the opportunity. Of course the stage was hard work and I had to preserve my energies. I was told that it was ridiculous that I was paid only £10 a week for playing *The Widow*; then Edwardes put up my salary to £20, but even that was not enough. When, at last, I screwed up my courage enough to go to see him about another rise, he talked so hard about everything else that I could not get a word in edgeways, and he bustled me out of his office saying: "And remember for your health to eat an apple every morning for breakfast." Of course £20 went a long way in those days; in *The Count of Luxembourg* I got £100 per week and that was like having £1,000 today. But I was never good about making money. Gabrielle Ray used to sell me her dresses secondhand. She was very clever, and was always paid much more for posing for the postcard photographers than I was. In *The Count of Luxembourg* – the last thing I played in before my marriage – I wore a blue osprey hat made by Mrs Ansell. It must have looked well from the front, but it was a beast: it weighed a ton.'

She remembered her honeymoon. 'We felt like Royalty, but we didn't want to go out – we felt too shy. When we returned to Scotland, I had to learn how to ride. One took lessons from a place in Knightsbridge, and I had only just got the rise in the seat when I went into the hunting field.'

The motor car took us through crowded traffic to Richmond and we sat by the river. Elsie had eaten one tea already at the hospital, but now ate a cucumber sandwich with two cups of coffee.

Surprisingly enough she allowed me to photograph her. 'I never thought I would be photographed again, and certainly not by you. Do you remember when you were a little boy and we met at the Carlton and you were shovelling up artificial snow? You must have been six or seven?' 'Surely not! Surely three or four?' Two rolls of snapshots were taken and it was time for Elsie to get back to her hospital. 'They'll kill you if I am late,' she laughed. 'We have dinner at six o'clock, and of course I must have my glass of port beforehand.' Her life was now comfortable and easy, but perhaps because those fifteen theatre years had been so exciting this long phase was something of an anti-climax. Yet how much worse it could have been if she had had no money. ('I must go one day to the bank to see my jewellery, and have the safes burnt open as I have lost the keys. And there are still some old-fashioned notes that must be changed; I kept them' – in a hush – 'in case a Socialist government came in!')

We passed a fairground and Elsie remarked: 'Oh, they're getting ready for the Whit holiday fair,' and she gave a macabre laugh when she said: 'You seem to be taking me past a great number of cemeteries today.'

The traffic was appalling at this busy time, and Elsie panicked a little because it was 6.30 on her return. She was in a hurry to get back to her life of habit and her glass of port. The nurse was there in attendance, and Elsie stepped into the old-fashioned ironwork lift on her way up to Room 34.

A few months later, among the accumulation of Christmas cards, letters to be sent off and various messages on my desk was a note to say that Dr Gould had telephoned from St Andrew's Hospital, Dollis Hill, to say that Lily Elsie was quite seriously ill. I telephoned and spoke to Jenny, her nice Australian nurse, who had made the last months easy and pleasant for Elsie. 'We don't know what to think. She may pull through, but it will be a long road to recovery. Mrs Bullough didn't like those terrible fogs at all – they upset her; and, of course, she had that pneumonia, but now she is very restless. Last night she did sleep a little, but we are all very upset – it's very sad.' I sent some flowers and rang again. 'We told her you had sent the flowers and she seemed very pleased. We keep telling her her friends are asking after her: that makes her feel less depressed.'

Two days later, on 16 December 1962, I saw the small obituary notice that I had for so long feared to see.

Lily Elsie was a born star. Despite her ignorance of life, she always had an instinctive knowledge of the stage, and it was this that brought her the acclaim that she fully deserved. Although success never spoilt her, she took her ascendancy as her right. But she was always delightfully natural, with a sense of humour and no affectation. She never said anything she didn't mean or believe. The newspapers told us she was seventy-six years old, but this fact did not make my personal feeling of loss any the less acute, for it was for the passing of much of my childhood as much as for her that I was now strangely and strongly affected. Whenever I hear the Lehár melodies, and see the misty colours of sweet peas, the houses with white-painted balconies and Dorothy Perkins ramblers trailing over trellis, or whenever I see a certain full-hearted rose, I remember my early love for Lily Elsie. And there are many other hidden subconscious currents that excite me like a half-forgotten, but sweet memory that can, no doubt, be traced back to the legendary figure who dominated those formative years. Lily Elsie was mourned by only a few trusted friends, for the present generation has never heard of her, and it was news of the death of Charles Laughton on the same day that filled all the newspaper headlines.

The Role of the Reasoner

(Charles Wyndham and George Alexander)

by George Rowell

L ET us begin by asking two questions about the matinée itself: when was it introduced and why did it get its name from a time of day at which it never took place? The second question is the more easily answered. Like so much else in the English theatre of the nineteenth century, the influence of France was decisive, and to the French élite morning was when they rose, whatever the hands of the clock declared. As early as 1696 a character in Regnard's comedy, *Le Joueur*, affirmed:

> De nos jours on étend souvent la matinée
> jusqu'à l'heure du dîner, c'est à dire
> jusqu'à six ou sept heures.

(Nowadays one often stretches the forenoon until dinner time, until six or seven o'clock)

The extension of the term to mean an afternoon performance belongs to the nineteenth century, and originates, as might be expected, with music rather than drama. Thackeray in *Vanity Fair* writes of a *matinée musicale*, since the English élite of his period would patronize an afternoon concert where they would eschew a play at any hour. It is an interesting reversal of the predominant theatrical trend, however, that when plays in the afternoon did make a tentative appearance, they were first termed 'morning performances', not matinées. The application of the term 'matinée' to the English theatre occurred in the 1880s, a decade when English drama was struggling to free itself from French influence. A programme for Irving's *Macbeth* at the Lyceum in April 1889 uses both terms, 'morning performance' and 'matinée', about the same occasion. By the 1890s the term matinée has taken over.

The evolution of the performance itself, whether 'morning' or 'matinée', was much more gradual and difficult to detect. For some forty years two distinct purposes were served by what appears to be the same phenomenon: one was an occasional afternoon performance of a play already in the evening bill, particularly a pantomime or some such family entertainment, the other was a specially mounted performance of a piece for afternoon audiences only. Rather surprisingly, in view of his reputation for light-hearted entertainment, the pioneer of the 'intellectual' morning performance was John Hollingshead at the Gaiety in 1871. The breakthrough to regular afternoon performances of a piece playing simultaneously at night is generally attributed to the Bancrofts with their Robertsonian repertoire at the Prince of Wales's, although even they made one false start during the run of *School*, which met 'with only a moderate and not sufficiently encouraging result', until 1878 when 'what are now called matinées – afternoon representations of the regular evening performance – were really established' with their production of *Diplomacy*.

The emergence of the matinée and the matinée idol are perhaps best illustrated from the career of the Bancrofts' contemporary, Charles Wyndham, the only English actor-manager to give his name to a surviving West End theatre, just as the rechristening of another of his theatres, the New, as the Albery, makes his step-son, Sir Bronson Albery, the only English impresario to be named amongst London's theatres. Wyndham established himself as a leading comedian at the Criterion in the 1870s by presenting a series of 'daring' farces, usually of French origin, at which London Society strove to be seen and shocked. Clearly such a repertoire did not lend itself to regular matinée performances, directed then and since at the unescorted female. Wyndham's matinée policy for the first ten years of his management was purely pragmatic; he would announce 'morning performances every Saturday' until he had assessed whether the play had any matinée appeal, and if not, drop them unceremoniously. Thus *Pink Dominos*, perhaps the most *risqué* and certainly the most successful of his farces, opened at the Criterion on 16 April 1877, received its first 'morning performance' on 28 April, but was restricted to the evening bill from June 1877. Occasionally during its extraordinary run of 555 performances Wyndham would experiment with a matinée, but at this stage of his career he evidently felt regular matinées were not for his public.

Wyndham's fame rested on his skill as a 'bustling' or 'rattling' comedian in the style of Charles James Mathews, several of whose parts he played, and he was appropriately known in the 1870s as 'the electric light comedian'. But by 1886 he was 49 and his motive power might be described as switching from direct to alternating current. He showed much self-knowledge and contributed materially to the evolution of the matinée idol when in that year he decided to revive T. W. Robertson's costume piece, *David Garrick*, lifted from the French. It belonged to an era immediately preceding Robertson's 'cup and saucer' comedies for the Bancrofts, and is much closer in spirit to, say, Taylor and Reade's *Masks and Faces* than his own original play, *Caste*, so that Robertson might be described as having written the last early Victorian as well as the first late Victorian comedy. Contrived and commonplace though *David Garrick* now seems, it provided the right vehicle at the right moment for Wyndham. This fictitious account of Garrick's complicity in a father's plot to disillusion a stage-struck girl by feigning drunkenness at a dinner-party, only of course to find himself responding to her adoration and marrying her, allowed Wyndham to graduate from bustling philanderer to romantic idol, and the Criterion to be transformed from an English Palais Royal to a rendez-vous for leisured ladies. He reinforced this new romantic reputation with several 'old English' classics (*She Stoops to Conquer*, *The School for Scandal*, *London Assurance*), but it was *David Garrick* to which he turned whenever the box office flagged.

The term *raisonneur* derives from that school of French nineteenth-century drama which succeeded the Romantic outpourings of Hugo and others, and which is appropriately labelled *théâtre utile*. Its foremost exponents were the younger Dumas and Emile Augier, playwrights whose work reflected Parisian high society and its conventions in the mid-century years. The *raisonneur* in this drama was a character standing apart from the main action and voicing the predictable (but therefore all the more powerful) judgement of polite society: in *La Dame aux Camélias* the elder Duval; in *Le Demi-Monde* (which appeared at the Criterion in 1892 as *The Fringe of Society*) Oliver de Jalan; in *Francillon*, the inspiration of Wyndham's great success, *The Case of Rebellious Susan*, Stanislas de Grandredon. The *raisonneur* is above all the spokesman of marriage and its sacrosanctity; the fact that he is rarely married himself doubtless enables him to view his friends' matrimonial problems with complete detachment.

The partnership of Charles Wyndham and Henry Arthur Jones produced five plays, three of which figured significantly both in the establishment of his theatres as 'society' theatres and in the emergence of Wyndham himself as a 'society' spokesman who in 1902, following the precedents of Irving and

Bancroft, became the third actor-knight. The earliest of Jones's pieces at the Criterion, *The Bauble Shop*, has no larger claim to consideration than as a first sketch for the finished portraits to follow. One other play, *The Physician*, lies outside what might be termed 'the Criterion category', and in fact resembles more a play for the St James's with the part of Dr Lewin Carey designed for Alexander. There remain three key pieces: *The Case of Rebellious Susan*, *The Liars*, and *Mrs Dane's Defence*, the last-named being first staged in 1900 at Wyndham's own theatre, largely built from the profits of the Criterion.

All three are examples of what Shaw describes as 'the usual formula for such plays. . . . A woman has, on some past occasion, been brought into conflict with the law which regulates the relations of the sexes. A man, by falling in love with her, or marrying her, is brought into conflict with the social convention which discountenances the woman'. In *The Case of Rebellious Susan* Lady Susan Harabin, stung by her husband's repeated infidelities, takes advantage of the attentions of a young diplomat under the Egyptian moon, and the rest of the play is concerned with concealing what those attentions were and how much advantage she took. In *The Liars* Lady Jessica Nepean, similarly slighted, totters on the brink of adultery in darkest Africa with the attentive explorer, Edward Falkner. In *Mrs Dane's Defence* the lady of the title has won the (strictly honourable) attentions of Lionel Carteret by changing her name and concealing her passionate past as a governess in Vienna. In each Wyndham played a bachelor-knight with a genius for friendly warnings.

But though the plots and people of these plays coincide, the history of *Rebellious Susan* distinguishes it clearly from its successors. Evidently Jones at first intended to convey that Lady Susan had paid out her inconstant husband in kind. Indeed the dedication 'To Mrs Grundy' concludes: ' . . . If you must have a moral in my comedy, suppose it to be this – "That as women cannot retaliate openly, they may retaliate secretly – and *lie*!" . . .' But this brand of sexual algebra was excluded from the Criterion curriculum in the 1890s, whatever kind of sums may have been totted up there in the *Pink Dominoes* days. Wyndham therefore embarked on a campaign to persuade Jones to modify the play for matinée audiences. Writing from St Moritz two months before the production, he confessed:

> I stand as bewildered today as ever at finding an author, a clean-living, clear-minded man, hoping to extract laughter from an audience on the score of a woman's impurity. I can realise the picture of a bad woman and her natural and desirable end being portrayed, but that amusement pure and simple should be expected from the sacrifice of that one indispensable quality in respect of womanhood astonishes me.
>
> I am equally astounded at a practical long-experienced dramatic author believing that he will induce married men to bring their wives to a theatre to learn the lesson that their wives can descend to such nastiness, as giving themselves up for one evening of adulterous pleasure and then returning safely to their husband's arms,

provided they are clever enough, low enough, and dishonest enough to avoid being found out.

This difference of opinion continued throughout rehearsals, and shortly before the first night Wyndham proposed a compromise in the crucial recriminatory passage between Lady Susan and her diplomat.

I want you to expunge the line 'I should kill myself if anyone knew' and 'never boasted', (he wrote to Jones) leaving the line: 'You have never spoken of me to any of your men friends?' These in no way interfere with your plans, but they afford me an opportunity of overcoming my strong repulsion to the whole idea which must be as evident to you as it is painful to me – and will allow me to go into the part with good will. Failing this, I am beginning to feel that my participation in the piece will not only be useless, but positively dangerous.

It was in fact in this ambiguous form that the play was produced and published, with the result that the text of the crucial scene between Lucien and Lady Susan is riddled with inconsistencies. But if the box office never lies, Wyndham was proved right, for the piece ran 164 nights, and was several times revived during his later years.

Certainly Jones thereafter accepted the matinée idol's creed and the public's adherence to it. The parallel situations in *The Liars* and *Mrs Dane's Defence* are resolved in a manner both orthodox and explicit. The last Act of *The Liars* finds Lady Jessica and her explorer planning their socially suicidal flight to Africa. Sir Christopher, himself heading for the Dark Continent, puts off his packing long enough to discourage them by the following argument:

Now! I've nothing to say in the abstract against running away with another man's wife! There may be planets where it is not only the highest ideal morality, but where it has the further advantage of being a practical way of carrying on society. But it has this one fatal defect in our country today – it won't work! You know what we English are, Ned. We're not a bit better than our neighbours, but, thank God! we do pretend we are, and we do make it hot for anybody who disturbs that holy pretence. And take my word for it, my dear Lady Jessica, my dear Ned, it won't work.

By 1900 Jones's conversion to orthodoxy was complete. Mrs Dane is not the spoilt wife, piqued by her husband's behaviour into retaliation, like Ladies Susan and Jessica. As a humble governess in Vienna she was the object of an infatuation which led to her employer's suicide and her bearing a son. What made her an outrageously fatal female in the eyes of the matinée public was her concealment of her maiden name and shame by assuming her cousin's identity and history. In the famous 'cross-examination scene' Wyndham as Sir Daniel Carteret broke down her story piece by piece, until he cries in triumph: 'Woman, you're lying. . . . You are Felicia Hindemarsh!' and, with Lionel's acquiescence, packs her off to Devonshire, where pasts, it would seem, are two a penny.

This exercise of a strictly Victorian *droit de seigneur* is all the more arbitrary, since at the outset of the play Sir Daniel has confessed that he once persuaded Lionel's mother to leave her husband and come to America with him and the child. Illness supervened, but he asserts: 'I've been successful and happy after a fashion; but there has never been a moment since I lost her when I wouldn't have cheerfully bartered every farthing, every honour, every triumph I've scored in my profession, to stand again on that platform at Liverpool and know she was coming to me.'

A modern playgoer might echo John Worthing's protest about poor Miss Prism: 'Why should there be one law for men, and another for women?' Even Sir Daniel's irreproachably correct friend, Lady Eastney, is moved to speak up for Mrs Dane: 'Oh, aren't you Pharisees and tyrants, all of you? And don't you make cowards and hypocrites of all of us? Don't you lead us into sin and then condemn us for it? Aren't you first our partners and then our judges?' but Sir Daniel is inexorable: 'The rules of the game are severe. If you don't like them, leave the sport alone. They will never be altered'; and the audience were heard to respond: 'Wyndham's in Wyndham's; all's right with the world'.

Mention of Lady Eastney leads to a different aspect of Wyndham's status as a matinée idol, for it is her hand Sir Daniel claims in marriage at the end of the play, once his task of preventing his foster-son's marriage to Mrs Dane has been accomplished. As has been suggested, the three 'key' parts Wyndham played for Jones were all bachelors, albeit mature bachelors: Wyndham himself was fifty-seven when he first played Sir Richard Kato, sixty when he created Sir Christopher Deering, and sixty-three when he appeared as Sir Daniel. The lyric strain was not part of his equipment. He never played Shakespeare in the West End, and only in his youth elsewhere. As actor-manager, however, he had a privilege which as matinée idol was also his duty: to start the play single and end it at the altar. Thus a companionable widow or childhood sweetheart was always on hand to make him the happiest of men and his audience the happiest of audiences.

Whether a matinée idol could acceptably play a married man is a leading question where George Alexander is concerned. Alexander was only thirty-two when he took the St James's; he had played Faust to Irving's Mephistopheles, and his greatest successes included such romantic roles as François Villon and Klaus Heinrich, though neither Orlando nor Benedick (his only Shakespearean parts at the St James's) was among his happiest performances.

Yet of the six crucial roles he played for Wilde and Pinero, two (Lord Windermere and Aubrey Tanqueray) were married, a third (Hilary Jesson) shows no signs of committing matrimony, and since he only tackled Lord Goring, one of the three 'curtain-call grooms', in a revival, his marriage to Mabel Chiltern could be regarded as *en deuxièmes noces*.

There were personal reasons for Wyndham's and Alexander's differing approaches. Wyndham had formed an artistic partnership with Mary Moore, and all Jones's plays for him contained a role for her equally important to the actor-manager's. Florence Alexander played a leading part at the St James's, but behind the scenes, dressing both the company and the stage, so that Alexander's independence of a regular leading-lady allowed a different balance in his ensemble. Another explanation could be that both Alexander and his authors knew what his public chose to ignore: that his acting had more authority than ardour. Alexander staged half a dozen of Pinero's plays at the St James's. In one of these (*Mid-Channel*) he did not appear; in another, *The Thunderbolt*, his part as an impoverished (and hen-pecked) music teacher living in 'a city in the Midlands' was so unflattering that the comparative failure of the play, in fact one of Pinero's most compelling, was largely attributed to this neglect of a matinée public's susceptibilities; while the last play on which they worked together, *The Big Drum*, was staged a couple of years before Alexander's death and added nothing to either man's reputation. The three Pinero plays central to this argument are therefore *Mrs Tanqueray*, *The Princess and the Butterfly*, and *His House in Order*; while the relevant pieces by Wilde are *Lady Windermere's Fan*, *The Importance of Being Earnest*, and (to a less degree) *An Ideal Husband*, in which Alexander appeared only on its revival in 1914.

In offering *The Importance* to Wyndham and Hawtrey (amongst others) before Alexander, Wilde gave weight to the view that Alexander lacked the lightness of touch of an ideal Jack Worthing. Similarly, in pressing *Pygmalion* on Alexander before reluctantly surrendering it to Tree, Shaw indicated that Higgins (as unromantic and authoritarian a figure as English comedy affords) was emphatically in Alexander's 'line'. Indeed Alexander himself might well have concurred, had not Shaw written the part of Eliza for Mrs Patrick Campbell. Hesketh Pearson reports (or perhaps reconstructs) Alexander's reaction as follows: 'That play is a cert, a dead cert. Now listen to me. I will get any actress you like to name for the flower girl. I will pay any salary she asks. You can settle your own terms. But go on for another play with Mrs Campbell I will *not*. I'd rather die.'

But another explanation could be Alexander's conception of the *raisonneur*'s role as compared with Wyndham's. It should first be noted that Alexander, as the younger man, only gradually assumed this role. In *Lady Windermere's Fan* it is shared by some half dozen 'swells', descending in age and rank from Lord Augustus Lorton to Mr Cecil Graham; in *The Second Mrs Tanqueray* the *raisonneur* is Cayley Drummle, not Aubrey; in *The Importance* his function is more Algernon's than Jack's. But when, in such roles as Sir George Lamorant in *The Princess and the Butterfly* and above all Hilary Jesson in *His House in Order*, Alexander graduated to *raisonneur*, there was a delicacy and a measure of flexibility about his interpretation which contrasts strongly with the rigidity (however triumphant) of Wyndham's bachelor-knights.

The 'problem plays' with which Alexander established himself at the St James's conform closely to Shaw's 'usual formula'. The women who have 'on some past occasion been brought into conflict with the law which regulates the relations of the sexes' include Mrs Erlynne and Paula Tanqueray, with honorary membership accorded to Miss Prism, whose offence is admittedly not sexual but literary, since she has committed 'a three-volume novel of more than usually revolting sentimentality'. In these plays the role of the *raisonneur* is a good deal less ponderous than that performed by Wyndham at the Criterion; one might expect Algernon Moncrieff to proclaim that 'girls never marry the men they flirt with', which 'accounts for the extraordinary number of bachelors that one sees all over the place'. But Cecil Graham is almost as flippant in pronouncing 'There's nothing in the world like the devotion of a married woman. It's a thing no married man knows anything about.' Even Cayley Drummle affects the epigrammatic: 'You may dive into many waters, but there is *one* social Dead Sea,' and describes himself as waiting there 'for some of my best friends *to come up*'. Meanwhile Alexander, as Windermere, Tanqueray, and Worthing, contented himself with dedication to matrimony. He seems to have conceived the actor-manager's role as supplying the romance rather than the reason.

But with *The Princess and the Butterfly* both author's and actor's points of view appear changed. Indeed this play marks more than one transition. Despite its elaborate cast and setting, it represents a departure from the problem play, for its tone is nearer fantasy than Society drama: the loves of 'the Butterfly', Sir George Lamorant, for the child Fay Zuliani, and the Princess Pannonia for young Edward Oriel, seem scarcely flesh and blood, and at the end one of their friends is moved to ask: 'Are you sane, all of you – any of you? Are you real? To me you appear like dream-people – fantastic creatures.'

Although as Lamorant Alexander accepted the judgement seat of the *raisonneur*, his pronouncements steer significantly clear of the relations between 'our courts of law and private juries of matrons' which Shaw identified as the subject matter of the problem play. Instead he concerns himself with the relations between youth and age, especially love across the age-gap. Confronting his protégée on her return from a masked ball, Sir

George comments: 'How pale and haggard you are! Some of you women squander your beauty, as some gamblers do their money, for mere excitement. You are rich – but don't play so recklessly, Fay.' Acknowledging his infatuation with her and the Princess's with Oriel, he asks: 'Love may give perpetual youth to the heart, but can love, in one no longer young, secure in perpetuity the responding love which it may have chanced to waken?' and concludes a little too glibly: 'Those who love deeply cannot age, nor perceive age in those they love.'

The whole play reflects the uneasy mating of reason and romance, and the St James's audience rejected the double wedding of May and December at the end, no doubt observing that if Charles Wyndham had been playing the part, Sir George would have claimed the Princess and taken her off to explore the Pannonian plains, leaving Fay and Edward to their common interests. Not surprisingly its production placed a great strain on Alexander's collaboration with Pinero. After the St James's had been substantially reconstructed in 1899, its licensee invited the playwright to contribute the reopening play. Pinero's response was unequivocal:

> Frankly, dear Alec, I don't think that you and I go well together in harness; or, rather, I do not feel happy in running tandem with you, myself as wheeler to your lead. I know you take a pride in being an autocrat in your theatre; it is a natural pride in a position you have worthily won for yourself. But I have also won – or have chosen to usurp – a similarly autocratic position in all that relates to my work. I hope I do not use my power unfairly or overbearingly, but I do exercise it – and any other condition of things is intolerable to me. In my association with you on the stage I have always felt that you have resented my authority. In the case of our last joint venture the circumstances which led up to it were of so unhappy a character that I resolved to abrogate this authority – to reduce it, at any rate, to a shadow. But, at the same time, I did not relish my position and determined – even before I started upon a campaign which I foresaw could not be otherwise than full of discomfort and constraint – that I would not again occupy it. To put the case shortly, there is no room for two autocrats in one small kingdom; and in every detail, however slight, that pertains to my work – though I avail myself gratefully of any assistance that is afforded me – I take to myself the right of dictation and veto.
>
> In face of this explanation, my dear Alec, (longer than I intended it to be) I trust you will forgive me for declining your offer, and will believe that this prompt candour on my part is exhibited in a spirit of fairness to yourself as well as from a desire to explain my own attitude.

Pinero's decision held until seven years later when these differences were healed in the greatest success of their partnership: *His House in Order*. Outwardly Alexander's part in this play had much in common with Sir George Lamorant. Both are in their forties; Sir George has retired from the Colonial Office, Hilary Jesson is on leave from the Foreign Office. But there is one crucial difference. Sir George is infatuated with Fay Zuliani; Hilary is not infatuated with the former governess, Nina Graham, fortunately since she is now married, albeit unhappily, to his brother, Filmer. In consequence the role of Hilary Jesson marks a significant (and successful) refinement of the function of the *raisonneur* at the St James's.

Hilary voices the dictates of social convention, as Cayley Drummle, Cecil Graham, and Algernon Moncrieff did before him, but these dictates are softened by tolerance and sympathy. Not for him the doctrine of one moral standard for men and another for women. Instead of Mosaic law he employs doggerel and fable. When Filmer complains of Nina's domestic failings, his brother improvises:

> If I had a little wife what wouldn't go,
> D'you think I would wallop her? No, no, no!
> I'd sack all my servants and live in hotels,
> And spend all my days gaily in ringin' the bells.

while his response to an invidious comparison between Nina and the first Mrs Jesson is to take a leaf from La Fontaine's book and tell the fable of the two cooks, Henri, who was perfection, and Adolphe, who was only less perfect than Henri but attempted suicide on that account.

The plot of *His House in Order* has much in common with Daphne du Maurier's *Rebecca*, for Annabel, the first Mrs Jesson, seems closely related to the first Mrs Maxim de Winter: a paragon of all the virtues, she met her death in a riding accident, leaving her husband to marry their son's governess but still controlled by Annabel's family, the Ridgeleys, in particular by her sister, Geraldine, an Edwardian Mrs Danvers, who keeps his house in an order Nina cannot even exercise over her dogs.

From the start Hilary radiates tolerance and *laisser vivre*. His approach on meeting his new sister-in-law is boldly informal for the St James's:

HILARY   We're relatives. We should get there sooner or later. My name's Hilary; yours is Nina.
NINA   Oh I – I am agreeable. (*He approaches her*) You are not a stickler for formalities, then, either?
HILARY   I! Lord, no!

But tolerance and informality are put to their sternest test when Nina discovers under the floorboards of Annabel's boudoir letters establishing incontrovertibly her liaison with Major Maurewarde, of which Master Derek is the issue. In the crucial scene, therefore, Hilary has to persuade Nina to join 'the people who have *renounced*', to surrender Maurewarde's letters and with them her chance of revenge. She does so, and although Hilary tells his brother the truth, the Ridgeley family never learn why their presence, above all Geraldine's, is no longer needed to keep Filmer's house in order. The contrast between Sir Daniel Carteret's treatment of Mrs Dane, denied a happiness which might have been hers and Lionel's, and Hilary Jesson's handling of the adulterous Annabel's reputation is marked.

An equally marked contrast is apparent between Wyndham's handling of Henry Arthur Jones, and Alexander's of Pinero. At an early stage in their collaboration Jones's assertion of rebellious Susan's right to pay out her husband in kind met with Wyndham's inflexible resistance. The playwright capitulated, and his work for Wyndham then described a graph of increasing orthodoxy, culminating in the glaring 'dual morality' of *Mrs Dane's Defence*. Alexander's partnership with Pinero began in the conventional Victorian key of *The Second Mrs Tanqueray*, survived the stresses of *The Princess and the Butterfly*, and reached its zenith in the tolerance shown by Hilary and Nina Jesson in *His House in Order*, a play which ran for four hundred and thirty performances and was followed by knighthoods for both author and actor. The opposed curves of these graphs suggest that Wyndham's theatres offered intelligent entertainment without controversy, whereas the St James's under Alexander aspired to be high-minded as well as high class.

One thing at least both actor-managers had in common: commercial as well as artistic success. Wyndham was the *raison d'être* of the Criterion from 1875 to 1899, and controlled it until his death in 1919. Alexander ran the St James's from 1891 until his death in 1917. These records of sustained popularity tell a very different story from their predecessors'. Squire Bancroft, for example, the leading actor-manager of the 1870s, retired from management in 1885 and rarely acted again, although he lived until 1926, while Henry Irving, head of his profession in the 1880s, was driven from the Lyceum by his creditors in 1902 and killed himself by overwork within three years. The fact that the heyday of Wyndham and Alexander was the years 1890 to 1914 when the matinée established itself as an important feature of the theatrical scene may not have been the sole reason for their success, but it was certainly crucial. These two matinée idols were not only loved; they prospered.

Edwardian Idols of My Youth

by Ivor Brown

During the height of the matinée age at the beginning of the century there were plenty of rich women with servants in their homes and no need to be their own house-bound housekeepers, cooks and housemaids. While their husbands were at their offices, they liked to lunch with a woman friend and 'do a play' with tea laid on. Their taste in drama was not exacting, but it was not limited to light comedy. They could accept a solid play with a 'problem' plot, and that might involve a long session. Pinero's *His House in Order*, produced at the St James's Theatre in 1906, took three hours. But there on the stage at all the big moments was the smooth, suave and enchanting George Alexander, the perfect gentleman perfectly tailored, the true matinée idol of his day whether after lunch or after dinner. That piece ran for over a year, which was then an exceptionally long run. It could not have done so without his contribution of masculine charm.

I was there as a schoolboy in the pit. My age made afternoon excursions compulsory. I queued with a sandwich packet, paid my half-crown and frequently got a seat in the front row, 'the best place in the house,' it was said. But it was not always the best place if a grand lady in the back row of the stalls had a particularly large hat to remove, which meant a long business with the formidable hatpins that skewered this creation to the coiffure. Hats were not always removed to oblige those behind them.

The ladies of St James's
Go swinging to the play

wrote Austin Dobson, whose light verse was so well fitted to the period. Were they so nimbly buoyant? The adjective 'swinging', applied for no good reason to London in the 1960s, did not suit the stately Alexandrian dames who arrived sumptuously in their private carriages, with massive millinery which became even larger and so more tiresome in the auditorium when *The Merry Widow* was being played at Daly's in 1907. There the star was Lily Elsie. She brought into fashion a feminine hat so monstrously broad (as Cecil Beaton has told us) that it made getting in and out of a brougham or the new-fangled taxi-cab an awkward manoeuvre.

There are various contributors to the making of an idol. Most important of course is a mysterious gift known as 'star quality'. When its owner takes the stage he or she rivets and retains the eyes and ears of the audience.

Personal magnetism on the stage is assisted by good looks in a man and by the conventional type of beauty in a woman. But that need not be conspicuous, and perhaps not there at all. Marie Tempest's features were not faultless. She was not a Helen of Troy but she sparkled inimitably. Gerald du Maurier was not an Adonis, but he was an irresistible in his quiet stage-craft. Both were sovereign in their kind. Sex appeal is a precious asset, not an essential. Sway over an audience has been exercised by some who did not infatuate. They seemed more likeable than lovable and were good companions and not erotic stimulants. But idolisation came their way.

The first of my matinée pit-trips to a West End theatre took me to see the great idol of the time, Lewis Waller, then actor-manager at a long-vanished theatre, the Imperial in Westminster. He was then to be seen as a model of gallantry and glamour in a piece called *Miss Elizabeth's Prisoner*. It was set in the America of the 1780s, which had already provided Bernard Shaw with a brilliantly contrived and sharply witty reshaping of a melodrama theme in *The Devil's Disciple*. At the age of fourteen I knew nothing of that play. I was entranced by the panache of the star appearing as a captured British officer who has to save his life by vibrating Miss Elizabeth's heart-strings with only a few minutes to spare. Of course he sued with such eloquence and elegance that he survived.

Waller was in his element. In modern dress he usually failed to fascinate, but in period silken splendour and with a sword in hand he was irresistible. He made a mark in Somerset Maugham's *The Explorer*. 'See him as he paces the drawing-room carpet,' said Max Beerbohm 'and admit how inadequate is the inevitable simile of the caged lion!' His voice turned tushery into passionate prose. His greatest success came in a piece of romantic and richly costumed fustian set in Georgian Bath and called, like its hero, *Monsieur Beaucaire*. After he had been wounded in a duel, his beloved beauty, to whom he had given flowers with some flowery talk of devotion, seeing a red stain on his shirt inquired tearfully about his wound. Centre-stage with his eye on the gallery he spoke the curtain line: 'It's only a r-red, r-red rose.' (He slightly rolled his r's.) It was tosh delivered to perfection. When he had an occasional failure he revived Beaucaire and the charm of voice, added to the élan of the actor, always kept the box-office busy again.

Rather, it was said, to his resentment, he attracted a band of worshipping gallery girls who called themselves the 'KOW' which seemed to suggest 'Keen on Waller' but was explained to stand for the less crude 'Keen Order of Wallerites'. They were all aflame on his first nights. Their idolatry was hysterical, very different from the mannerly and restrained adoration of George Alexander among the ladies of St James's.

Waller had done well in Shakespeare with Herbert Beerbohm Tree, and not only in the flamboyant 'into battle' roles. On his own he chose and excelled as the *beau sabreur*. As Conan Doyle's Brigadier Gerard he scored in typical form. Yet such are the oddities of star quality, that he was, off the stage and out of costume, a small and not strikingly handsome man. It was a habit of the idolaters to hang about at stage-doors to see their darlings emerge. I once waited there to gaze in rapture at the heroic Lewis. I got a shock, not a thrill. Could this little chap in a rather dingy grey suit be he? On the stage he had seemed as large as he was lustrous, dynamic and debonair. But I continued to pay my holiday half-crowns and feel that I was getting good value. In the lime-light he was enlarged, magnetic and magniloquent. The voice lifted the most ordinary lines to the level of inspired writing.

Henry Ainley was large, handsome and could walk the street as he did the stage – as one of nature's grandees, commanding worship. There was a roll of great music when he spoke. A young man from Yorkshire, he had become instantaneously an idol in 1902 when he had appeared with Alexander in *Paolo and Francesca* by Stephen Phillips, who wrote much-esteemed plays in verse of a bland, Tennysonian kind. Unlike Waller, Ainley could wear a lounge suit without loss of his stage presence. Being omnivorous in the theatre I hungrily followed the New Drama of realism in Harley Granville-Barker's productions of Shaw and others at the Royal Court Theatre as eagerly as the old romantic routine in the West End. As much a Shavian as a Wallerite, I went there to a matinée of a revival of *You Never Can Tell*. The play was the primary reason for my well-rewarded journey. There was a bonus added to my joy by the presence of Ainley in the part of Mr Valentine, the dentist. P. G. Wodehouse, then emerging as a master of school stories, has called the members of that profession Fangsters. Ainley, drawing fangs with his forceps, drew hearts with his power to fascinate.

That piece, showing Shaw in his lightest and least doctrinaire form, might have contributed much earlier to the annals of idolization. The very popular and versatile Cyril Maude, a sure 'draw' in any play, was then actor-manager at the Haymarket Theatre. He took a fancy to it, agreed to produce it, and then backed out when two important but imperceptive members of his company said there was 'not a laugh in it'. The rehearsals became a mess and a misery. If Maude had stuck to his choice and played either Valentine or the waiter, since he was a master of elderly as well as junior comedy, he might have made money for all concerned, including G.B.S., who still needed it. The play was published the following year in *Plays Pleasant*. Turning elsewhere, Maude was an idol in a variety of roles, most effectively in naval uniform in *The Flag Lieutenant* and in the title part of a frothy little comedy from the French called *Toddles*. His public doted on him, whether he was nimbly adroit in a frisky piece or sedentary in one of his almost Methuselah-like roles, in a play, for example, called *Grumpy*.

Ainley marched on through the first age of the idols. He was a clever all-round actor as well as a good-looker who caught and held the eyes of those most susceptible to sex appeal. His range of skill was abundantly proved when he appeared in Arnold Bennett's play *The Great Adventure*, which ran for two and a half years at the Kingsway Theatre just before the First World War. His part was that of a famous and fashionable portrait painter who loathed being lionized in high society and disappeared to enjoy a quiet and anonymous life in hiding. There was no scope here for the grandeur of his looks and voice. Brilliantly directed by Granville-Barker, his character study of a shy, secretive man delighted the connoisseurs of subtle acting without losing the loyalty of those who were later given the nasty little name of 'fans'. His last great success was in St John Ervine's *The First Mrs Fraser* (1929), in which he starred with Marie Tempest. For idolatrous star-gazers here was a dazzling partnership.

Very different but with an equally large following was Charles Hawtrey, whose voice and features were not his principal attraction. He nearly always displayed a small moustache, then unusual in masculine idols, and on the only occasion when he appeared clean-shaven the play disappointed. The son of a master at Eton and himself an Old Etonian, he was very much the gentleman in the parts he played, but he was also much liked when cast as one whose morals were less exalted than his manners. His strength was a sly, smooth, quiet humour; he was at his best in parts where he had to practise a discreet duplicity. When he fibbed he could not fail. Supreme as a gay deceiver, he had an early and enormous success in 1899 with a completely different part in *A*

Message from Mars. As the title implies, this mysterious space-traveller had something serious to tell the wicked world. He was a most virtuous counsellor. In this age of the idols, the censor was a rigid dictator of decorum and, if impropriety crept in, it had to do so by a *double-entendre*, the nuance of an actor's naughty use of a winking eye or the insertion of an unscripted gag.

Preaching by an idol could be popular if the moral medicine was sugared in sentiment, and Hawtrey delivered his message triumphantly. So, some years later, did the austerely handsome Johnston Forbes-Robertson in *The Passing of the Third Floor Back* by Jerome K. Jerome, another sermon superbly spoken with Forbes-Robertson's classic style and voice adapted to shabby lodging-house surroundings. Audiences could then relish hours of up-lift. For the opposite moral effect Hawtrey could be seen briefly at the end of his career in a farce called *Up in Mabel's Room*. That play was hardly consistent with the information provided in *The Oxford Companion to the Theatre* that Hawtrey was 'a keen student of the Bible with a text for every occasion'. This addiction to the Good Book did not make a good bargain for his creditors. But he could charm his way out of trouble and ended his life of lavish spending and tardy paying with a knighthood conferred in 1922. He had little time to enjoy it, since he died in 1924.

During the war years from 1914 to 1918, while London was a lodging-house between life and death, the men on leave looked only for cheerful consolation in the theatre. There were then much larger audiences for entertainments providing this escape. The plays which pleased had runs of previously un-paralleled length. A farce called *A Little Bit of Fluff* had over a thousand per-formances at the Criterion and the musical spectacular *Chu Chin Chow*, staged at His Majesty's in 1916, stayed on after the Armistice to run up a record with over 2,200 performances. (The audiences then were mostly nocturnal seekers of an easy chortle or a sumptuous eyeful.)

There was one piece of that period which created another matinée idol. He was Owen Nares, who appeared at the Duke of York's Theatre in 1915 as leading man to the American actress Doris Keene, playing as a love-lorn clergyman with amorous propensities. The soulful man of God exposed to the temptations of the flesh is a certain success, as Hall Caine, that master of a blend between the sensuous and the sentimental, had discovered when his novel *The Christian* was dramatized. Nares was too intelligent a man for this type of part, as he proved in many of his subsequent roles. But his good man driven to distraction by a less virtuous woman established him as top of the class in the charm school. His approach to the public was not the attack of a flamboyant romantic. He was a natural star in the portrayal of the 'good sort' characters, smoothly handsome and essentially 'well-graced', to use the adjective which Shakespeare had chosen to describe the star who made things difficult for those of lesser radiance. I never saw him in a costume piece, but he made a fine return to the clerical cloth in St John Ervine's play *Robert's Wife* in 1937.

The venerated idols of religion have images and there is much talk now of the 'images' of important people. The word is applied to their characters and reputations as well as to their appearances. The images of the Edwardian matinée idols took the eye and were made available for admiration by the copious sale of picture postcards. These were not limited to the feminine beauties. Such leading men as Henry Ainley and Lewis Waller were plentifully on view in the shops. At a higher level of the commerce were cabinet-size photographs handsomely framed. I remember one in my own home. It was not an autographed present, but a purchase made by a matinée addict. The image was that of George Alexander, looking soulful and serene. The phrase 'pin-up' had not come in, but the practice of pinning was being added to the happy filling of an album. The majestic cabinet-size article was a prop-up on a piano or a mantelpiece.

The chosen images were not limited to the beaux and the belles of the musical stage. The ownership of heart-appeal brought in, for example, the delicate features of Martin Harvey, who toured continually in *The Only Way* and *The Cigarette Maker's Romance*, mingling these with some highly praised but less rewarded excursions into the classics in London. But the biggest sales were of the feminine adorables. One favourite was a trio of Zena Dare, her no less decorative sister Phyllis and their brother Jack. It was in fact a family group since it included their mother and father. And it was a good idea to add to the glamour of the great and a reminder to the public that they had homes, pets and untheatrical relatives. One who became top of the pictorial tops as well as having her name in lights in Shaftesbury Avenue and playing leading parts on the stage was Marie Studholme. I never saw her in a play or musical piece, but I could not look at a shop without seeing her more often than any of those who topped the bill. She did not seem to outshine the others in loveliness, but her image became ubiquitous, a 'must' in every album of the image-collectors.

Actors and actresses had been climbing the social ladder when the age of the matinée idol began. In Pinero's *Trelawney of the Wells* the players are comprehensively dismissed as 'gipsies' by Sir William Gower when they enter his mansion in Cavendish Square. Soon, having struggled up from scum status, they could be summoned to Buckingham Palace and return as Sirs. The honours began with knighthoods for Henry Irving in 1895 and for Squire Bancroft in 1897. They were followed by Charles Wyndham, who had the

looks and magnetism of an idol, in 1902, John Hare in 1907, Herbert
Beerbohm Tree in 1909, and George Alexander in 1911. All had carried the
financial risks and professional cares of management when no theatres were
subsidised. Gerald du Maurier had been actor-manager at Wyndham's
Theatre for twelve years when he was knighted in 1922. And so it went on,
with titles for Barry Jackson and Nigel Playfair in 1925 and 1928. Since then
the acknowledgement of supreme quality as an actor has been steadily ex-
tended, with Sir Ralph Richardson, Sir Godfrey Tearle, Sir John Gielgud,
Sir Alec Guinness, Sir John Clements and Sir Michael Redgrave as examples.
At last came a coronet when Sir Laurence Olivier took his seat in the House of
Lords in 1970. What would Sir William Gower have said to that?

The women were stupidly overlooked when the giving of titles began. There
was no chivalry in their case. Ellen Terry, who had a host of idolators, including
Bernard Shaw, was not made a Dame until 1925, thirty years after Sir Henry
Irving, with whom she had been an equal attraction at the Lyceum. Oddly,
she was not the first of those honoured for acting. Her predecessor was an
American, Geneviève Ward, who first appeared in London in 1874 and had
taken leading Shakespearean parts with Irving. She had also been in management, starring in a great success, *Forget-Me-Not*. Her DBE came in 1922, a
year before her death at the age of eighty-six. Ellen Terry had not received the
title of Dame until three years before her death at eighty-one. When titles were
concerned, the great ladies were indeed kept 'waiting in the wings'. There was
less hesitation when Sybil Thorndike became a Dame in 1931. Her immediate
successors were Marie Tempest, Irene Vanbrugh, Lilian Braithwaite and
Edith Evans. After that there was a continuing regard for equality of the sexes
in the tributes to the highest talent. These questions of equality certainly did
not trouble the young idolators as we made a long climb up steep stairs to the
shilling gallery, and an uncushioned seat at the end of it. A place in 'the gods'
was hellish hard. At His Majesty's there were only bare boards. After some
misery there during a Shakespearean afternoon I always saved my small silver
to raise half-a-crown for a place in the pit. The seats there were covered, but
not padded. Since the matinées were usually packed when an idol was on view
we had to sit close together. In the case of a great success the attendants would
order us to move up in order to let more in. That was cruelly unfair, since
some wedged into the front row were latecomers who had not queued for the
coveted place.

For half-an-hour after admission we looked at a handsome curtain, then
listened to the overture provided by a small orchestra. Edward German's
Merrie England melodies were frequently the dulcet consolation for delay.
At last the moment came. Our endurance had been eased by expectation. The
practice, deplorable to me, of coming in to see the stage and the scenery
exposed was unthinkable at that time. The theatre was unashamedly theatrical.
That adjective was not then contemptuous. Illusion is now sneered at by the

progressives. We had come for just that, for excitement, suspense and for escape into a different world. When the second great moment came with the entry of the idol, who was worshipped, wonderful, and to put it crudely the reason why we had parted so eagerly with our money, we had compensation in full. Puerile? But I was, after all, a boy and my neighbours on the crowded benches, whatever their age, were as simple-minded as myself and no less entranced.

Father's Footsteps
(Gerald du Maurier)

by Daphne du Maurier

M Y father Gerald was born on 26 March 1873, so if he were alive today he would be over a hundred years old. The words make no sense to me, and by no possible feat of the imagination can I conjure up a vision of some lean and slippered pantaloon sitting in a wheelchair propped up by pillows, deaf, perhaps, mouth half-open, fumbling for telegrams of congratulation.

When he died on 11 April 1934 at the comparatively early age of sixty-one, after an operation for cancer – and I have it on good authority that with the surgical skill and medical treatment of today they could have saved him – he knew, despite plans for convalescence and smiles of reassurance to my mother, sitting by his bedside (he died on the thirty-first anniversary of their wedding day) that his time had come. Ripe old age was not for him. The weeks and months ahead held no promise. He had neither the energy nor the inclination to read plays which he would be bored to direct and equally bored to perform in; and as for hanging about a film studio all day waiting to speak half-a-dozen lines that would later be cut, this might serve to pay off what he owed for income tax, but would only increase the sense of apathy within. To what end? An expression he often used in those last years, half-joking, half-serious, and then would follow it up with his favourite quotation: 'Now more than ever seems it rich to die, to cease upon the midnight with no pain.'

Well, he had his wish. He had no pain. My aunt, who was with him at the time, told me he had a curious, puzzled look in his eyes, as if asking a question. I can believe it. He had the same look when I smiled at him from the doorway and waved goodbye before his operation.

This is no way to start a chapter about a matinée idol. The end before the beginning. The trouble is that, as his daughter, I never saw the beginning, only grew up through childhood and adolescence when the tide of his popularity was running at full flood. He was thirty-three in 1906, a year before I was born, when he made his first big success as Raffles, the cricketer turned cracksman, in a play packed full of action from start to finish, a novelty in those days, which delighted his Edwardian audiences as much as a similar theme about a footballer of renown turning out to be one of the Great Train Robbers would enthral a pack of shouting teenage fans in 1974. In 1906, however, his applauders were not children – except on half-holidays: they were respectable fathers of families, middle-aged matrons, wide-eyed spinsters, stolid businessmen, sisters and aunts up from the country, anyone and everyone who had money enough in his pocket to pay for a seat in gallery, pit or stall, and desired above all things not to be made to think but to be entertained. It was exciting, and rather shocking, to have the hero of a play a burglar – and not an obvious burglar, the spinster ladies told themselves, who wore a cloth cap and a muffler, but a gentleman strolling about with his hands in his pockets. It gave them a *frisson*. And the men in the audience nodded in agreement. Nonsense, of course, but jolly good fun, and how easy du Maurier made the whole thing look, from lighting a cigarette to handling a gun. No wonder the women were mad about him.

Easy, perhaps, but in 1906 this sort of acting was new, and a critic of the day was even more impressed than the audience. 'To play such a scene as this, slowly but surely working to a tremendous emotional climax, with few words and the difficulty of an assumed calmness which needs much subtlety, is the achievement of a tragedian of uncommon quality.'

I wonder if Gerald read this notice and whether, for a moment, he thought, 'Tragedian? Me? Could I ever? Dare I ever?' Then, with a smile, he threw the thought away with the newspaper, and continued to give his public what it wanted, Arsène Lupin, a French crook and a duke, Jimmy Valentine, the safe-opener, one impossible con man after another, and the greatest crook of them all, Hubert Ware in George Bancroft's *The Ware Case*, who murdered his brother-in-law by drowning him in a lake, and lied his way out of the witness-box with the help of a down-at-heel accomplice. Immoral, if you come to think of it. No message to the masses. It did not send the audiences home pondering about world problems (it was first produced in 1915, and the men who shouted their applause were all in khaki), but it allowed them to forget what they were going back to in the trenches – the murder of a brother-in-law in a lake made sense and war did not.

Lists of plays that were popular successes between the years 1906 and 1918, all produced at Wyndham's Theatre, where Gerald had gone into management in 1910 with a non-acting partner, Frank Curzon, would be of little interest to the reader of 1974. He will never see them. None, except those of J. M. Barrie, is likely to be revived. Suffice it to say they were of their era, and Gerald, who had a genius for knowing when the moment was ripe for something old or something new, a revival once popular and acclaimed a second time or a novelty catching the passing mood, never failed to 'bring them in', as the saying went. 'House Full' boards went up outside the theatre, the queues lengthened, the taxis rolled.

This, it could be argued by the young of today, sounds somewhat tame. Bourgeois, middle-class. Nothing like a Pop Festival in Hyde Park or the Isle of Wight, where boys and girls will sleep out in the open and wait twenty-four hours in the rain to hear the beloved reach for his mike or twang his guitar. Football-players are mobbed as they leave the ground, film-stars (and they grow fewer every day) besieged outside their hotels, disc-jockeys accosted in the streets; anyone who happens to hit the headlines in the morning appears on television that same evening and is seen by millions. Instant fame is the order of the day. Herein lies the difference between our time and forty, fifty, sixty years ago. There was no hysteria then, Applause, yes, and plenty of it, and boos and cat-calls too, when a play had offended, reviews the following morning written by critics of repute who did not hesitate to damn author and cast alike if they deserved it, yet at the same time spared the newspaper reader the cheap gibe or flourish of wit.

Dignity, perhaps, was the operative word. Dignity, and ease of manner. Recognition of talent, and technique, and training, and understanding on the part of critic and playgoer alike that the men and women on the other side of the footlights had worked long and hard during the weeks of rehearsal to bring pleasure to those who sat and watched. If they had failed, too bad; the play would be withdrawn, the cast dismissed, the management lose money, and a start must begin all over again to find a play that would please the audience better.

A point in favour of the old actor-manager of the past was that those he endeavoured to entertain connected him with one particular theatre. The play-goers from 1910 to 1925 did not have to search the newspapers to discover where Gerald du Maurier was performing: it could only be at Wyndham's Theatre. (And after 1925, when the partnership with Frank Curzon ended and Gilbert Miller took his place, the St James's Theatre became the new home.) The cast changed, of course, from play to play, but there was continuity in the theatre staff, the commissionaire in front of the theatre, the stage door-keeper, the cleaners, the dressers, the stage-manager, the manager in the box-office. Thinking back, after all too many years, I can feel the swing-doors with the bars across them under my hands; surely I had to reach up to them? And Bob, the stage-door keeper, smiling down from his stool. The stairs to the dressing-room, stage entrance on the left, stairs to the other dressing-rooms on the right. The musty, indefinable, theatre smell of shifting scenery, with stage-hands moving about and Poole, Gerald's dresser, who had rather a red face and mumbled as he spoke, hovering at the entrance to the dressing-room.

The colour of the room, in retrospect, seems to be green. There were play-bills all over the wall on the left. A large mirror on the right, and a flat sort of divan beneath it on which my sisters and I used to sit. It was good for dangling our legs. A curtain, seldom pulled, divided the inner sanctum where Gerald changed and made up. A different smell came from it, not musty – grease-paint (I'm told they don't use it today), but eau-de-cologne and something else, cool, clean, that must have been Gerald himself. To us children there was nothing singular or surprising that in a moment he would come bursting in from the door that led directly to back-stage, calling for Poole, and that he would hear the distant sound of applause which meant that the audience was still clapping after the final curtain, before 'God Save the King'. This was his life. Other children's fathers, perhaps, went to an office; ours went to the theatre. Then, perhaps, friends or acquaintances who had been to the matinée would come round to see him, which meant standing up and shaking hands on our part, and listening, yawning, while the chatter passed over our heads. The people who came always seemed excited, thrilled: entering the star's dressing-room was an event. It was a relief when the exclamations and the congratulations were over and we were just ourselves, with Gerald sitting down and taking off his make-up at the dressing-table. Pity, though, I sometimes thought. He looked nicer with it on, bolder, somehow, and his eyes very bright. Still, it was all part of the game of make-believe that was his, and ours as well. Life was pretending to be someone else. Otherwise it was rather dull.

I suppose I must have been about six or possibly seven when I first realized that Gerald – Daddy, as we called him – was recognized, known, by strangers outside the theatre. We were entering a restaurant – it was probably the Piccadilly Hotel, because he had not yet started his custom of going to the Savoy, and for some reason or other he was taking us out to lunch; perhaps it was my elder sister Angela's birthday. There were several people standing about and I was lagging behind. Then a tall woman – all adults seem unbearably tall to a small child – nudged her companion with a knowing look and said, 'There's Gerald du Maurier.' She sounded excited, and there was a gleam in her eye. The escort turned and stared, and a knowing look came into his eye too. Both of them smirked. Somehow, I don't know why, I found this offensive. I looked up sharply at my father, but he was humming softly under his breath, as he often did, and took not the slightest notice of either the tall woman or her escort, but I knew that he had heard the exclamation, and he knew that I had heard it too. Waiters suddenly approached, bowing, pulling back chairs from our table. Heads turned. The same gleam, the same nudge. We sat down and the business of the lunch proceeded, and the whole scene sank into a child's unconscious mind, but the penny had dropped.

From then on I knew that strangers, people we should never know, never speak to, were in some curious way gratified when he passed by. The applause, the clapping of hands, the little knot of men and women, mostly women, waiting outside the stage-door when we left the theatre to go home after a matinée, was all part of the same thing. Because Gerald – Daddy – had pleased them by pretending to be someone else, like Raffles leaping out of the grandfather-clock in the last act, he also pleased them by going into a restaurant and having lunch. And the strange thing was that it made *them* feel important, not him. He didn't care. And somehow, to a child of six or seven, this was tremendously important. If Gerald had smirked back, or thrown them a glance over his shoulder – those two in the restaurant – or in any way shown himself aware . . . *my* idol would have crashed.

This cool disregard on the part of the well-known towards the pointer, the starer, was not, I think, peculiar to Gerald, but was characteristic of his fellow-stars as well, half a century and more ago. They were not concerned about their image. I suspect that it is different today. With rare exceptions, a public figure who does not wave, grin, exchange jokes with his admirers and continually show himself conscious of his fans would be accused of having a swollen head. The fact that Gerald ignored nudges and whispers in the street or in restaurants did not mean that he despised the crowds who came to applaud him in the theatre, nor indeed the many fans who wrote to him or waited outside the stage-door, autograph-book in hand. Letters were answered promptly, though I have no recollection of who did the secretarial work before my aunt Sybil – Billy, my mother's sister – took it on around 1919. Hands were shaken, autographs written, and all with a good grace, after the matinée in that dark passage between Wyndham's and the New Theatre; then to the car drawn up at the front of the house, with Dan – or was it Martin? – throwing open the door, and so back home for an early dinner at a quarter-to-seven, then twenty minutes' shut-eye before the evening performance. Eight performances a week, bed never before midnight or later, but first supper – eggs and bacon or sausages – cooked by my mother, who had waited up for him in her dressing-gown and now listened to the gossip of his day.

Stage, film and television stars nowadays have marriages that come apart with the first row. An absence for a few weeks on tour or on location is asking for trouble. Somebody's eye wanders, is caught, and the curious modern custom of telling all to the innocent partner so as to appease personal guilt is followed through to its inevitable conclusion, and the innocent partner, pride outraged, sues for a divorce. Everyone marries again. Perhaps it will be second or third time lucky.

Gerald, who had learnt the facts of life as a young actor from Mrs Patrick Campbell and others, fell in love with my mother, Muriel Beaumont, when they were acting together in Barrie's *The Admirable Crichton* at the Duke of York's Theatre in 1902. She was very pretty, rather naïve, had a will of her own and adored him. Adoration was mutual, and continued unchanging until his death thirty-one years after their marriage in 1903. How fully my mother was aware of his wandering eye I shall never know. Perhaps she closed her own, realising, with the wisdom of her particular generation, that he would always place her first. Not a marriage of convenience, but a marriage of love and understanding. Twice I saw my mother really roused, with a high colour and stamping foot. The first occasion was when she opened her bill from Fortnum & Mason and saw, in the middle of a list of items she had herself ordered, a large case of tea that had been sent round, on Gerald's instructions, to the apartment of his current leading lady. Let him order goods on the side if he must, she told him, but not put them down to his wife.

The second occasion was more serious. Driving into London from Hampstead in her own small car she noticed, with astonishment, Gerald's Sunbeam parked outside a terrace-house on the fringe of St John's Wood. The house was inhabited by a young actress who had a small part in his current production. My mother – Mo, as she was always called – drove on to town, whether to shop or to visit friends I don't know, but on the return journey, a few hours later, she saw that the Sunbeam was still there. Crisis threatened. Dinner before the theatre that evening was an ordeal. I know, because I was there. What passed between my father and my mother in the way of accusation, denial, acknowledgement, contrition, I shall never know, except for the quick whisper in my ear from Gerald on his way to the theatre, 'Mummy's so angry with me, I don't know what to do.' How old was I? Nineteen, twenty? I don't remember; but I felt then as if he were my brother, or indeed my son. The father-daughter relationship had entered a deeper phase.

Ten years or so previously the relationship had been more personal, more emotional. If Gerald's most popular successes to date – and I am now speaking of 1917 – had been chiefly those of what we should now call the cops-and-robbers variety, the thrill of the chase, it took J. M. Barrie to draw the finest acting out of the matinée idol of the day. In *Dear Brutus*, surely Barrie's best play, the least sentimental, the most perceptive, Gerald took the part of a jaded, spoilt, successful painter, at odds with his wife and with the world. The title – taken from Cassius in *Julius Caesar*, 'The fault, dear Brutus, is not in our stars but in ourselves, that we are underlings' – gives the theme of the play; a group of people, the painter amongst them, as they wander in an enchanted wood, are shown, by their host magician, what they would have done with their lives had they been given a second chance. Gerald, as Will Dearth, is still an artist, but unsuccessful, with no possessions except a single daughter in her teens, whom he loves, and who loves him. The transformation of the jaded, successful man in the first act to the happy-go-lucky father in the second saw Gerald at his peak. He was himself, yes, but also every man who carries in his soul a seed of discontent, of wishing that his world was other than it had turned out to be. There was nostalgia, too – memories of his own artist father, who had known success but had remained his generous, unspoilt self.

The third act brought realisation. The second chance was nothing but a dream. He was Will Dearth, who had conquered the artistic world, but he had no daughter. 'When I was in the wood with Margaret,' Gerald said, 'she . . . she . . . Margaret . . . ' and then he lifted his head and looked about him, at the walls of the house enclosing him, no wood, no child, and it was as though he shrank into himself, and the expression in his eyes, bewildered, lost, anguished, was something that his real daughter, a child of ten, has never forgotten, can never forget. Filial identification? Possibly. But the hushed audience identified also, and this is surely the whole meaning of communication between the actor on the stage and those who sit and watch him; they have a bond in common, they see themselves.

The natural school of acting that Gerald founded had much to answer for in later years. Mumbled speaking, sloppy gestures, actors with small talent believing that, without years of training and hard thought, they could walk an easy road to success. It was not so. Either they achieved a temporary popularity, or they fell by the way. Only those with real genius knew how to develop the technique and build upon it, and I do not think it is fancy on my part, or filial pride, when I think of the two greatest actors of our day, Laurence Olivier and John Gielgud, who, in their youth, must have seen *Dear Brutus* and watched Gerald in his prime. *

It can be argued, or course, that when Gerald appeared on the stage for the first time in 1894, at the age of twenty-one, without any training, he did so through favouritism. John Hare happened to be a friend of his father, and was pleased to give the lad the humble part of Fritz the waiter in Sydney Grunsby's *The Old Jew*, with little to do and still less to say. His only experience until then had been in amateur theatricals during school holidays from Harrow, and at Harrow his sole claim to distinction had been his ability to imitate Sir Henry Irving up and down the corridors, to the amusement of masters and boys

---

* Since writing the above I have been told that John Gielgud *did* see Gerald in *Dear Brutus*, when he was thirteen. He was taken by his father at Christmas, and the visit was repeated in January. Two programmes exist in the Mander and Mitchenson Collection with his manuscript comments upon them 'charming – Faith Celli and du Maurier excellent' and on the second visit 'again – charming as ever'.

alike. Possibly an added inducement to John Hare was the fact that two years previously the boy's father, George du Maurier, had published his novel *Trilby*, which had proved to be the literary event of the season in both England and America. The *Punch* artist, a celebrity anyway, was now world-famous. Nothing succeeds like success, and it is doubtful if the critic who wrote of Fritz the waiter, 'Mr du Maurier in a very few words showed that he had probably found his vocation', would have noticed the young man but for the familiar name in the programme.

A familiar name on its own, however, does not carry its bearer far unless the talent is there, and the will to work, and Gerald possessed not only talent but determination too, qualities that were developed in the following years under the brilliant tuition of Beerbohm Tree and Mrs Patrick Campbell. From Fritz the waiter to Will Dearth may not have been a hard road or an uphill climb, but it took three-and-twenty years to achieve, which is a fair step, if you come to think of it. Charm and ease of manner may win popularity in a night, but artistic genius within a man must be nurtured by perception, experience, and integrity, if it is to survive for more than a decade.

'Why was Daddy knighted?' I asked my mother when, after his death in 1934, I was making notes for his biography. She looked up from her embroidery with a thoughtful expression in her eyes. 'I don't think we ever knew,' she replied, which seemed to me then, and now, a delightful attitude to honours, and one that was undoubtedly Gerald's own. I assume that the knighthood was laid upon him in 1922 not because of the wild popularity of Bulldog Drummond, a very different role from that of Will Dearth, nor for the somewhat quixotic gesture which he made in his mid-forties in 1918 by throwing up *Dear Brutus* and joining the Irish Guards as a cadet (a tribute, I suspect, to his beloved brother Guy, who had been killed in action in 1915), but plainly and simply 'for services rendered to his profession'. He was president not only of the Actor's Orphanage but of a number of other charitable organisations, never sparing himself when he could make money for those less fortunate than himself. Wasn't it Will Dearth in the enchanted wood who had said to his daughter Margaret, 'We lucky ones, let's always be kind to those who are down on their luck, and when we're kind, let's be a little kinder?' No one ever asked Gerald for a loan and was refused, and needless to say the money, if any attempt was made to return it, was not accepted. He was never a rich man, as riches are known today in the world of film and pop star, but what he earned was generously spent, needy relatives taken care of, friends paid for on holiday. Make other people happy while you have the means to do so, and to hell with the future and the Inland Revenue . . . .

If the matinée idol of the war years was now Sir Gerald with added responsibilities, he carried the burden lightly; and although in the 1920s he was the undoubted head of his profession, and had turned fifty, he was still youthful in appearance and young in heart. No one who remembers *The Last of Mrs Cheyney* – Freddie Lonsdale's witty comedy at the St James's Theatre – in which he co-starred with Gladys Cooper, will forget the brilliance of these two, their consummate ease and grace, their timing, the sense of fun that pervaded the whole production. Now there were two sets of fans waiting at the stage-door after a performance. His and hers. And if nobody screamed or fainted when Gladys finally emerged, I do recollect the murmur that arose from her excited adorers, gradually swelling in volume as she passed between them, and hands would be stretched out to touch her coat as though the very texture had magic properties. Gladys smiled, and waved, and made a dash for her car, and if by chance I scrambled in her wake, being an adorer in my own fashion, I used to wonder how swiftly a waiting crowd might be moved to anger, the murmur of approval turn to a roar of hate, the hands outstretched to touch, reach down for stones. Anyone who has heard boos and groans and whistles at a first night after a flop will understand me.

The great day for the fans, of course, was the annual Theatrical Garden Party, in aid of the Actors' Orphanage, originally held in the Botanical Gardens in Regent's Park, but in postwar years in the Chelsea Hospital Gardens. This would be the nearest thing, fifty years ago, to the pop festivals of our own time. The whole theatrical profession would be there, stars, supporting players, understudies. The sight was something between a circus and a fun-fair. Walk up . . . walk up . . . Come bowl for a pig with Owen Nares. Dig for buried treasure with Phyllis Dare. Buy Gladys Cooper Face Cream from her own hands. The biggest draw, as might be expected, was a vast marquee at the end of the grounds covering a built-up stage, with a curtain and rows of seats for a paying audience, where Gerald, with a picked cast of actors and actresses, gave a knock-about performance known as *The Grand Giggle*. If memory serves me right, the skit or farce would last about thirty minutes, the action proceeding at a cracking pace to whoops of laughter. Then the audience would troop out to allow their successors in the queue outside to take their place. An exhausting afternoon for the players, but a field-day for the fans. Even the performers' families basked in reflected glory. My mother, with a bevy of helpers, would preside over a hoop-la stall with all the grace of a queen consort, with my sisters and myself as a doubtful added attraction, the whispered, 'Ooh! aren't they dears?', bringing blushes to our cheeks. It was much more fun to roam the other stalls incognito than to pose as prize exhibits.

Well, it's all over now. Grand Giggles and hoop-la stalls belong to a bygone age. Some of those who drew the crowds in the Twenties now live in Denville Hall for retired actors and actresses, of which Gerald was also president in his prime. The art of acting is ephemeral, especially in the theatre. We can see the film stars of yesterday in yesterday's films, hear the voices of poets and singers on a record, keep the plays of dead dramatists upon our bookshelves, but the actor who holds his audience captive for one brief moment upon a lighted stage vanishes forever when the curtain falls. The actors and actresses of two generations ago live on in the memories of those who had the good fortune to watch them and applaud, and if this is poor consolation for the absence of voice, and smile, and gesture, at least something of their presence lingers still, to bring courage and inspiration to their successors.

When a young player today glances intuitively over his shoulder, alters position, changes tone and speaks with greater clarity – none of which has been laid down for him in the script or urged upon him by the director – is it fanciful to believe that something of the talent possessed by others has brushed off on his shoulders, and that as he treads the boards of a well-worn stage the very dust of a predecessor rises to become part of him? Sentimental, perhaps, but your born actor has sentiment bred in the bone, and superstition too. He feels, he is aware, and no matter how many theatres fall on the scrap-heap – the St James's is no more and other theatres are threatened; Wyndham's may one day give place to an office block – the few square acres of London where he works, from Covent Garden to Piccadilly and beyond, are haunted by a happy breed of men who one and all were strolling players in their time. Applause was theirs for a night and a day in their world of make-believe, but the emotion they engendered in themselves and in those about them was for posterity.

When I think of Gerald – and scarcely a day passes without some reminder, from the photographs and mementoes round the house down to his signet-ring, which I wear upon my finger – it is not as a father that I see him most clearly, bowling to us children at cricket on the lawn at Hampstead and assuming a different personality with each delivery of the ball, nor as the producer, directing rehearsals of a play with intense concentration from a corner of the stage or from the stalls, nor yet as the actor, putting every ounce of energy and thought into a first-night performance and then standing, with the cast beside him, to take his bow and receive the shouting acclaim at the final curtain. No, he has pottered downstairs to the drawing-room one fine morning in search of cigarettes, while Mo is upstairs having a bath, and he is wearing silk pyjamas from Beale & Edmonds of Bond Street, topped by a very old cardigan full of holes that once belonged to his mother. He switches on the gramophone and the hit-song of the day, a sensuous waltz, floats upon the air. He holds out his arms to a non-existent partner, and, closing his eyes, circles the room with the exaggerated rhythm of a musical-comedy hero, languid, romantic, murmuring with mock passion,

> I wonder why you keep me waiting,
> Charmaine, Charmaine. . . . '

Unseen by friends or fans, and unobserved, so he imagines, by any member of his family, Gerald obeys the instinct of a lifetime, and is acting to himself.

▐▐

THE period that was epitomised in literature by T. S. Eliot's vision of The Waste Land and in life by economic depression, mass unemployment and the rise of different totalitarian regimes throughout Europe with their evil idolatry of the state and the leader was remarkable in the London theatre for an insouciance, a playfulness, a frivolous gaiety the like of which has not been seen before or since. It was, in the words of Noël Coward, 'On with the Dance'. The matinée flourished throughout these uneasy years of entre deux guerres when there were many with time on their hands to attend it; so did musical romance, intimate revue, light comedy and other escapist genres. Idols in the du Maurier mould, a Hicks, a Tearle, a Massey, had their shining hours upon the stage but in retrospect the period seems to be dominated by geniuses of astonishing versatility and élan, Ivor Novello and Noël Coward. Sandy Wilson looks in this section at some of the musical plays of the former and Micheál Mac Liammóir recalls the life-enhancing personality of Novello as a man and an artist. Whether Noël Coward was a matinée idol in the strict sense of the phrase is a question that Sheridan Morley answers at the start of his consideration of the several faces of the Master. Part of Coward's career was inseparable from that of Gertrude Lawrence who is remembered by Cecil Beaton among other successors of Lily Elsie. Vivian Ellis conjures back the musical theatre over a quarter of a century, its many leading ladies and its two great impresarios, Charlot and Cochran. Then there were the vehicles for the idols, all those sensations and box-office winners, that lie for the most part in unrevivable oblivion; Philip Hope-Wallace remembers their impact on him as he looks back on the rewards of a lifetime spent as a professional theatregoer.

A.C.

From Gladys Cooper to Gertrude Lawrence

by Cecil Beaton

WITH Lily Elsie's retirement from the musical comedy stage, London looked in vain for a star replacement. At Daly's her immediate successor was the Hungarian, Sari Petrass. Sari had a slightly oyster-like face with circular nostrils, round glassy eyes, and though by no means unattractive, had a homely, oatmealy personality. Her singing voice was stronger than Lily Elsie's and Lehár approved of her as his choice for rendering his *Tzigane* melodies in *Gipsy Love*, even though, when tired, she could be accused of an occasionally flat note. Lehár had composed no waltz tune that could be easily recognized or whistled by the proverbial butcher boys, and Sari Petrass had no theatrical glamour or legendary quality. London did not take her to its heart. She died in a most hauntingly horrible way when on a motoring tour in Austria with her friend, Lady Allen Horne. Their driver mistook the boundary of a jetty and the two ladies drowned in their car.

Winifred Barnes, almost excessively pretty and petite, then became the leading lady at Daly's in *Betty*, a Cinderella story of a housemaid who became a beautiful bride. 'Baby' Barnes, as she was known in the profession, had infinite appeal, and all the rich men in London wanted to nurture her. Her wide scylla-blue eyes, nut-brown hair and little bun-like features were adorable, and her dimpled daintiness won her a large public across the footlights. But she was made only of the stuff of youthfulness, and she did not develop as an artist. Although remaining popular within rather social circles, and accordingly painted by the fashionable Ambrose McEvoy, who captured her untidy allure in a ravishing portrait, she took to taking one nip too many, the dimples increased, and the little waif evaporated, if not into thin air, into some sort of haze.

After the first night of *After the Girl*, an inconsequential musical at the Gaiety, Isobel Elsom, a pale flaxen blonde with the mythical features of the unicorn, was hailed by the morning newspapers as 'the new Lily Elsie'. But the title was not apt. The flashlight photographs showed Miss Elsom's dressing-room transformed into a grotto of floral tributes, but the public did not flock to see the newcomer. Soon this dreamy young lady with junket-white complexion, strongly forward-thrust chin, but inexpressive limbs, progressed to the legitimate stage. This she adorned until the earliest British films and Hollywood claimed her, eventually making her into a Chaplin figure of fun in *Monsieur Verdoux*.

Iris Hoey then succeeded as a somewhat unusual leading lady in *The Pearl Girl* and *Oh, Oh, Delphine!* Her voice was small, but, more extraordinary, she was without the quality of vulnerability, and seemed quite capable of coping with the inevitable catastrophe at the end of Act II. But she had a great sense of fun and an unusual beauty which was appreciated by postcard fans: her mouth wide and curling into arabesques of amusement, her eyes atwinkle and her profile like that of a Minoan serpent.

Ina Claire, from America, dazzled London with her sparkling vitality and sharp sense of mischief in *The Girl from Utah*. She, like Lily Elsie, had begun her career as a child giving impersonations of famous actors and actresses, and to this day she can evoke Sarah Bernhardt, of the brown velvet voice and the courage always to appear on the wave's crest, in a devastating caricature that is at once full of *diablerie* and compassion. With the declaration of war in 1914, Ina Claire returned to New York where she originated *The Quaker Girl*, adorned the plays of Maugham, Behrman and Lonsdale, and became America's most brilliant comedienne of this century.

Nellie Taylor, who had played *Betty* in Birmingham, came to London and she, too, developed a plaintive attraction which gained her a devoted following. She somehow brought out the innate gallantry of the young London bloods, and when later, in a revue, she sang 'The Blue Boy Blues' in a Gainsborough suit, they all wanted to love, honour and cherish her till death. It was, however, Herbert Buckmaster, the former husband of Gladys Cooper, who married this appealing little creature with the features of an eighteenth-century doll, who named a flower shop after her. This delicate little sprite expired at a dreadfully youthful age.

Gladys Cooper had been, in the minor capacity of Sadie Van Tromp, an added adornment to Lily Elsie and *The Dollar Princess* cast. Soon she became, together with Ivy Close, the wife of the photographer Elwin Neame, the greatest picture postcard beauty of the lot. Her popularity even outclassed that of Gabrielle Ray, Zena and Phyllis Dare, Julia James, or Gertie Millar. And not only on postcards was her long, wavy, fair silken hair, her peach-blossom pink-and-whiteness, her bold almond-shaped nostrils, and 'sugar cushion' lips, seen in every household, but also on the mud walls of the dug-outs in Flanders.

Gabrielle Ray, a very high favourite in the 'Picture Postcard Stakes', was a high-kicking dancer with a squeaky voice and an aura of Marie Laurençin prettiness. But the effect she created was of her own making. Lily Elsie used to marvel at the stage make-up that 'Gabs' Ray invented where she made of her face a *pointilliste* painting with little dots of all colours to give highlights and shadows to eyes, nose, cheeks and chin. Likewise, she was a forerunner of today's 'sun streak' hair-dyeing by choosing clusters of curls of slightly varying colours. But perhaps her greatest innovation was to arrange that her photographer should stretch an invisible thread of cotton in front of his sitter so that she could rest the tip of her small parrot's beak nose on it, thus pioneering, in her impromptu manner, the days of plastic surgery.

Both 'Gabs' Ray and Julia James were surrounded by ambiguous auras of off-stage romantic activities which only added to the fervour of their public. Julia James, with her russet silk hair and huge hare's eyes and a flair for 'artistic' self-adornment, was at her popular peak in the First World War. It was widely known that she was the simultaneous favourite of Lloyd George and Admiral Beatty.

Gertie Millar, who had started life as a Lancashire mill girl, became a great favourite at the Gaiety. Critics and audiences alike were bewitched by her Pekinese piquancy and her 'lighter than air' dancing. Gradually she migrated to the Palace for *Bric-à-Brac*, one of the best wartime revues; but when she became too plump for the stage, she settled for the family emeralds and a cosy marriage to the Earl of Dudley.

Even when at Daly's, Gladys Cooper was ambitious to become something more than the perfect 'Pear's Soap Beauty'. The rather bossy girl who stood in the wings learning the lines of the rest of the company was determined to teach herself as much as possible about the craft of the theatre, so that she could succeed as an actress. Soon she turned to the non-musical stage and, at one time, was appearing in two plays at neighbouring theatres in the course of one evening. But for many years because of her marvellous classical beauty, Gladys Cooper tended to be regarded just as an embellishment to any cast and it was not until she was given the chance to play many varied roles in *My Lady's Dress*, a melodramatic play by Edward Knobloch, that she revealed her qualities as a capable actress, and a matinée idol.

In 1921, in *The Betrothal* by Maurice Maeterlinck, she appeared as a draped figure, unveiling her face only in the last act. This long-awaited revelation was for all who witnessed it such a supreme moment of beauty that a gasp went through the entire house. For me the emotion was so intense that the memory of it will remain with me until I die. At the St James's Theatre in *The Last of Mrs Cheyney* Gladys gave a performance that was more than a match for her opposite player, Gerald du Maurier. In 1927, she became actress-manager of the Playhouse and enjoyed the happiest phase in her life. Appearing in the company of Charles Hawtrey, Allen Aynesworth, and Dennis Eadie, she produced plays by Pinero, Lonsdale, and Maugham.

When she decided on a revival of *The Second Mrs Tanqueray*, it was a foregone conclusion that the cream-and-roses blonde would be inadequate in the name part that was considered to belong for ever to its creator, the Beardsleyesque Mrs Patrick Campbell. But Gladys decided that she would chalk-whiten her face, darken her stag-like eyes, wet her hair and drag it back into a huge tight chignon. In this startling disguise she had never looked more nobly beautiful; nor had she been acknowledged to possess such profound depths as an actress.

In spite of the fact that the shop windows of Selfridge's store were filled with her likenesses advertising facial cream, Gladys Cooper was oblivious of the effect her appearance had on the public. In private life she was un-interested in the art of self-adornment, but being a true woman of the theatre, she knew the value of having the best designers work on her costumes. When she started to revive earlier plays in the modern idiom, she gave her trust to Edward Molyneux. This choice was a brilliant one, for he knew exactly how she should appear at her most glamorous. Gladys admitted that it was Edward Molyneux who taught her about clothes. In later life she acquired that most rare talent of buying, from the most unlikely places, garments at very small cost which, on her, became *chic* and stylish.

The picture postcard stands continued to revolve and Gladys Cooper remained favourite. She had gained a deserved *réclame* as a forceful actress, and proved at her best in parts worthy of her written by Enid Bagnold or E. M. Forster. Later she became much sought-after for movie and television screens. Even at the time of her death at the age of more than eighty Gladys Cooper's name remained 'a household word'.

The world of English operetta came out of its eclipse with *The Maid of the Mountains*. José Collins was no picture postcard beauty, but her full-throated notes became an anodyne to pain during the terrible years of the First World War. But the days of Daly's were nearly over.

Admittedly the talented and delightful Evelyn Laye adorned its last stages.

She could sing, act within the confines of the medium, and had a stage appearance that resembled beauty. But that most dreadful of all theatre phenomena prevented her from ever being given the true success she deserved – for her the timing was wrong. If she had appeared ten years later or earlier, she would have become the great star that she merited to be. It was many years before, in New York, she appeared in Coward's *Bitter-Sweet* and was acclaimed fully, followed by, of course, the blandishments of Hollywood.

Focus now switched to the largely American musicals at Drury Lane. There the leading lady, the Canadian Edith Day, had a fervid following, for her voice was of an exceptional purity; but the new favourites were mostly those who hardly came in the category of classical beauty. The latest stars to shine were those whose talents and intelligence brought them their fame, and most of them appeared in the new form of 'revue'.

When the American Jewess, Ethel Levey, appeared in *Hello Rag-time!* in 1912 at the Hippodrome she sounded, in her deep *basso profundo* voice, the deathknell of all the pink and white soubrettes who had lingered on so long. Although she could not claim to have picture postcard looks, to me she was of a startlingly exotic beauty. She had, what is surely the ultimate test, an appearance that could not in any way be improved upon. The bold features within the lithe, sensitive framework of her face created an entity. With ram-like profile, her nose a perfect crescent, the raven's wing hair, the violent black eyes, her lascivious mouth suddenly stretching into a wide, catlike grin, she presented quite a new picture to the scene of popular entertainment. Married to the American, George M. Cohan, one of the greatest entertainers Broadway has ever known – dancer, singer and playwright – his brilliance must have been an inspiration to his wife.

The critics called her the 'Sarah Bernhardt of Revue', yet if any woman was her prototype perhaps it was the American Norah Bayes. But instead of blonde voluptuousness, Ethel Levey was a bird-thin creature with a coal-heaver's voice, animalistic high kicks and acrobatic dances. She made her audiences feel that they were in the slipstream of an aeroplane belonging to her second husband, the pioneer aviator, Claude Graham White. With *Hello Tango!* Ethel Levey was established as an English institution, which perhaps in terms of the theatre is another name for matinée idol. She was the first to wear stage costumes – other than for ballet – designed by Léon Bakst, with his predilection for top hats, tricornes, Turkish trousers, fringes, hobble skirts slashed by colour – all worn with her gold bangle on an ankle, it was no wonder that the poet, Rupert Brooke, brought his love, Cathleen Nesbitt to see the revue thirteen times. The impact that Ethel Levey had on me, in terms of style, humour and decorativeness, was my preparation for the Diaghilev ballet and much else of the theatre that I subsequently learnt to love.

Under the brilliant aegis of Charles B. Cochran, Alice Delysia became the next great revue star. Delysia is an artist of impeccable taste. Her voice was exquisitely trained, and she knows all the ways of putting a song across the footlights. Alice Delysia is a big, handsome, large-chinned Frenchwoman. In her blue button eyes there is a twinkle of amusement at the way she over-plays the sex game. When she smiles her upper teeth are seen to be too short, and her features, though strong and effective on stage, are altogether too heavy for the camera so that she could never claim the advantage of being a 'pin-up'; her one attempt at filming in Rider Haggard's *She* was of no lasting consequence. But the theatre-loving bourgeois flocked to see her, and enjoyed the extra *frisson* that they were being subjected to 'glamour' in its most pleasantly Gallic form. They knew she was only pretending to be wicked, was perhaps naughty but was most certainly nice. And they were right: Delysia was, for all her allure and her daring dresses, a jolly good sort. During the two world wars she worked unsparingly – and sometimes in extremely dangerous conditions – to entertain the troops in many remote parts of the world.

Also in revue, and also French, was the lovable Gaby Deslys. Plump, pullet-like Gaby had a pear-shaped nose, cherry lips, and bosoms like early melons, but her sex appeal was not oppressive. Her eyes were sadly smiling, and even the women in the audience loved her for her audacity as she doffed a porcupine hat of osprey and threw it roughly into the wings before performing an acrobatic dance with her partner, Harry Pilcer. Gaby was said to have little stage talent except that, as she said, she could not dance or sing, but she could 'do it'. Gaby Deslys with her famous Royal love affair and yards of pearls which the King of Portugal gave her, her fantastic feathered hats and jewels, was able to cast her spell upon Jean Cocteau who wrote a prose poem about her when, in the tremendous arc lights of the Casino de Paris, she danced *le jazz* for the first time. Another unexpected victim of Gaby's was the pipe-smoking elf from Thrums, James M. Barrie. When Gaby Deslys first called on him in his eyrie in the Adelphi, she won his heart. Out of sheer *joie de vivre*, on leaving him she ran down the many circles of staircases ringing the door bells of each flat as she passed. He was besotted enough to write an entertainment for her, which she graced, named *Rosy Rapture*. But it is said that Gaby's heart – and whose was not? – was touched by the 'gentleman-actor' Basil Hallam. This most adorable 'Gilbert the Filbert' had an attraction that was devastating to all ages and sexes. His voice was husky and small, he was not a good dancer, but he had a charm that endeared him to the whole of the generation that was to be wiped out by the world war. Too delicate of health to be accepted by the Army he continued to appear (with Elsie Jamis) at the Palace, but white feathers drove him to become a balloonist and in a tragic accident he fell from the skies.

Gaby Deslys was the 'queen of glamour', and part of her great prestige was provided by publicity. Her every appearance added excitement to her myth: the crowds waited for her at the stage door and they were never disappointed. They gasped as she appeared clad from head to foot in magenta with a wind-mill of paradise feathers on her head, or dressed entirely in black and white furs, to step into the Rolls-Royce of 'elephants' breath' that awaited her.

She died of cancer of the throat at an early age. Her legacy is to be found not only in some early Paramount films but in theatrical history, for she chipped a niche for herself as a flamboyant personality – the embodiment of frivolity, excess and luxuriousness. Many, with the help of great publicity, organizations, have tried to emulate her, but none has had her original flair.

Beatrice Lillie, who appeared in London's early intimate revues, can be said to be the outstanding female comic genius of the stage in our time. At first her unique humour and subtle fun were only appreciated by a few, but she has elevated the taste of the public to appreciate the most delicate forms of wit and humour. In spite of her penchant in later years for appearing in large scale revues in huge theatres, her subtle effects have never been swamped. Neither were they dimmed in the films she graced, and her performance in *On Approval*, has become a cinema classic. Is it not startling to think that Bea Lillie has, always with the same individual style, represented a lanky spirit of hermaphroditic youthfulness for over a period of fifty years?

With her in the early days of revue was the equally incomparable Gertrude Lawrence. Without a strong voice, without classical beauty, and with only little training, she had everything: 'style, beauty, glamorous charm, gaiety, heart-throb'. At her revue peak in Noël Coward's *London Calling!* she made 'Parisian Pierrot, Society's Hero' into the signature tune of the late Twenties. As a singer of Cole Porter's lyrics no one was her equal. She migrated to the drawing-rooms of comedy. Her length of limb, short, silky brown hair, her shining apricot skin and fruity pout, were all part of an irresistible allure and her voice, both arrogant and full of pathos, gave style to even the tritest phrase. In competition with her even the brilliance of Coward was well-matched. Audiences both sides of the Atlantic vied for her presence, and it is sad that London never saw her in Kurt Weill's *Lady in the Dark*, said by all who saw her in New York to have been the highest point of her career.

As an actress Gertrude Lawrence lacked discipline: this affected some of her later performances when she was prone to over-emphasis. Sometimes she would listen to the advice of the last person who visited her in her dressing room, thereby often ruining many an effect that she had already instinctively perfected. But she was that very rare and wonderful theatre phenomenon – a young person who came from out of nowhere: with no known background and without roots, she intuitively presented an entirely new and original variation to the accepted standards of feminine appeal. With her curdled voice, limited in its range, she was able to suggest the quality of heartbreak, or the sadness of laughter. Her façade could be *mondaine* and *chic*, but you knew her feelings were deep and sincere. Gertrude Lawrence was generous to the point of recklessness, and it was only to be expected that New York managements should take advantage of her. But when they stuck knives in her back she sailed gaily on – even to her early death, which then was vulgarly exploited by those who had shown their disloyalty and venality. The night Gertrude Lawrence died they put out the lights for her on Broadway – but they never succeeded in dimming the brightness of her spirit.

Twenty-Five Years of Leading Ladies (and Gentlemen)

by Vivian Ellis

The Birth and Death of Musical Comedy

THE nowadays despised theatrical art form once known as musical comedy originated with George Edwardes first at the Prince of Wales, then at the Gaiety Theatre, in the Strand. It continued to amuse the public, if not the critics, until comedian Leslie Henson (undoubtedly the reincarnation of a frog) together with the cast of *Running Riot* of which I happened to be the composer, performed the final obsequies at the selfsame theatre due for demolition shortly before the outbreak of the 1939 war.

Since the war this predictable but innocuous form of entertainment, with its melodious misunderstanding at the end of Act I and final reconciliation at the end of Act II, has been superseded by a series of highly efficient American importations. All are remarkable for their vitality and the fact that they are never referred to as musical comedies but as musical plays in which, it is emphasized, the songs arise out of the story.

In musical comedy no one bothered much about the story but the songs went round the world and are still being sung today. In content those musical plays bear a remarkable resemblance to their British predecessors. Book, lyrics and music; hero and heroine; light comedian and soubrette are assisted by a sprightly chorus who no longer have the leisure for conversation during their more strenuous dance routines.

Only three ingredients are missing:

I.   Elegance.

II.   The string section of the orchestras, formerly drowned at matinée performances by the percussive clatter of tea cups.

III.   That indescribable something once known as star quality and now rechristened with that loathsome sobriquet 'charisma'.

This last deficiency is not so much the fault of the artistes but the fact that responsibility for their behaviour, on and off stage, no longer rests with managers such as George Edwardes, Robert Courtneidge, André Charlot and Charles B. Cochran who gradually groomed them for stardom. The advent of television has not only done away with provincial tours where fledgelings could spread their wings, but frequent appearances have destroyed their mystique so that yesterday's *avant-garde* soon becomes tomorrow's *déjà vu*.

The role of the impresario was clearly defined. As Charles B. Cochran observed to me, 'I start with a blank sheet of paper.' (Too often his successors begin by acquiring the reproduction rights.) On this sheet and reams more paper would go the names, addresses and phone numbers of his author, composer, director, designer, choreographer, conductor, each and every member of his cast, staff, wardrobe and current mistress, rehearsal pianist and press agent (especially the latter), all working under his anxious scrutiny and, no doubt, that of his backers.

Lady Cochran was renowned for her wit. During our long association covering a similar period, she told me of a book she had begun but never finished entitled *Twenty-Five Years of Leading Ladies*. By the addition of the words *And Gentlemen* I hope to embellish the picture, realizing that excepting for the inevitable cascade of tears when other forms of female cajolery have failed, the tantrums of a leading lady and a leading man are almost identical. Without these histrionics, let me hasten to add, they would probably be no good at all.

André Charlot and Charles B. Cochran Present . . .

During approximately the second quarter of the present century, two West End managers were outstanding in the realm of revue and musical plays. First, André Charlot who discovered practially everyone with the exception of myself, although I gave him ample opportunity. Jack Buchanan, Beatrice Lillie, Gertrude Lawrence, June – once Gertie's understudy at £4 a week – and Jessie Matthews spring instantly to mind. Then along came Cochran, who would annexe Charlot's artistes, giving them that additional glamour that hung like a golden aureole around what everyone alluded to as a Cochran Show. Cochran may not be credited with as many discoveries apart from the incomparable Alice Delysia, made in France. Nevertheless, it was Cochran, the showman, who was instrumental in bringing over to this country the great international companies of the *Chauve-Souris*, *Blackbirds*, the Guitrys and Eleonora Duse. Making far less noise than Sarah Bernhardt with her *voix d'or* – by then a trifle tarnished – Duse, speaking in Italian with the minimum of gesture and make-up, held at least one youthful member of her audience spelbound during her matinée season at the New Oxford Theatre in 1923.

Charlot did everything on a shoestring. Indeed, in one of his revues featuring Frances Day, the cast were tastefully attired in sacking. Cochran, in contrast, did things in the grand manner and in still better taste. The one extravagance they had in common was a fondness for expensive cigars. Neither were strangers to bankruptcy, but this only served to bring out the unswerving devotion of all with whom they came into contract. For years I worked for Cochran without one. Actresses pledged their jewels and actors played for nothing which they sometimes did in any case. During each lean period Cochran retired to write his reminiscences. Both went to stay with friends in Hollywood. Cochran returned to England before the last war, to arise, phoenix-like, from the rubble of the London blitz to produce his longest run, *Bless the Bride* by A. P. Herbert and myself, after a slow start and a mixed press, ran for 836 performances.

Charlot was an imposing presence, with hornrims and a dry sense of humour. Because, for the one and only occasion, I asked for and received a lump sum instead of a royalty on his 1928 revue which I foresaw would be a flop, he'd allude to me, rather ruefully, as 'Mister Businessman Ellis', a title which, in the case of Charlot, I was justly proud. Everyone called him 'Guv' and his charming wife 'Flip'. As far as I could discover, Charlot, without the assistance of Elsie April who divided her time between him and Cochran, taking down composers' notes (never mine) while making a few of her own, appeared to be tone deaf. Cochran, despite statements to the contrary, had an ear for a tune, then considered an essential ingredient of a musical show. On one occasion, before the onset of the crippling arthritis so bravely borne in later years, Cochran danced to one of my tunes after an audition at Her Majesty's Theatre. It ranks as my favourite stage performance.

The most tragic sight before a musical is a vocal chorus audition. Author, composer and director sit huddled in the stalls, supposedly making notes. Across a darkened stage, lit by a single working light, walks a procession of protracted death. Shivering aspirants force a bright smile while their names are read out by the assistant stage manager, before breaking into the opening bars of Puccini's 'Oh, my Beloved Daddy'. Apart from the impossibility of engaging hundreds of applicants to fill a dozen places as my friend and collaborator Sir Alan Herbert would have wished, there comes that awful moment when, pressed for time, someone interrupts before they've finished. It used to make me cringe. Those who reached the end would be invited to return, when the whole weeding-out process would begin again.

Both Charlot and Cochran were laden with charm. Charlot's was vintage French, with rolled gold R's. 'My dear, I could not possibly afford to pay you the salary I know you are worth but if you'd care to accept . . . ?' And they accepted.

Cochran, who never knew the meaning of the word parsimony, whether with other people's money or his own, would paint so glowing a picture of the opportunities ahead that the listener, like the circus clowns he so admired, would tumble through the outstretched paper hoop. Cochran was tubbier than Charlot, with fair hair worn with a centre parting, a small nose and a rubicund complexion. He was immaculate in dress, wore a monocle with which he made great play and a trilby hat at a jaunty angle. He carried a cane, originally as a stage prop but latterly to lean upon. He'd seldom raise his voice. Instead he'd write the miscreant a long lecture, several of which I still cherish. With a combination of snobbery and showmanship he attributed his birthplace to Lindfield in Sussex, setting of *Bless the Bride*. Actually, he was born in Brighton and his sisters owned a laundry. By dint of constant reading, observation and sheer flair, he not only became Britain's greatest showman but acquired a genuine understanding of the arts – and artistes. He was a trifle short on humour and, like Florenz Ziegfeld, regarded comedians as necessary interludes before the next gorgeous change of scene. I remember A.P.H. and I having to demonstrate a funny song to him behind a bathroom door accompanied by the sound of splashing.

A Cochran first night was also a social occasion; that of *Big Ben* at the Adelphi Theatre in 1946, for instance, created a traffic block in the Strand. In addition to the Prime Minister, Mr Attlee (as he then was), members of the Labour Cabinet starting the fashion for lounge suits, Field Marshal Montgomery and Marina, Duchess of Kent, there was the added attraction of Princess Elizabeth – the present Queen – attending her first night sitting bang in the middle of the stalls with her fiancé Prince Philip, so there was no possibility of the audience being bored by the play. A.P.H. compared them to a well-attended church congregation. A few hours previously Cochran had received a message, purporting to be from the Palace, requesting that the start should be delayed by a quarter of an hour. Realizing its lack of authenticity, the consequent dislocation of the police, the press who had to meet a deadline for the next day's papers, to say nothing of those members of the audience who had last trains to catch, the curtain rose promptly on, as we'd guessed, the Royal Party already seated.

The opening performance of our revue *Streamline* at the Palace Theatre in 1934 fared even worse. Competition for first night tickets, at twice the normal prices, reached an all-time high. It also produced a resentful audience at having to pay so much for the privilege of seeing who had managed to be present. For once, A.P.H. seemed to be wordless. Not so another of my collaborators, Desmond Carter, who penned the poignant couplet:

'If Lady Colefax can't get in,
Then why on earth should I?'

The era of Sibyl Colefax is as dead as the dodo but the explanation of those lines is simple enough. Cochran's audiences, at any rate for the commencement of the run, were mainly drawn from the purlieus of Mayfair and Belgravia. If successful their ripples would spread, as he once said to me when I resided in the locality, to people living in the Finchley Road – the Finchley Road, of course, being a very long road. Today, that audience has vanished from the scene with Joan Clarkson (once a Cochran Young Lady known as the English Rose) and good taste, without the backing of the Arts Council, has become box office poison.

Cochran could blow himself up with success and deflate himself with failure. Then he would complain that his productions had a habit of coinciding with a calamity such as a Royal demise followed, in those days, by a period of strict Court Mourning; a severe illness of either himself or a prominent member of the cast; or a newspaper strike which, being nothing if not a publicist, drove him off the pages. But he always managed to bounce back.

Gaiety Girls

On Thursday, 27 September 1888, at the ramshackle Opera Comique off the Strand (home of the first Gilbert & Sullivan operas) the curtain rose on a comic opera entitled *Carina*. The libretto was the work of E. L. Blanchard of the literary staff of *The Daily Telegraph* and Cunningham Bridgman; the music by my grandmother Julia Woolf, reelected King's Scholar, Associate Member and Fellow of the Royal Academy of Music. *Carina* could and should have been played by Florence St John, comic opera star and according to Cochran and all who heard her the possessor of one of the loveliest voices that ever sung in operetta save, perhaps, that of Yvonne Printemps. Being a friend of the family's, my grandfather, who knew nothing about music, took it upon himself to instruct Florence St John on how to sing, with predictable results. Moral, never row with your leading lady until she is safely under contract.

My mother, as a child, remembered hearing Florence St John at a rehearsal at the Gaiety. She also heard Mrs St John's opinion of her understudy delivered in a Devonian accent. 'That pig-faced boogerr better not show herself on this stage while I'm here!' The understudy in question was Marie Tempest, one of the first if not the last of the matinée idols.

Before witnessing the teacup comedy's final death rattle, Marie Tempest sang the lead in *The Pirates of Penzance* in America as well as in four musical comedies at Daly's Theatre. Given such a training, she was eminently fitted to deal with a younger actress who tried to upstage her: with commendable ingenuity, this young actress overcame the disadvantage of being seated down-stage by altering the position of her chair until the fateful night when she discovered that it had been screwed to the floor. To Dame Marie is attributed that apocryphal remark, 'I always close my eyes when being driven through the suburbs.'

Red corpuscles among the blue. Years after they'd left the stage at a lunch at the Baronness Emile d'Erlanger's I challenged Julia James and the delicious Denise Orme (at that time Lady Churston) to come clean and give me an audition which they proceeded to do, singing 'Widows are Wonderful' and a medley from *Our Miss Gibbs* with such distinction that I quite forgot to take note of their voices. By the time I met the Marchioness of Headfort and the buxom Countess of Dudley at a Gaiety Girl Foyles luncheon in honour of Walter Macqueen-Pope, I found it hard to connect these ladies with Rosie Boote and the glamorous Gertie Millar. But Lily Elsie, silver-haired, cool and elegant, recalled a bunch of Cecil Beaton's parma violets. I did not mention to Lily Elsie the one occasion I'd seen her on the stage, during a comeback in the late Twenties with Bobby Howes in *The Blue Train* at the old Prince of Wales Theatre. On her first entrance she stood at the top of a flight of stairs expecting the applause she must have received at every performance of *The Merry Widow* or *The Dollar Princess*. Nothing happened until, with the experience gained from the non-reception of some of my own songs, I burst into a round of spontaneous hand-clapping taken up by the audience with the alacrity of a sheepdog trial.

Another Gaiety Girl who attempted a comeback, accompanied by a chorus of scowling Tiny Tots, was the winsome Gabrielle Ray. We rehearsed in the empty ballroom of the De Vere Hotel lined, for some extraordinary reason, by a row of empty champagne bottles. She struck me as a shy, bemused lady, surprisingly tall and with a surprisingly small voice. At one time Gabrielle Ray made a pretty penny from the sale of her postcards. I have one of her masti-cating a piece of mistletoe as well as one of Violet Loraine, later Lady Joicey, whose joy was hearing a quartette render 'A Japanese Sandman' at Tilly's Tearoom in Newcastle. The singer of 'If You Were the Only Girl in the World' chose to return in the ill-fated revue *Fanfare* in 1932 at the newly-opened Prince Edward Theatre, now the London Casino. I was involved in the composition of the song with which she stopped the show – always a bad sign for the show – entitled, optimistically as it turned out, 'Dreams that Don't Grow Old'.

Why do they do it? In stately home or semi-detached, the retired musical comedy artiste hears the siren voice of the call boy crying 'Overture and Beginners' and is utterly lost. Take away an actress's food and she'll survive.

Take away her audience's applause and in theatrical parlance, she'll die the death.

'In her Oriental splendour she is a peak in a chain of hillocks.' No description of José Collins could equal that, not even Binnie Hale's devastating impersonation in André Charlot's revue *Puppets* at the Vaudeville Theatre with her opening remark, 'I *am* the Mountain.'

Born in Whitechapel in 1887, José was the illegitimate daughter of Lottie Collins of 'Ta-ra-ra-Boom-de-aye' fame and Joseph Van den Berg. Much emphasis was placed on her Spanish antecedents, which suited her stage roles and suited José. Off-stage she was short, with tiny hands and feet despite a tendency towards what the Navy would describe as top-hamper. On stage she seemed to grow in stature until she dominated every scene but by the time she arrived at the Gaiety in 1922, each had seen better days. Whether as the Countess Vera Lizavetta in *The Last Waltz* with a score by Oscar Straus; *Catherine* (Tchaikovsky and a sprained ankle); or *Our Nell* in a golden wig subsequently discarded for her own raven hair, she was José, 'whom the crowd worships and can do no wrong'. At one time José was autographing 3000 postcards a week.

I was still at school in 1917 when *The Maid of the Mountains* was first seen at Daly's Theatre where it ran for 1352 performances. It would have run longer if José hadn't tired of her role, just as Cochran tired of *Bless the Bride*. In the theatre it is a mistake to withdraw a success. One never knows when it may happen again. Apart from José, *The Maid* was remarkable for its score, although few may know, or care, that the melody of the first four bars of the waltz song 'Love can Find a Way', is the first two bars of the waltz from *The Merry Widow* excepting that in the case of *The Maid* each note is played twice. Why, in the recent revival at the Palace Theatre, it was deemed necessary to interpolate songs from two other shows, I shall never understand. I sat through this performance hearing in my head those unforgettable songs as only José could render them when, during a blissful week shortly after the knell of *Our Nell*, I was her temporary accompanist in her Variety act at the Bristol Hippodrome.

As soon as the number of her turn was flashed on either side of the stage the orchestra would strike up the famous waltz, drowned by the cheers of the audience. Up went the curtain and down came José resplendent in her Reville dress with a long, long V, trailing clouds of tulle, wearing a triple row of pearls and waving an enormous ostrich feather fan. The whole scintillating effect was sheer stagecraft. There was that voice production that no amount of training could ruin, her experience as a leading lady at fourteen; singing *Fledermaus* in New York, singing 'Just a Little Love, a Little Kiss' for the Ziegfeld Follies at the New Amsterdam Theatre; singing for six years at Daly's, two at the Gaiety and goodness knows how many music hall dates between. To last out that amount of time a voice needs constant cultivation.

Never mind the scenes, the tears and the tantrums. (Her first husband, the late Lord Robert Innes-Ker, must have had some anxious moments.) Never mind the language on the night poor José was stuck in the Gaiety lift and missed her entrance. (They had to ring down the curtain.) Never mind the extravagance, the champagne parties in the dressing room, the eight fur coats, the hats and dresses that would be torn off and handed to anyone who admired them. Never mind those unfulfilled promises to sing 'my wonderful music', nor the occasions when some of us wondered whether José would be 'all right'. All would be redeemed from the moment she opened her mouth, emitting a string of notes as carefully graded as her own precious pearls.

José Collins was everyone's idea of how a musical comedy actress should look and behave. And sing. Let us leave her in Bristol, taking her innumerable curtain calls and then, with a typically flamboyant gesture, leading forward her accompanist to share them while murmuring, between smiles and bows to the audience, 'I hope it's fish and chips for supper tonight.' More bows. 'And pickled onions.'

Evelyn Laye, C.B.E., or Nothing Like a Dame. Why this great-hearted, gorgeous-looking creature has been kept waiting in the wings until recently while other members of her profession have had honours showered upon them, is quite beyond my comprehension. Her work for the Royal Navy during the last war which I saw at first hand as Command Entertainments officer deserves recognition even if she'd never been a star of the first magnitude.

From the age of 19 when, chaperoned by her parents, she played Ada Reeve's original part in the 1920 revival of *The Shop Girl* at the Gaiety, Boo Laye has been a star. Star at Daly's in *Madame Pompadour* (it took months of practice to acquire that French accent and years to lose it); star of Noël Coward's *Bitter-Sweet* where she made a furore in New York and later over here, as well as innumerable other Cochran shows. In the title role of *Helen* her face would have launched a thousand ships without the slightest difficulty but, as I afterwards pointed out, her bone structure would last a lifetime, which it has.

Although we've never been associated professionally, (if one discounts our joint appearance accompanied by a choir of 300 naval ratings at an Albert Hall concert in aid of King George's Fund for Sailors) our paths crossed when Boo entertained the Navy during the Plymouth Blitz. She gave the right impression and did all the right things, insisting on visiting the Petty Officer's Mess prior to that of the high-ups until – alone at last – she said to me, 'And now may I unpin my face?'

Boo Laye hasn't always had cause to smile. In her stage career she's touched both the heights and depths. Admittedly, she's made her mistakes but who hasn't? After years of stardom she agreed to audition for *The King and I* at Drury Lane, scene of her former triumph in *The New Moon*. It was then that she heard the actress's death knell: 'Thank you, Miss Laye, we'll let you know.'

At fifty, if you're a star, this isn't fun. Shortly afterwards, she was again on top of the world, co-starring with Anton Walbrook in *Wedding in Paris* at the London Hippodrome.

In her private life she has known both happiness and grief when she lost her second husband, Frank Lawton, after a long illness during which she nursed him with utter devotion while struggling never to let her public down. If any-one would qualify for that much-abused description, the actress with a heart of gold, I'd nominate Evelyn Laye.

Entente Cordiale

There is something irresistible about a French accent, as Yvonne Arnaud knew. The longer she remained in England, the stronger it became. To Cochran, it was a magnet. Top of his list of Parisian imports I'd place Alice Delysia. It might appear ungallant to state her age, (84 – plus all her own teeth), had she not already done so in a recent broadcast on BBC's *Desert Island Discs*. Starting her career as a *midinette* – and what better a start for a little girl with her way to make in the world – she soon became a collector's piece, a saucy French actress who really could act, sing and dance. That is how Cochran first discovered her in Paris. In addition, she is fond of cooking and kind to strangers.

In 1925, I'd managed to get a song into *Still Dancing*, sequel to *On with the Dance*, after one of Cochran's little tiffs with Noël Coward. It introduced Alice in one of those sequined backless dresses (she has a beautiful back) that had previously shocked the Lord Chamberlain in Cochran's production of *As You Were* in 1918. 'Poppy' wasn't a very good song but Arthur Wimperis's lyric had two lines that went:

> 'Poppy's a popular person
> Poppy's a Peach – and a Pearl',

much improved by Delysia's pronunciation of 'Poppy's a Pitch – and a Pearl'.

In those days I was terrified of stage stars. Binnie Hale and Cicely Court-neidge frightened the daylights out of me but Delysia took me, a gawky un-known, shopping with her in the Berwick Market. Since then many actresses have taken me shopping but none so economically as Alice.

During Delysia's Second World War appearances in the 1940s, her stage was the desert and her backcloth the stars when not obscured by a sandstorm. To me, the spectacle of this by now mature but indomitable French actress, tramping all over North Africa and elsewhere singing 'If you Could Care for Me' to an audience of sex-starved combat troops, is the personification of

Marianne. Following the liberation of France, Alice joined the marchers down the Champs-Elysées. No wonder she was honoured by the French and British Governments for services so fearlessly rendered.

After the war I was in Paris with the Cochrans, searching for a male lead for *Bless the Bride.* Into our sitting room at the Hotel Scribe swept Alice. Proudly she introduced her husband, Capitaine René Kolb-Bernard, DSC and *Agent Consulaire* for France. Then they whisked me away to a *boîte* in a cellar to hear some dreadful *diseuse* sing at five hundred revolutions to the minute. How infinitely better Alice could have done the job herself!

On the last day of our stay in Paris when our hopes, francs and supplies of eligible actors were running out, Cochran and I found what we were looking for. I've already stated that leading men are almost as much trouble – and not nearly so much fun – as leading ladies. Georges Guétary is the exception. Never have I encountered a more conscientious worker. Like the other actors we'd seen, Georges could hardly speak English but by the time rehearsals were due to begin, he was practically word perfect. Being Greek helped. Greeks can master any language, including their own. Georges is what the French would term '*sérieux*'. He could have become a serious artiste had the money been equally serious. He'd render Brahms *lieder* as effortlessly as 'Ma Belle Marguerite' which originally he didn't want to sing because artistes aren't always the best judges of their material. On the first night of *Bless the Bride* it held up the show. Moreover, Georges was grateful and gratitude in our profession, as Cochran said, is a bonus.

Mention of Georges reminds me of Lizbeth Webb, 'discovered' by Cochran in the presence of the press at an audition at the Stoll Theatre on the site of the Royalty in Kingsway. Actually, she'd already been discovered when she arrived in Cochran's Bond Street office, with an introduction from Geraldo, for whom she's been a crooner. At the advanced age of nineteen, Liz took over the lead in *Big Ben*, outwardly without a tremor. As Lucy, heroine of *Bless the Bride*, she was a combination of luscious voice, figure and a beguiling air of innocence. In true Cochran tradition she is now also known as Lady Campbell.

Cochran used to tell me how he'd first seen Yvonne Printemps as a *figurante* at *Les Folies-Bergère* appearing as '*Le fils de Sacha Guitry*'. Sacha saw her from a box and subsequently married her. There were at least three Guitrys; Lucien the father, Sacha his son and Yvonne, Sacha's wife until she left him. They held a unique place in the French theatre, writing and acting in their own and other people's plays, as well as in London after Cochran brought them over.

Yvonne wouldn't describe herself as a great beauty. She had enormous eyes, the most expressive hands and a God-given instrument in her larynx. To preserve this gift she ate and drank sparingly, refused party invitations and would panic at the onset of hoarseness. Her turned-up nose acted as a sounding board and she sang like a bird.

Back again at the Gaiety, I can recall Yvonne dressed as the youthful Mozart, vocalizing that long-drawn-out penultimate note accompanied by the exquisite music of Reynaldo Hahn. Then, in 1934, Yvonne singing what in my opinion remains one of Noël Coward's loveliest songs, 'I'll Follow my Secret Heart' in *Conversation Piece* at His Majesty's Theatre. From my own experience I knew that although Yvonne might be speaking her part in English she was thinking in French. Off stage, I'd say something to her in English, to which she'd reply in her mother tongue and weakly (and who wouldn't be weak with Yvonne) I'd acquiesce.

Finally there came that fateful evening in December 1936, when I realized a lifelong ambition to hear Yvonne sing one of my own songs in a play by Ben Travers entitled *O, Mistress Mine* at the St James's Theatre. By a most unfortunate coincidence, the play bore a resemblance to the real-life drama being enacted by our late King Edward VIII at the time of his abdication and was foredoomed to failure. 'When a Woman Smiles', specially written for Yvonne, was technically difficult to sing. The only English singer I heard tackle it successfully was Vanessa Lee, now Lady Graves.

Afterwards, Yvonne sang it to me (unaccompanied on this occasion) in a blacked-out bistro near the Théâtre de la Michodière where she was acting with her present husband, Pierre Fresnay, in Marcel Achard's *Auprès de ma Blonde*. Fresnay, one of France's foremost actors, has since scored yet another success in Roussin's *La Claque* – all about a composer who slaps the face of a critic – a thought, I must admit, that hadn't occurred to me. Fresnay speaks perfect English but, *hélas*, has never succeeded in imparting it to his wife.

In all the years I've known her, I've yet to see Yvonne in anything but artificial light, even in my own home where she grew ecstatic about our *bidet*, then something of an innovation in this country. In her beautiful French she exclaimed '*Ah – un bidet!*' Well, she could hardly have been expected to know the English translation for *that*.

Jack Buchanan and Anna Neagle

In 1931, shortly before the ides of March, there arrived at the London Hippodrome an entertainment entitled *Stand Up and Sing* of which I was credited as being part composer – my part being the equivalent of the hind legs of a stage donkey. When, prior to its production, I was informed that my contribution was to consist of five songs, none of them to be sung by Jack Buchanan, I asked to be released from my contract. Fortunately for me as it turned out, my request was refused. Of the six shows I was engaged upon at the time, all of them on a royalty basis, *Stand Up and Sing* easily outran the rest.

The only thing I recall about this show was a haunting song by the American composer Phil Charig, 'There's Always Tomorrow', wherein a young woman with a face like a flower was given a brief opportunity to shine. I recognized her as Marjorie Robertson who did a sword dance in one of Cochran's Trocadero cabarets but on the programme she was billed as Anna Neagle. With that uncanny premonition that has served me so well in the theatre and so ill on the Stock Markets, I've always regarded Anna's stage and screen performances as those of a predestined Dame.

·Our next contact was at a naval base during the 1939 war when Anna appeared in an ENSA show devised and compèred by her film director husband, Herbert Wilcox, on which a naval rating commented 'Last night I saw Anna Neagle playing at Queen Victoria.' Perhaps her best performance was given when she wasn't playing at anything, while touring the naval hospital wards. With her sincerity and lack of affectation she established an instant rapport with the patients, never batting an eyelid at the sights that met her gaze and unhampered by the stilted dialogue of some of her films.

For one of them, *Piccadilly Incident*, I wrote some music that was so incidental when shown that I had difficulty in recognizing it, just as I had with Anna's voice during the preliminary try-out of *Charlie Girl* whose story – but not the music – reminded me of *Mister Cinders*. Owing to some mechanical fault with the mike, poor Anna's voice seemed to be emanating from her chest. Notwithstanding these and other private misfortunes I maintain that it was Dame Anna the draw, the consistent performer and seasoned trouper who was never 'off' except for holidays for over 2,000 performances, who was mainly responsible for the show's success.

Despite my denigration as a composer, there was never any friction between Jack Buchanan and myself because I seldom saw him. When I did, he'd be seated in his dressing room surrounded by silent gallery girls. These girls were quite a feature of the London theatre at the time and could help make or mar a star. They'd run after Carl Brisson, dimpled ex-boxing champion of Denmark, who played Danilo to Evelyn Laye's Sonia in a revival of *The Merry Widow* at Daly's in 1923. Coventry Street would echo to voices calling out 'Carl Brisson is coming, Carl Brisson is coming!' Whether they emanated from members of the gallery or his own entourage, I didn't wait to see.

In Jack Buchanan's dressing room not a voice was heard, and if there were any funeral notes they weren't mine. Nobody uttered. The girls were too overcome; Jack, exuding sex appeal, would be thinking out a new piece of stage business (his mind rarely strayed beyond the stage-door) and I'd be too embarrassed. Practically every one of his leading ladies was infatuated with him, not surprisingly. No man on the musical stage could wear clothes like Jack; no voice – and I've heard far better voices – could recapture his exclusive timbre and no one could have behaved more generously when we were once more associated after the last war and he pretended to have forgotten the whole incident.

Fifteen years is a long time for any composer to wait to hear his song sung but in the case of Jack Buchanan it was well worth it. With only a shimmering curtain to cover a scene change, he strolled on to the stage of the Prince of Wales Theatre singing to a hushed house what the critic of *The Times* described as 'a wistful plea for the liberation of London where the rule of fashion was still remembered and gay young noodles would sally forth on a fine spring morning to get themselves measured for a gold cigarette case, and the revues which Mr Buchanan led still sported with the airs and graces of the golden age'. Sad to relate, my song was banned by Auntie BBC before she'd had her hormone treatment, as being 'too controversial'.

My last memory of Jack Buchanan is seated in his office (naturally above a theatre); trilby hat tilted forward to disguise his thinning hair; perfectly shod feet on the desk next to that gold cigarette case and that inimitable cracked voice with its Scottish overtones saying, 'Well, old boy?'

Jack Hulbert and Cicely Courtneidge

This is the tale of a stage-struck Cambridge undergraduate who met and married the daughter of producer Robert Courtneidge and with a wave of his magic wand (done in slow motion) transformed a dainty soubrette into a great comedienne.

No comedienne over the years has given me more pleasure – and greater aggro – than Cis, and her husband Jack Hulbert. With my nose to the grindstone and feet fastened to the treadmill they made me work – an anathema – as only they were capable of working in order to achieve those seemingly effortless effects in a series of revues and musical plays covering a period of twenty years. When, after that, they went 'straight', I must admit to a sense of relief. Hypnotized by Jack's charm and Cis's blandishments I'd find myself back on the job, the treadmill hidden from view, happy at the thought – in the words of one of our songs – of being 'Together Again'.

I've a signed photograph of Jack Hulbert dated 1925 and inscribed 'To Vivian Ellis' (we were very formal at first) 'with Great Expectations.' Whether these expectations were ultimately fulfilled is not for me to say. But in a broadcast in 1972 Dame Cicely – for once omitting to rap me across the knuckles – mentioned that I'd written the hit song of one of her shows, thoughtfully given to Bobby Howes to sing just before she had to make an entrance. The song was 'She's My Lovely' which I hereby affectionately dedicate to her.

With the disarming candour that has characterized our relations, Cis has since confessed that her first impressions of me were far from favourable. She described me, with perfect accuracy, as spotty, tongue-tied, and in need of a haircut.

With equal verisimilitude I informed her that she is at her funniest when she 'dresses up'. Where she assembled her remarkable stage wardrobe is her secret, but those who saw them as I did in my capacity of composer and later lyric writer, are unlikely to forget Cicely's schoolboy kept in during a cricket match by form-master Jack in *By The Way;* Cis's village postmistress in *The House that Jack Built;* her respectable spinster trapped in a low French dive in *Folly To Be Wise;* her ultra-refined barmaid in *Hide & Seek* singing

> 'Maybelle, Maybelle,
> I'm both willing and abelle'

and the pair of them as a retired Anglo-Indian couple in *Under Your Hat*, with Cis declaiming 'The Empire Depends on You'. This was at the time of Munich and under the erroneous impression that the Empire was depending upon me, I cut a rehearsal and without consulting the Hulberts gave an audition at what the late George Black Senior designated as the Admirality. There a gold-braided gentleman informed me, just like the stage, that my services would not be required but they'd make a note of my name, which indeed they did. To be perfectly frank – a certain prelude to criticism – I found the Naval night watches less fatiguing than those of the Hulberts.

Displaying that hallmark of all true comedians, they were in deadly earnest about their work, on and off the stage. Night after night during their preliminary tours 'prior to London production', they'd hold midnight conferences in their hotel sitting room following supper after the show. I was unlucky, inasmuch as music came last on the agenda, by which time – longing to go to bed and already attired in pyjamas and dressing gown – their composer had to be aroused from slumber. I will not revive memories of those prolonged dress rehearsals, only exceeded by Cochran's and terminated by the arrival of the first night audience, because in my experience a smooth dress rehearsal has inevitably presaged a total disaster.

Jack Hulbert, unlike Jack Buchanan, has many outside interests ranging from geology to gardening. At their famous Christmas parties (where surely their daughter Pamela must have held a world record for the longevity of her belief in Santa Claus) Jack would give an off stage performance in full regalia. His arrival would be accompanied by sound effects and mounting excitement from Cicely, acting her head off for the benefit of the younger members of their family. Then Jack would climb down from the roof, covered with artificial snow and the debris from a few loosened tiles.

On Christmas Eves the shows would be played at breakneck speed in order that Cis, the actress, should rush home and complete her metamorphosis into Cis, the hostess. As meticulous in her home as on the stage, the hostess would be in a state of physical collapse by the time the party was due to start. So much nonsense has been written about the proverbial generosity of stage people that I hesitate to add to it. But at the Hulberts' Christmas parties nobody went short of a carefully chosen present and everyone was introduced. How often, on these occasions, the outsiders are left in one corner while the pros gather in another in order to talk shop.

One of my worst experiences was at Sophie Tucker's birthday party at the Kit-Kat Club. Not aware of that old Broadway custom of calling upon one's guests to sing for their suppers, Jessie Matthews was hauled on to the dance floor; Clarice Mayne footed it to the nearest door but poor Cis – no extempore artiste at the best of times – remained rooted to our floodlit table, unable to locate her shoes.

Dear Jack, the rehearsal demon king, who's a much better actor than most people realize; and dearest Cis (and let's cut 'Vitality' for this matinée performance) who taught me – among other things – the difference between the written and spoken word; I salute you, both in moments of triumph and adversity, for your mutual devotion – on and off stage – throughout the years.

June

'*You* and *I* remember that day of our meeting half way up those stairs in Poland Street and I shall always be grateful to you for writing one of my *loveliest* songs and feel happy that it led you on to such success.

Bless you – and thank you for 'Little Boy Blues' *and* for coming to my party yesterday – I kept looking for you and suddenly saw you – then the evening was complete!'

This inscription on the fly-leaf of June's autobiography refers to an incident in 1927 when June was rehearsing for one of the few Hulbert shows they hadn't invited me to compose. Under my arm (and I nearly wrote Under Your Hat) was the manuscript of a song specially written for her that I'd been told she'd rejected. In the theatre it is a mistake to believe all one hears, especially when I'd already been successfully associated with June in a song from *Mercenary Mary* called 'Over My Shoulder'.

I said to her 'I hear you turned this down.' Peering at the manuscript with those limpid myopic eyes (off stage she wore reading glasses and she read constantly), she replied 'I've never even heard it. Play it for me.' So in that dusty and deserted rehearsal room during the lunch break, my song 'Little Boy Blues' was started on its way to being one of the hits of *Clowns in Clover*.

A composer's relations with an artiste are comparable, or should be, with a love affair. With some there's that mutual spark; with others mutual distrust. Neither my music nor June's interpretation of it were assertive; each complemented the other. (The Hulberts would complain, with justification, that in order to hear me play they had to put their heads inside the piano.) For myself when young, June possessed a magic that must once have been Lily Elsie's. By all accounts Edith Day had it when she first appeared in London in *Irene*, recently revived on Broadway. Likewise another Day, Frances, a platinum blondeshell who rocketed through four of my shows during the thirties and with whom I often rehearsed at her launching pad. The one thing that matters on the musical stage is personality. If proficiency in singing, dancing and, as an afterthought, acting were all, the star system would have vanished long ago. When June, for instance, made her first stage entrance, starry-eyed, hands on one hip and shoulder raised in a characteristic pose that had inspired one of my earliest compositions, you could have heard one of her diamond pins drop.

June would be the last to claim that her success was due to her voice that critic James Agate once compared to the twittering of half-awakened birds. But this 'bird' was exceedingly wide awake. Her voice, admittedly small in volume, was true; her diction (and often her gaze) would travel to Marie Lloyd's boy up in the gallery, unassisted by amplification. Her dancing was of so high an order that had she continued with Pavlova instead of more lucrative engagements she might have become a great ballerina. In excuse – and this may sound as corny as it is creditable – much of her salary went towards helping out at home. All the same, she didn't do too badly. Each time we met she seemed to be wearing an additional diamond bracelet.

June's career can be divided roughly into three acts. (I regret being too late for the prologue). Act One, set in the Twenties and ending with a peal of wedding bells on her marriage in 1929 to the late Lord Inverclyde whom I first met in her dressing room. It depicts June the dancer; the girl who danced with the (then) Prince of Wales; the sawdust doll being thrown about the London Pavilion stage by Clifton Webb in 'Whose Baby are You?' from Cochran's *Fun of the Fayre;* sedate leading lady for Jack Buchanan who proceeded to lead her up the garden path; or floating across the vast stage of the London Hippodrome in *Mercenary Mary*.

Act Two takes place in the Thirties, following a sensational stage comeback in 1932 which lasted until her second marriage to California-based Eddie Hillman in 1937. June, still on her points, in my hatshop ballet choreographed by Frederick Ashton in a Charlot show at the Vaudeville Theatre. Ever a watcher on the sidelines, enters June the mimic, or Bergner without tears.

And lastly Act Three in 1960 at her party, which is where we came in. Centre stage is June, the Beaverbrook journalist and author of a stage autobiography that actually wasn't ghosted. June, with her undyed hair and still incredible figure wearing one of those indispensable little black dresses and the only musical comedy necklace extant that wasn't about to be stolen. I asked her whether she thought she might have repeated her success if she'd started her stage career today? Her answer was a definite 'No' and I'm inclined to agree.

June was a product of her time, even as to her name, shingled by Cochran from June Howard-Tripp. Hers was an era belonging to the heyday of P. G. Wodehouse and the Bright Young Things, Skindles and Le Touquet; the Who's-for-Tennis? set; the Embassy Club crowd foxtrotting to the sweet music of Bert Ambrose's band; those Years of Grace and favours; of weekend country house parties with ladies' maids and gentlemen's relish. Where has all the glamour gone?

It's a mistake to be the last to leave a party. Let us make an exit before the curtain falls.

Jack, Bobby and Ivor

by Sandy Wilson

'Or else a dreary matinée' – thus complains Beatrice Lillie in a Noël Coward song about a blasé lady of the Thirties. For myself, a far from blasé schoolboy of the Thirties, matinées were never dreary, although I did prefer to go, if possible, to an evening performance because it felt more 'grown-up'; but any opportunity to visit the theatre was welcome, for once term had begun it became a forbidden pleasure and at my school at any rate a subject hardly fit for decent chaps to discuss.

Perhaps it was her awareness of this that prompted my mother to sweeten the pill of returning to school by taking me to a matinée on the last day of the holidays, which meant our setting out before lunch, me dressed in the regulation costume of grey tweed suit, Eton collar and grey tweed cap, carrying what was known as a 'first-night case,' containing pyjamas and a 'spongebag', which in turn contained not a sponge but a face-flannel, a tooth-brush and a tube of Gibbs' Dentifrice. Thus prepared, we would proceed by underground to the theatre of our choice and reserve, for sixpence each, two stools in the gallery queue, and then repair to the Coventry Street Corner House for lunch, either in the first floor marble restaurant, the mezzanine Old Vienna or, if we were feeling adventurous, in the newly opened brasserie in the basement, where a *Tzigane* orchestra accompanied the clatter of cutlery. Returning to the theatre at one-thirty we would occupy our stools and be diverted for a while by the 'buskers', street entertainers who sang, gave recitations or performed tricks such as tearing up a sheet of newspaper and unfolding it to reveal an intricate pattern or a row of chorus girls. Usually the mysterious 'Long-Haired Man' who visited every queue in the West End, would stride swiftly past with his furled umbrella, pursued by jeering street-urchins, and then at two o'clock the box-office opened and we would buy our tickets and make the long ascent by stone staircase to the gallery. At last we were inside the theatre, with the murmur of voices from below as the stalls and circle filled up. We passed the time remaining before the curtain rose by reading and re-reading the programme, and some theatres at that time sold a 'Magazine Programme' which thoughtfully included a Theatre Quiz to enliven the waiting.

Finally at the appointed time, or shortly afterwards, the house lights were lowered and the show began.

Much as I savoured every moment of them at the time, I am afraid that I can remember very little about the shows that we saw at those end-of-the-holidays matinées. There was *Blackbirds of 1934* at the Coliseum, starring a lady trumpeter called Valaida. There was *Viceroy Sarah*, a play about the Duchess of Marlborough and her fateful friendship with Queen Anne. And there was – a strange choice – Nancy Price in Zola's *Thérèse Raquin*, being paralysed with horror at hearing of her son's murder and eventually managing to trace the guilty name in the dust. And then there was – and now at last I introduce my first matinée idol – *Mr Whittington*, a musical comedy at the Hippodrome, the star of which was Jack Buchanan.

I would like to be able to say that it was I who chose, or rather demanded, to see *Mr Whittington*, because of my already burgeoning fascination with the musical. In fact it was almost certainly my mother's decision, and so far was I at the time from being fascinated with the musical that I would probably have preferred a play. But Jack Buchanan had a special place not only in my mother's heart but in the heart of almost every woman between the age of eighteen and eighty-five who had ever seen him on the stage. My mother would excuse her admiration by explaining that he came from a 'perfectly ordinary' family in Helensburgh (my father came from a fairly ordinary family in Stirling) and had worked his way up from nothing. But what really appealed to her, and to all his other female admirers, was that Jack Buchanan was well known to be secretly fighting a losing battle against tuberculosis – or 'TB' as it was referred to, in hushed tones – and that of course was the reason why he would never marry. To make the whole thing more poignant, Elsie Randolph, who usually played opposite him, was also well-known to be secretly in love with him but of course quite unaware of his approaching demise. So every woman in the audience, while outwardly laughing and applauding, would be inwardly choking back a sob. What more cast-iron formula could there be for success? I never discovered when, if ever, since Mr Buchanan persisted in remaining alive until well over the age of sixty, this romantic illusion was dispelled and what effect it had on his popularity. Perhaps it was lucky for him that the war intervened and impending death rapidly lost its sentimental attraction.

Jack Buchanan was unusual for a funny man in that he was strikingly, almost extravagantly, handsome: tall, slim, with glossy black hair and finely moulded features, the word 'debonair' might have been invented to describe him. 'He is the model of the new comedians,' said St John Ervine in his review of *That's a Good Girl*, 'the happy, handsome, well-dressed sort who contrast so startlingly with the old-fashioned, red-nosed, ugly, ill-dressed and incredibly vulgar sort.' His elegance was legendary and never deserted him, no matter how undignified the situations in which the plot landed him. 'He was so immaculate,' says Elsie Randolph, 'it made *me* fastidious about people.' He also possessed, *par excellence*, the ability to make all he did seem easy, a casual event in which he invited you to participate at your leisure.

The shows he appeared in were, like his clothes, tailor-made and, with the odd exception, ran very much to form. As in most musical comedies of the Twenties and Thirties, the plots revolved round the search for money or its equivalent in the shape of stolen jewellery, mislaid documents or a runaway heiress. This necessitated rapid and arbitrary journeys to various locales: the south of France in *That's a Good Girl*, Egypt in *Stand Up and Sing* and Epsom in *Mr Whittington* (where the Derby was run onstage, with real horses). While the setting might vary, the character Buchanan played hardly did. 'It had to be the same part in every show,' Elsie Randolph recalls. 'They expected it. He could be called Dick or Bill or even Jack. I've called him Jack onstage by mistake.' The plot of *Stand Up and Sing* is characteristic, as described in *Theatre World*: 'He appears as one Rockingham Smith, a gentleman of leisure, who . . . is engaged as valet to Count Maxim Dupont, and accompanies that unscrupulous person to Cairo, where there is much ado about certain concessions involving that legendary fruit of human delight, the banana.' 'We always had an ingénue,' says Miss Randolph, 'and sometimes she was the girl Jack ended up with.' In this instance she was called Lady Mary Clyde-Burkin and was played by Anna Neagle. Also on hand, as a princess, was Vera Pearce, an actress of majestic proportions but astonishing agility. 'There was a scene where "Rocky" and the princess, under the influence of a potent drug, exchange amorous pleasantries and indulge in a duet and dance entitled "Hiccup Time in Burgundy".' 'Was there a plot?' asked James Agate rhetorically. 'Not that you minded. Was there music? Not to annoy anybody. Was the show a "wow"? Overwhelmingly so.'

Earlier on in his career Jack Buchanan had also made a success in New York in *André Charlot's London Revue of 1924*. He was a little overshadowed by his co-stars, Beatrice Lillie and Gertrude Lawrence, the *New York Times* merely referring to him as 'a lengthy gentleman with an amiable stage presence and first-rate dancing ability, but hardly remarkable otherwise.' But when they all returned the following year in a new edition, he received equal acclaim: 'When the principals walked onto the stage . . . each was greeted in turn for a few moments while the music stopped.' And when he appeared again in Cochran's *Wake Up and Dream*, the *New York Times* was unrestrained in its praise of 'the dainty, wry touch of comedy which only Jack Buchanan can supply'.

But it was in England that he achieved his greatest popularity, particularly in partnership with Elsie Randolph. He had spotted her at the Queen's Hall roof cabaret in 1923 and invited her to join the cast of *Battling Butler* in a couple of small roles. She graduated to understudying one of the leads and after playing the part successfully was rewarded with third billing in his next musical *Toni*, in which the leading lady was June. Next came Jerome Kern's *Sunny*, in which she co-starred with Buchanan and Binnie Hale, and finally in 1928 at the Hippodrome she played opposite him in the first of their big successes together, *That's A Good Girl*. The genesis of this show is typical of the time. Douglas Furber, Buchanan's pet scriptwriter, had shown him the book of an operetta in which there was the role of Wilhelmina, a German telegraph girl – a part which appealed to Miss Randolph. Some time later, while working on a new show, Buchanan and Furber remembered Wilhelmina and incorporated her into the scenario as a disguise for the heroine, a detective called Joy Dean, and offered the part to Miss Randolph. But up until two weeks before rehearsal, she relates, the show had no score. 'We'd heard Gershwin's "The Man I Love" and adored it, and Jack said, "If only we could get hold of it and alter the lyric, it would make a lovely number for us".' But Ira Gershwin refused, and it was only after a cabled SOS to Max Dreyfus, the New York head of Chappells Music, that a potential composer appeared. 'It was Phil Charig, who arrived off the boat and played three hit numbers straight off: "Chirp, Chirp"; "Sweet So And So," and "Fancy Our Meeting".' The latter song is probably the one most closely associated with the partnership, and when they danced to it on the first night, *The Times* critic felt that 'as we listen to the slow flip-flop-flap of two pairs of shoes caressing the stage in harmony, it seems that the dancers are diversifying the silence with an exquisite pattern'. From then on they were established as a team. 'Very often people would come from the provinces without knowing what we were in. They'd just say, "Let's go and see a Jack and Elsie show".'

Buchanan deserted this successful formula at his peril. In 1935 he appeared at the Alhambra (now the Odeon, Leicester Square) in an elaborately staged period piece called *The Flying Trapeze*. The gallery booed the leading lady, June Clyde, and shouted 'Where's Elsie?'. The show closed shortly afterwards.

As on stage, so off, life in the neighbourhood of Jack Buchanan tended to resemble a party. Post-West End tours, nowadays shunned by the stars, were done in style in those days. 'It was lovely. We were like a family,' says Miss Randolph, and as paterfamilias Buchanan indulged his offspring in frequent 'treats'. 'We were playing Liverpool when the Grand National was on. He booked a coach on a train and took the entire company. He gave all the chorus kids a pound each to back a horse, and we were all given drinks and then taken to the buffet car for lunch on Mr Buchanan.' That evening a theatrical agent who had also been at Aintree came round to Elsie's dressing-room for a chat: 'Wasn't that a wonderful thing of Jack to do? There's only one other star who'd do that for the whole company. Ruth Draper.'

And what about that well-known secret passion? 'We had no illusions about each other,' says Miss Randolph today. 'I loved him dearly, as everybody did, and I know he loved me. Some people do jell, and we did – fortunately. I miss him sadly, I must say.'

If 'debonair' was the word for Jack Buchanan, the word for Bobby Howes was 'winsome'. Short of stature, with bright blue eyes and an endearing grin, he was the original 'little boy lost' whom women long to mother. His appeal is exemplified by Buttons, the devoted and put upon page-boy who loves Cinderella in vain, and one of his most successful shows was *Mr Cinders*, an adaptation of the fairy-story with the sexes reversed. According to *Theatre World*, 'Cinderella here becomes Jim Lancaster, the down-trodden cousin of the snobbish Lancasters of Merton Chase. Ordered about relentlessly by his two cousins . . . and squashed by the massive Lady Lancaster, Jim's life is hardly worth living until the whirlwind arrival of Jill Kemp . . . daughter of a millionaire, [who] is being pursued by the local police for exceeding the speed limit . . . Jill plays the fairy godmother and sends Jim off to the ball in a heavy fancy-dress disguise, following discreetly after in her Rolls-Royce.' Jill was played by Binnie Hale, a silvery, volatile comedienne who partnered Howes perfectly, particularly when they sang and danced 'I'm A One-Man Girl Who's Looking For A One-Girl Man' and, in the words of Vivian Ellis's hit number from the show, 'Spread a Little Happiness' throughout the audience. They were not as inseparable as Buchanan and Randolph and did not co-star again until five years later in *Yes, Madam?* at the Hippodrome. James Agate, less tolerant of musical comedy conventions than other critics, wrote, 'Is it a trick of the mind that one seems to have plenteously beheld Miss Binnie Hale masquerading as a pert yet loving chambermaid, Mr Bobby Howes disguised as a winsome valet or chauffeur and various other capable ladies masquerading as dragonsome châtelaines in whose establishments elderly fribbles surreptitiously carouse?' He conceded however that 'Miss Hale gives us generously of her tenuous charm and Mr Howes is again so winning as perilously to approach the point where there will be nothing left to be won'.

Because of his size audiences loved to see Bobby Howes at the mercy of large women, and here Vera Pearce again graces the scene. 'It is wildly funny,' said the *Daily Mail*, 'when Miss Vera Pearce, as Pansy, flings Mr Howes about in a romp which sends him flying into a bed of flowers. The whole audience shouted with joy at this.' He was also matched with an actress of monumentally forbidding aspect called Bertha Belmore, and in *Big Business* the three of them joined forces in 'an interpolated masque of Robin Hood, with Miss Pearce superbly majestic in green tights, Miss Belmore as Will Scarlett and Mr Howes as Little John' – of course.

The plot of a Bobby Howes show owed very little to probability, but a great deal to the necessity of involving him in ridiculous physical situations or outrageous disguises. Ivor Brown wrote of *Bobby, Get Your Gun!* in 1938, 'Of course the life and the soul of the party, which flits from somewhere near Cambridge to somewhere near Cuba, is Mr Howes, who, like all good clowns, is a really good actor too, and will present you with a true image of anything from a colonel to a penguin, from a racing cox to a gangster terror. The best song,' he adds, 'is one of the gown in the jazz age, "Veni, Vidi, Swing It, Baby" –a modern classic indeed.'

Perhaps Howes's most unlikely vehicle was an importation from Broadway called *Sons O' Guns*, full of fun on and around the Western Front, 'on which' commented *The Times*, 'bombs only fall when it is time for a hard-working chorus to rest. . . . It is the persuasive innocence of Bobby Howes that makes the plot of this piece almost credible.' The review ends: 'Upon the love-making Miss Mireille Perrey and Mr Howes together bestow a whimsical grace that commends some scenes that in affairs of this sort have often no more than a formal interest.' This rather verbose tribute highlights the reverse of the Bobby Howes coin. As *Theatre World* remarked in its review of *For The Love of Mike*, 'There are few comedians who can combine broad comedy and wistfulness in the manner of Mr Howes,' and one had to be very hard-hearted indeed to remain unmoved when he sang what virtually became his signature tune, 'She's my Lovely'.

Noël Coward is often cited as a total Man of the Theatre, but in fact he has diversified his career considerably between theatre, cinema and cabaret, with a little light literature thrown in. Ivor Novello, on the other hand, apart from his early film star career, was almost entirely devoted to the stage. 'It's the only thing I care a damn about,' he told a reporter on the first night of *The Dancing Years*. 'It's my whole life, and I want to go on writing and acting till I die of old age.' He did precisely that, although he died, not of old age, but of a heart-attack when he was only fifty-eight. His greatest contribution to the theatre was a series of musical extravaganzas which he master-minded between 1935 and the outbreak of the last war, and the melodies he wrote for them are his memorial.

In his choice of leading ladies he divided his allegiance equally between two

American emigrées: the flashing-eyed brunette opera singer turned actress, Mary Ellis, and the rose petal blonde star of *Sally* and *The Cabaret Girl*, Dorothy Dickson. Miss Ellis had first impressed London critics in Eugene O'Neill's *Strange Interlude* and then proceeded to make an equal but totally different impact in Kern's operetta, *Music in the Air*. 'I suddenly saw this exquisite young man sitting in a box,' she remembers, 'No, not young; Ivor must have been eight years older than I was. He came to a matinée, and that night I got a box – it looked as though it was a coffin – full of lilies, with a great message on it.' The 'great message' included an impassioned request that she and Novello should do a show together. She had to turn it down temporarily because of a two-year Hollywood contract; but in the meanwhile he was approached by the management of Drury Lane, one of London's largest theatres, to write a piece which might restore the house's declining fortune. He outlined a story on the spot, which was approved, and shortly afterwards Miss Ellis began to receive his home-made records of the score. The company had to start rehearsals ten days before she was due back. 'Don't worry,' she cabled. 'I'll learn the whole first half and walk off the boat into rehearsal' – and did.

He called the show *Glamorous Night*, and the first night lived up to the title. 'Cheers, shouts, yells and a tornado of clapping greeted Mr Ivor Novello's first entrance,' wrote the *Daily Mail* critic, ' . . . beyond all doubt *Glamorous Night* is wildly, inspiringly, intoxicatingly triumphant.' What he had achieved is hard to describe because it literally beggars description. 'They hadn't had anything like that at Drury Lane,' says Miss Ellis, 'or anywhere.' Novello took as the springboard for his story the affair of King Carol of Rumania and Madame Lupescu, but added a great deal besides. He played Anthony Allen, inventor of television, who is bribed to keep quiet by Lord Radio and departs on a Mediterranean cruise. He finds himself in a country called Krasnia, where he saves the king's mistress, a gypsy opera singer called Melitza, from assassination. They fall in love and escape aboard the cruise vessel, ss *Silver Star*, which is promptly sunk, in full view of the audience. Cast ashore, they meet up with gypsies and undergo a ritual marriage ceremony; but duty to the Crown recalls Melitza to Krasnia and Anthony returns to London and watches the Royal Wedding on a gigantic TV screen.

It was nonsense of course, but done with total conviction and vanquishing panache. 'I lift my hat to Mr Novello,' wrote Ivor Brown. 'He can wade through tosh with the straightest face: the tongue never visibly approaches the cheek.' And this was far from being a pose. 'In a funny way he was a terribly unsophisticated person,' says Mary Ellis, 'not that he wasn't mischievous and naughty and everything under the sun, but his saving grace was that he was utterly sincere.' Despite its absurdity, she found that *Glamorous Night* 'achieved a quality that was better than *it* was. I spent my wits and my spirit on a scene that, if it had been done less well, would have been ghastly.'

Also in the cast was another American, Elisabeth Welch, who had scored a hit singing 'Solomon' in Cole Porter's *Nymph Errant*. 'I was just there because Ivor wanted this one song, "Shanty Town". I was a stowaway, but no one ever discovered where I stowed away from! They find me during the cabaret and drag me on. There was I, in rags, with a darkened stage and all the company, including Ivor, Mary and the dancing girls. So how could you fail?' But arbitrary as the situations sound on paper, on stage they all worked: Novello saw to that, with the able assistance of a woman director, Leontine Sagan. 'There wasn't one night that the three of us didn't meet and talk over the next day's scenes,' recalls Miss Ellis, while Miss Welch says, 'He was the conductor of the symphony and Leontine was the first fiddle.'

Glamorous Night was a howling success, but the theatre management had booked a pantomime for Christmas, and it had to close in December. Novello was hurt and angry, and returned to the straight theatre and a version of Max Beerbohm's *The Happy Hypocrite* in which he played the bloated debauchee, Lord George Hell, who is transformed by true love into an angelic youth. 'He makes the transition with high ability,' noted Ivor Brown, but the run was short, and Drury Lane begged him to return. This time the leading lady was Dorothy Dickson.

'We first met at a party in New York. The hostess said, "May I present Mr Novello?" I looked up and I thought I had never seen anything more beautiful in my life. We clicked – just like that. Then when I came over to London to do *Sally* we became great, great friends: we were all in the same divine sort of circle.' The show Novello wrote for himself and Miss Dickson was in a lighter vein and it was called *Careless Rapture*. He was Michael, illegitimate brother of a diplomat who is engaged to Penelope (Dorothy Dickson), a musical comedy star.

Like everyone else who worked with him, Miss Dickson was impressed by his total command of the diverse elements of a production. 'To me the most attractive moment that he ever had was at the musical rehearsal, when the whole orchestra was there, the stage-hands, everyone. If people had seen him then, they would have seen all his talents come together at once.' But, for all his dedication, Ivor could see the funny side of his creations. 'He rang me and said, "Can you come to the theatre at ten o'clock on Thursday morning? They're delivering the earthquake." So I went, and there it was, all collapsed. It was magnificent, and we all passed out laughing. I had a scene on a Chinese balcony in which I had the line: "My maid says it's earthquake weather." It went into our language from then on.'

While he may have been an object of worship to his fans, to his company he was an equal and a friend. 'Being a matinée idol only meant to him that the gallery was full,' Mary Ellis emphasises. 'As for personal delight in it, that wasn't in his nature. He had no "side" at all.' – a sentiment echoed by all who worked with him, and which, according to Dorothy Dickson, overflowed into the audience. 'They can tell whether you are a person who loves his friends – and he really did. That was his secret.' And for the friends, as for the chums of Jack Buchanan, there were numerous jaunts and outings, particularly on weekends to Redroofs, his country home. They would all ride down there on Saturday night after the show and return to Town on Monday, with Ivor doing *The Times* crossword. 'It was a merry gathering from beginning to end,' says Miss Dickson. 'We would play tennis or go in the swimming pool. Then he would call out, "Come here a minute!" and sit at the piano and say, "Have I written this or have you heard it before?" He had no discipline, unlike Noël, who was one hundred per cent disciplined. But he *could* write his own music down.'

In this carefree atmosphere the next Drury Lane show was born. It was called *Crest of the Wave* and its plot certainly rode to a crest of improbability. Ivor played Don Gantry, heir to an impoverished estate, who according to *The Times*, 'having rejected the determined advances of a millionairess, is very rudely shot by her four times in the back.' This only delays him momentarily from embarking on a cruise – yet again – in company with Honey Wortle (Dorothy Dickson), a film extra who, at the end of the second act, announces, 'I'm getting off at Hollywood. I've got a marvellous picture contract waiting for me.' Don's own film career is nearly cut short by Otto Fresch, 'a star embittered by his waning popularity', (also played by Novello in a modified Lord George Hell make-up), who engineers a train crash – in full view, etc. – which Don and Honey survive, returning to the ancestral mansion in time for Christmas Eve. 'How bare the narrative seems! How richly Drury Lane has clothed it!' enthused *The Times*, while James Agate described the first night in his best ironic style: 'Outside . . . cordons of police held back hundreds of autograph seekers. Inside hundreds of autograph givers had congregated. . . . As the conductor advanced to his rostrum, a Parsifalian hush reigned, broken only by the crackle of a too-stout shirt front and the rustle of an ill-mannered ruby.' The curtain rose and the gallery waited breathlessly for Ivor's entrance, almost applauding another actor, Peter Graves, by mistake. 'But anticipation was not long in fulfilment, for now a figure in riding-breeches haughtily descend the stairs. . . . It was Mr Ivor Novello and, as they say at film receptions, in person. Very little older, not a whit more rotund, with chin aloof as of yore and the aristocratic gaze of Mr Beerbohm's Lord Byron.'

'A boyish and simple evening,' *The Times* concluded; but the vein was wearing thin. Instead of following up with another musical, Novello took an enormous gamble. Dorothy Dickson was in any case having trouble with her singing voice: 'He told me he had this plan to do *Henry V*, and asked me to play the Princess. I thought "How lovely!" So we all went off to Venice and had a wonderful holiday, and then he came back to start the production.' Critics were sceptical, but in the event even Agate stayed to praise, although, like other reviewers, he pointed out that the vast and realistic production made nonsense of the Chorus. 'He [Novello] has fire where fire should be: the prayer before battle and the reading of the list of the dead are beautifully done, and the soliloquy beginning "Upon the King . . . " has an entirely admirable cogency.' But it was September 1938, and the public had enough war-talk in the newspapers without listening to martial speeches at Drury Lane. *Henry V* ran just over two weeks.

What was going on in Europe could no longer be ignored, even in the wonderland of Drury Lane, and through the plot of his next show, *The Dancing Years*, Novello for the first time wove the thread of a contemporary theme. Basically the story of the rise to fame of a composer and his love for an opera-singer (a role which Mary Ellis returned to play), it dealt in its later stages with the Nazi occupation of Vienna and the persecution of the Jews, although *The Times* felt that 'the shadows are hardly more than pretexts for easy sentiment', and Agate called it merely 'an excellent example of that form of entertainment which should be called Magnoperetta'. This time the show relied less on spectacle than on its endlessly melodious score. 'A more solid piece,' Mary Ellis calls it, 'less beautiful to look at, but a more dramatic story', and it was certainly his most successful show commercially since, although the outbreak of war ended its run at Drury Lane, it continued to play at other theatres for most of the duration.

In 1951, while acting in his latest operetta, *King's Rhapsody*, another variation of the Lupescu affair, with a touch of the Duke of Windsor, Ivor Novello was suddenly taken ill and died. Would there have continued to be a place for his kind of show in the theatre of today? 'He wrote modern fairy-tales,' says Elisabeth Welch, 'and I don't think the public want fairy-tales any longer.' 'He wanted only the lovely things,' says Dorothy Dickson, 'but people like that are pop stars now – not that any of them are like him.'

No one could be like Ivor Novello. But when the management of *King's Rhapsody* sought a star to replace him, it seemed only fitting that their choice should fall on – Jack Buchanan.

The Light of Many Lamps

Micheál Mac Liammóir

M Y first sight of Ivor Novello was not on the stage but in the flat of Anew McMaster, the Irish actor who had just married my sister Mana, transmuting us both, to our mutual amazement, from old and established friends into brothers- in-law.

The year was 1924 and I, inescapably the same age as the century, was also twenty-four. Of course I had heard of Ivor – who had not? – but I had never seen him on a stage or on a film because my home, or homes, during the Twenties was divided between Ireland, France, and Switzerland. And I was, therefore, totally unprepared for the astonishing figure who bounded into the room with all the suddenness and all the swiftness of a pagan god. Not a faun – there was nothing puckish or impish about him – a god, incongruously though elegantly clad in a lounge suit, a striped silk shirt and a dazzling smile.

It may be that Ivor was really more Roman than Greek: his dark hair, his clear, faintly sunburned skin, his magnificent brown eyes were more Italianate perhaps than Hellenic; but I had never seen – before or since – such an exaggeratedly handsome young man, or one with so genial and glowing a personality. He reminded me, in some curious way, of a high-spirited and affectionate child, although he was already in his mid thirties and already too among the most popular and distinguished figures on the London stage. Childlike, perhaps, because everything seemed to charm him: almost (though not quite) all people seemed delightful to him, and one of the curious enchantments he flung over almost everybody he met was that whomever he was addressing at the moment seemed just then to be the only being in the world who held any interest for him.

Nobody could or ever did attempt to deny his personal charm but there were always, here and there, a few doubters. His numerous talents, said these (usually envious) people, were terribly facile. So they were. His music, they continued, was over-sweet. So it was. He was not by any means a great actor. Nor was he. His taste was uncertain and inclined to the superficial. So it was: he never claimed otherwise. His mind was sparkingly entertaining but un-profound. So is champagne. His plays were chatty and fluttered over the sur-face of things. So did Molière's and Congreve's and Wilde's. His kindliness was a pose and all done for the sake of effect and popularity.

This was a black lie. He was one of the most truly kindly of human beings the world has known. Perhaps his hatred of discord, his fear of any ominous shadows that threatened the honey-coloured light of his view of life was a form of weakness. If anything went wrong, if actor or actress or technician dis-pleased him there would be a brief, whispered suggestion to his splendid friend, secretary, manager and fellow Welshman known on earth as Lloydie, and the offending party – actor, actress, electrician or cook – would be dealt with by Lloydie and disappear, and poor Lloydie, with the expression of a worn-out diplomat, would say, 'It's all arranged.' Then Ivor would sail through his next triumphant episode with a blissfully unconscious smile, and Bobby Andrews would say with that velvet gravity that always draped his wickedest cracks, 'So our dear Miss X will be seen no more. Ivor is feeling much happier now about the opening night.'

This trick of escaping from anything embarrassing or unpleasant was, if you will, a form of weakness, but it sprang as I think from his innate kindliness which was applied to himself and to others alike.

Indeed the charm that emanated from him had its roots in this benevolent quality as surely as the rose-tree has its roots in the nourishing soil, and the popularity he enjoyed was the result, as inevitable as the unquestioned popu-larity of the rose, whose supremacy among lovers of flowers is only denied by the most avid of seekers after originality.

The great friends of his life, those who knew him far more intimately and more truly than I – Robert Andrews was chief among these – would agree, I think, with me about this. To me, as to many others who saw him only occasionally, his most striking quality was *radiance*.

He had merely to appear on the stage or walk into a room for that stage and that room to glow with what seemed to be the light of many lamps. One felt happier merely by looking at him or listening to him, whatever sense or non-sense he talked, and he talked plenty of both. He also listened with apparently concentrated delight to what other people were talking about. And this, in the world in which chiefly I encountered him, was mainly nonsense: scintillating, sardonic, subtle, or merely silly in turn, but always nonsense. Brilliant, brittle, benevolent and bitchy in turn, but still nonsense. And to this he would contribute his own share and be as scintillating, as sardonic, or as subtle in turn, but seldom silly and still more seldom bitchy. In fact whenever the last adjective applied it would invariably be modified, be dulcified, if you will, by some half-terse, half-tender rider.

'Yes, you're perfectly right,' I heard him say one evening about some actress beloved by her public but not by her profession: 'What a cow. What a cow. What a *cow*. But what a *dear*. . . . '

He was the only actor I have known who looked forward to everything: even to rehearsals and matinées. 'We're having our twentieth rehearsal tomorrow at ten,' he told me once. 'And we've arrived at last to the really thrilling stage when we're all catching fire.'

And on another occasion after one of his shows I had seen and told him how much I had enjoyed it, he answered: 'Oh I'm so glad, and do you know we're having a *matinée tomorrow*!' as if it were the one unique and glorious event he'd been waiting for for years.

The last time I saw him was when Hilton Edwards and I were playing in one Glasgow theatre and he starring in another. After our shows we were having supper at his hotel with himself and Bobby Andrews, and Hilton, filled with wonder at his slimness, his chin-line, his apparently inexhaustibly handsome face – for he was already in his fifties – said, 'How do you do it, Ivor? Do you take lots of exercise?' And he answered seriously, 'Oh no, Hilton. Never. Health is fatal.'

That was after a performance of *Perchance to Dream* and when we saw it at a matinée, noting his grace, the charm of his voice and presence, the magic of that smile that seemed to illuminate stage and auditorium, we said to each other: 'What an Oberon he could play if he wanted to!'

Fay Compton is another of those who had and thank God still has the magic of the mantle of Harlequin, under which she undoubtedly was born. But Fay has too important a place in my affection and my admiration for me to speak of her from an unbiased view. For one thing she is so profoundly personal. It is one of her many secrets. Beautiful in her youth as an *à la France* rose, nimble as a dancer, swift as a flash of lightning, decisive as a gun-shot, bitter as gall, sweet as honey, measured as a T-square, ceremonious and gay as a Viennese waltz, unpredictable as a Chopin prelude, she is the most bewildering of the children of Harlequin. That is her great quality of her acting and of herself: it is also her curse.

For a London actress she is far too versatile. She can do anything at all. Happy are those great actresses of the English stage, from Mrs Patrick Campbell and Sybil Thorndike to Peggy Ashcroft and Maggie Smith, of whom one always knew, or knows, the quality, the style of the enchantments for which to prepare. With Fay one can never tell: her abundant, her almost absurd versatility, has already been touched upon, and this quality is at once her triumph and her tragedy. I have seen her myself in a variety of parts where sheer contrast takes the breath away: from the days when she played glittering juveniles on both sides of the Atlantic in such productions as *The Pearl Girl*, *Tonight's The Night*, and *Innocent and Annabel* to the *Prisoner of Zenda*, *Hamlet*, *The Bells*, *Candida*, *The Tempest*, *Dick Whittington* and just a few more. In all of these plays she changed, chameleon-like and yet without losing one light or shadow of herself, into a different woman: she could, it has always seemed to me, do anything in the world from playing one of the most moving Ophelias the world has known to the most comical and debonair of Dick Whittingtons: the fact that I never saw her as Mary Rose sits frequently at my door-step like an importunate ghost and haunts me with regret.

Besides acting, singing, and dancing she can also, I must add, give imitations of monkeys, parrots, her own beloved and lamented brother Compton Mackenzie, as well as of her own dogs or of other people's cats so uncannily accurate that one cannot believe they are not in the room: one feels inclined to fling a bone into a corner or place a reverent saucer of cream under the table.

I never worked with her until 1949, the year when, in Orson Welles' film of *Othello*, she played Emilia and I Iago. Indeed, until that year, although I had applauded her so often, we had never met at all. Since that first encounter we have been great friends and my love and admiration have increased, for I have discovered not only a great artist – that I knew long before 1949 – but a great woman as well. I wrote about her then in a diary I published about the making of that film:

What I found about her most unexpectedly were the two small Angels, one at each side of her head about a foot and a half above her shoulders. They are very small angels indeed and rather stiff like the angels in a French primitive, but they are there all right, rolling their pale blue eyes up to heaven and puffing out their cheeks, one of them blowing a little golden trumpet and the other fiddling away like mad. The angels . . . are indubitable and follow her everywhere.

And I see another account, briefer yet fuller, in a sort of cast list that forms an abbreviated foreword at the beginning of the story: 'Fay Compton. A lovely Actress, accompanied by Angels and Demons, with musical instruments, playing Emilia.'

I was quite serious when I wrote those words but I am puzzled by the demons. If they were ever there I am certain that she is slaying them as Saint George slew the dragon. Because, as I have noted, she can do anything at all. But I will of course admit: I am a little prejudiced in her favour.

The Master

(Noël Coward)

by Sheridan Morley

STRICTLY speaking, Noël Coward was not a matinée idol at all; although a chronology of his career would show that the years of his early fame (1924–1930) were still those of the matinée stars in their greatest glory, it became clear from the very beginning that the young Master was all set to break most of the ground rules which governed the making of more orthodox idols.

In the first place, Coward's face was, unlike Ivor Novello's, never his fortune; the early photographs show a less than commanding profile and, in place of the moody stare then believed to denote romanticism and an artistic temperament, a look of stark ambitious intensity. Sir Noël himself was under no illusions about his photographic image in the Twenties:

At the time of *The Vortex* I was photographed, and interviewed, and photographed again. In the street. In the park. In my dressing-room. At my piano. With my dear old mother, without my dear old mother – and, on one occasion, sitting up in an over-elaborate bed looking like a heavily doped Chinese illusionist. This last photograph, I believe, did me a good deal of harm. People glancing at it concluded at once, and with a certain justification, that I was undoubtedly a weedy sensualist in the last stages of physical and moral degeneration, and that they had better hurry off to see me in my play before my inevitable demise placed that faintly macabre pleasure beyond their reach.

Secondly, where matinée idols generally soothed and reassured their audiences, Coward often irritated and annoyed his: *The Vortex*, (1924) his first major success and therefore inevitably the one which cast the image, appeared after all to be about drug addiction at a time when alcoholism was scarcely mentionable on the London stage. True, precisely because of that, the 'bright young things' flocked to it first at Hampstead and later at the Royalty; but they were as far removed from a matinée audience as were the Royal Court theatregoers of the late 1950s removed from regular patrons of the Theatre Royal, Haymarket.

Coward himself always maintained that *The Vortex* was not written to shock or offend ('neither of which exceedingly second-rate ambitions had ever occurred to me') but the fact remains that it did. That the play may in its innermost heart not be about drug addiction at all but about homosexuality, something infinitely closer to Coward's own private existence and at that time even more theatrically unmentionable than drugs, is virtually unprovable even with the wisdom of hindsight; but for the time of the play's first production drugs alone were bad enough: 'A dustbin of a play!' shrieked the *Daily Express* in 1924 and the cry was taken up by the then doyen of the matinée idols Sir Gerald du Maurier himself: 'The public are asking for filth . . . the younger generation are knocking at the door of the dustbin . . . if life is worse than the stage, should the stage hold the mirror up to such distorted nature? If so, where shall we be – without reticence or reverence?'

There, if anywhere, was the moment when Coward and the matinée idols parted company; he replied to Sir Gerald's attack in an article published by the *Daily Express* early in 1925. It began:

Sir Gerald du Maurier, having – if he will forgive me saying so – enthusiastically showered the English stage with second-rate drama for many years, now rises up with incredible violence and has a nice slap all round at the earnest and perspiring young dramatist. This is awful; it is also a little unwise. Art demands reverence much more than life does – and Sir Gerald's reverence so far seems to have been entirely devoted to the box-office.

In 1961 Coward was to write a series of articles for the *Sunday Times* deploring the 'decline' of the modern theatre in almost precisely Sir Gerald's phraseology . . . but that was nearly forty years later, by which time the angry young man of the Twenties had moved along with his audience into a more conservative frame of mind.

At the time of *The Vortex* the up-and-coming matinée idol was not Coward but Ivor Novello, who more readily conformed in profile and production to what was expected by middle-aged ladies in hats at two-thirty in the afternoon. 'Darling Ivor' seldom, if ever, shocked anybody, at least in public, though one of the rare occasions on which he did so was suitably enough in a play by Coward entitled *Sirocco* which flopped with a resounding thud at Daly's in November 1927. The failure did the star rather less harm than his author however, not only because the critics were more or less fair in apportioning the blame but also because Novello was already far more deeply embedded in the public's affection than was Coward. Ivor had already passed most of the tests of the matinée idol; what's more he was already into films, where his romantic profile had made him a star capable of carrying any production on his name alone. In contrast Coward, though he had first filmed under the aegis of D. W. Griffith as early as 1917 (*Hearts of the World*) did not actually star in a picture until *The Scoundrel* in 1934 and then had to wait for a real screen success until *In Which We Serve* which was made during the Second World War.

So thirdly, if you're still with me, Coward failed the test of the matinée idol in that his name alone, though by the end of the Twenties familiar as that of an actor, playwright, composer, lyricist and director, was still seldom seen alone above a title in the way that designated a matinée star like Novello or du Maurier or even Owen Nares. Coward, realising perhaps that his public image was 'too clever by half' ever to have an unadulterated romantic appeal, took care to be billed in the company of other stars like Gertrude Lawrence, Yvonne Printemps or the Lunts.

Not until after the war did he feel confident enough of his own drawing power as an actor to bill himself alone above a title, and by that time the British theatrical climate was much changed. Novello smiled on until 1951, offering romantic melodies for the palm court trade, but the matinée idol business really collapsed towards the end of the Thirties, leaving Coward – originally its sworn opponent – to fill one of the gaps created by its demise.

To go back to the very beginning, Coward's early childhood lacked both the romantic squalor and the air of vague mystery which were the prerequisites of the ideal matinée idol. Early pictures show a somewhat stolid, surburban child which is very largely what he was – born in Teddington just before the last Christmas of the nineteenth century (hence the Noël), brought up in Clapham and Battersea, educated briefly at the Chapel Royal school and then, at the age of eleven, sent off to Lila Field to make his stage début in *The Goldfish* along-side another somewhat unlikely juvenile novice, Micheál Mac Liammóir.

Coward quickly learnt the lessons of the child actor: discipline, endurance, efficiency, a certain respect for his elders and betters both in the company and in the audience, and a healthy ability for self-criticism: 'I was a talented child, God knows, and – when washed and smarmed down a bit – passably attractive; but I was I believe one of the worst boy actors ever inflicted on the general public.'

Throughout the early years of his career, Coward's theatrical masters were craftsmen – Charles Hawtrey, with whom he appeared in *The Great Name* in 1911, George Bernard Shaw to whom he turned for advice on the writing of *The Young Idea* in 1921 (having borrowed its two principal characters from *You Never Can Tell*) and André Charlot under whose aegis he learnt the elements of revue and for whom he wrote most of *London Calling!* in 1923.

What they taught him, one suspects, had a little to do with personal glamour but everything to do with professional polish.

As a result, by 1925 Coward had not only *The Vortex* but also *Hay Fever*, *Fallen Angels* and a second revue, *On With The Dance* running concurrently in London – and that was also the year of his triumphant New York début as Nicky Lancaster. But although *The Vortex* did not live as long on Broadway as it had in London (even then its author was a fervent believer in limiting his runs as an actor to around three months in order to get back to the writing as quickly as possible) it gave Coward his first jump ahead of his British contemporaries. Of them all, perhaps only Jack Buchanan, Gertrude Lawrence and Beatrice Lillie could claim equal American success during the 1920s, and they were purely performers. In Coward, and particularly in the intensity of *The Vortex*, American audiences seemed to recognise something closer to their own theatrical tastes than either the Victorian melodramas or the languid Edwardian comedies which had made up the bulk of previous imports from London.

In any event Coward returned to England bathed in the rosy glow of transatlantic success; like Cole Porter, the songwriter he already most closely resembled in the meticulous arrangement of his lyrics, Coward straddled the gap between showbusiness and the social aristocracy on both sides of the Atlantic. But he still lacked the massive popular support granted to the idols; his talents to amuse, various and remarkable as they were, did not lend themselves to fan clubs or indeed the fan mentality. Many of those who stood lovelorn at Novello's stage doors could not forgive Coward for the 'shocks' of *The Vortex*, nor for the way he had publicly reviled du Maurier, nor above all for the way he quite clearly represented a new generation . . . one too young to encompass the average theatregoers of the time and too sharp to give them much in the way of cosy reassurance. It was Ivor Brown who, writing in 1930, best summed up what Coward stood for in the 1920s:

Ten years ago we were all looking for that 'new world after the war'. Everybody had his eyes on the horizon and scanned it for the rising walls of a New Jerusalem. We had grand hopes of peace and plenty, of democracy fired by a common sympathy, of a new and kindly social order. People trumpeted the word 'reconstruction' as though it were magic. We have had our disillusion. Reconstruction withered where it grew. New Jerusalems never rose from their fanciful foundation. Bravery of thought was replaced by bitterness of mood. It was easy to doubt everything: hard to find acceptable faiths. The younger generation may have been dismayed; but at least it could dance. It turned its back on solemn creeds. It was light of toe, light of touch. Of that period and temper Mr Coward is the dramatist . . . what he has done is to record the laughing way of a generation which is hiding its disenchantment under a smile.

But disenchantment was still not the safest or most enduring box-office material, and when Coward came off the crest of his early success, as he did in 1927 with the consecutive failures of *Home Chat* and *Sirocco*, it was with a certain unattractive glee that a number of people spat at him outside the theatre . . . not something which tended to happen to the idols.

It was in 1929, after Coward had retrieved his prestige with the success of a revue for Cochran called *On With The Dance*, that he first decided to make a play for the gallery. The one he made, *Bitter-Sweet*, remains among the most schmalzy and triumphant operettas of the twentieth century and is only separable from the best of Novello on account of an occasional stringency in the lyrics. But for all its success and, allowing that it rates second only to *Cavalcade* in the efficiency and versatility of Coward's one-man showmanship (in this case he was author, composer, lyricist and director), *Bitter-Sweet* remains apart from the body of his later work.

Having shown once that he could turn out operetta along with the best of them (and to those who remembered the furore over *The Vortex* and *Fallen Angels* less than five years earlier it must have seemed roughly akin to the idea of John Osborne following up *Look Back in Anger* with *The Great Waltz*), Coward never quite managed to do it again. The musicals that were designed to recapture the *Bitter-Sweet* market (*Conversation Piece* in 1934, *Operette* in 1937, *Pacific 1860* in 1946) never fully did so, and it became increasingly clear that Coward's safest bets were to be the intimate, sophisticated comedies of the Thirties and Forties – plays which demanded a reasonably urbane, liberal and adult audience of the kind not usually to be found on the registers of fan clubs or hanging about outside chilly stage doors in the hope of autographs.

Nevertheless, within two years of *Bitter-Sweet* (and at the end of a remarkable twenty-four-month output which also included *Private Lives*) Coward had written and staged the one show which was to put him squarely into public favour on all levels. The novelist G. B. ('Peter') Stern later recollected:

> . . . I had gone down late one afternoon to see Noël Coward at his studio in London and found him in a state of excitement, surrounded by a litter of old illustrated volumes of reference: 'Peter, do you know anything about the Boer War?' for he had just had the idea of writing a revue on a big scale that would cover the events of the first thirty years of the twentieth century. He was going to take one family, he said, and their servants, and show the same people going through it all, and I had ten years start of him, for he was only just going to be born when the Boer War broke out. I told him about the newsboys down the street, about the siege of Mafeking, about Bugler Dunne . . . We found the title the same evening. I kept on saying 'You want something like Pageant or Procession' . . . and then Noël shouted 'Cavalcade'!

More than thirty-five years after the first, and to date the only professional full-stage production of *Cavalcade*, Coward found himself at a fork luncheon in London the only man in possession of a knife. 'But of course, dear boy,' he explained to an impressed reporter, 'after all I did write *Cavalcade*.' And indeed if Coward is to be considered in the light of any single technical achievement in the theatre then *Cavalcade* is undoubtedly the one. Not because it is a very remarkable play, nor because it offers to the literature of the theatre any new or staggering thoughts, nor yet because it has much chance of survival (its size and scope have so far defeated any thoughts of professional revival on the stage) but purely because of the massive, almost numbing scale on which it is conceived. From Coward's one ambitious idea, confirmed and clarified by the pictures in back numbers of the *Illustrated London News*, grew a grandiose show in three acts and twenty-two scenes that was to cost an almost unprecedented thirty thousand pre-war pounds and that was to keep a cast and backstage crew of well over four hundred people employed at the Lane for more than a year, playing to a total box-office take of around three hundred thousand pounds. It was, in short, an epic.

After a week of endless, crisis-ridden dress rehearsals, *Cavalcade* had its first public performance at Drury Lane on 13 October 1931, soon after Britain came off the gold standard and a few days before the general election threw out the Labour party to return a true-blue National Government in a mood of near-hysterical patriotic fervour. In the light of such feeling, Coward had a hard time afterwards explaining that the timing of *Cavalcade* was nothing more than a happy coincidence, and that he had not written this ultra-jingoistic epic to cash in on the national mood of the moment. Quite apart from the fact that *Cavalcade* had been conceived a full year earlier, Noël had been so involved in its elaborate production that he was barely aware of the election at all, let alone the likely result of it. He was, as always, bleakly uninterested in politics of any kind.

All the same, the appearance of *Cavalcade* – together with a first night speech in the course of which Coward declared his hope that 'this play has made you feel in spite of the troublous times we are living in that it is still a pretty exciting thing to be English' – seemed to find him a place in a good many theatregoers' hearts. The rebel of the Twenties had become to them, albeit unintentionally, the super-patriot of the Thirties and to the laurels already predicted for him by Laurette Taylor (marked 'Duty,' 'Perseverance' and 'Believe in Your Star') could now be added one labelled 'Popularity'. *Cavalcade* marked the beginning of an identification between Coward and England which, reinforced by the success of *In Which We Serve* a decade later, was to live on for the rest of his career despite a period of professional decline in the late Forties and then twenty years of tax-induced exile in Switzerland and the West Indies.

A jack of all theatrical trades and the master of most of them, Coward pursued his career long after the more orthodox idols had fallen. By using every available medium from the short story to the one-act ballet, and by seldom turning up in the same plays twice, he avoided the more obvious pitfalls of the matinée idols: unlike du Maurier he never bored himself and unlike most of the others he never bored his audience. Frequently he irritated them, driving his more devoted admirers to despair with the likes of *Home Chat* or *Ace of Clubs*, but as no two consecutive Coward productions were ever alike the legacy of the failures was as short-lived as that of the successes.

Consequently, although Kenneth Tynan maintains that 'in twenty years' time we shall all know exactly what is meant by "a very Noël Coward sort of person" ', I am not so sure. A clipped, suave Englishman with a gift for repartee? But then what about the sheer naked fury of *Post-Mortem*, the bitterness of *Peace in our Time* or the smug suburban pride of *This Happy Breed*? A satirical songwriter? But then what about the sentimental glories of 'Someday I'll Find You' or 'Zigeuner'? Though the image of cocktails and laughter is enduring, what comes after is actually a certain amount of confusion and contradiction. Coward's philosophy, though he usually denied that such a thing even existed, was subtle, tortuous, and made up of apparent inconsistences. A suburban child caught up in the jet set, a writer of love stories never publicly known to be in love, a master technician who originally sold himself as a gifted amateur, he was never an easy man to chart either professionally or privately.

His appeal, at least in the late Twenties and Thirties, was undoubtedly to high café society . . . but that was where London theatregoers of the time came from and anybody who did not appeal to that section of the community was likely to end up either in Shakespeare or on tour. In the Forties he cast his net wider, working in front of troop audiences around the world and making *In Which We Serve*, the naval film which was the only project of Coward's working life to equal the ambition, the scope and the eventual patriotic success of the epic that was *Cavalcade*.

But when Coward returned from the last of his wartime concert tours he found that the London theatre of 1945 was not exactly holding out its arms in welcome. In swift succession between 1945 and 1949 he notched up failures in revue (*Sigh No More*), musical comedy (*Pacific 1860*, *Ace of Clubs*) and straight plays (*Peace in our Time*). His only successes in those years came from a revival of *Present Laughter* and the script for David Lean's *Brief Encounter* and by 1951 the odds on a Coward renaissance must have seemed low indeed. Novello was dead, du Maurier was dead, Cochran was dead, the age of the actor-managers and the matinée idols was even deader, and Coward was beached by more than just his Jamaican home.

When he did manage to retrieve his career it was not only with the West End success of *Relative Values* and *Quadrille* (in neither of which he appeared) but, characteristically, with an entirely new departure. Encouraged by his wartime concert experience, and presumably realising that he who had sung sophisticated ditties to the Fourteenth Army in Burma and got away with it could thereafter sing anything to anybody, Coward set up as a midnight matinée idol in cabaret first at the Café de Paris and then more profitably at the Desert Inn in Las Vegas where he discovered that the audience were not so much café society as Nescafé society.

Romping fastidiously, Coward worked in twice-nightly cabaret through all the songs that, in John Whiting's phrase, 'we sang to our girls driving back in the red MG from the Thames pub on a summer night in 1936'. From 'Dance, Dance, Dance Little Lady' through 'Mad Dogs' and 'Mrs Worthington' all the way to 'The Party's Over Now' he presented a repertoire chosen from around three hundred of his own songs and in the process established himself as a solo entertainer on a level with his beloved Dietrich.

As Las Vegas proved yet again, Coward was a survivor . . . and, like all professional survivors, he was careful not to affiliate himself too closely with any one theatrical age. True, there is a hazy school of thought which exclusively identifies him with the 1920s, since that was the decade of his first success and his greatest news value; but anyone imagining that even by the 1930s he had it made need look no further than Cyril Connolly writing in that decade a review of *Present Indicative*, Coward's first autobiography:

What are we left with? The picture, carefully incomplete, of a success; probably of one of the most talented and prodigiously successful people the world has ever known – a person of infinite charm and adaptability whose very adaptability however makes him inferior to a more compact and worldly competitor in his own sphere, like Cole Porter; and an essentially unhappy man, a man who gives one the impression of having seldom really thought or really lived and who is intelligent enough to know it. But what can he do about it? He is not religious, politics bore him, art means facility or else brickbats, love wild excitement and the nervous breakdown. There is only success, more and more of it, till from his pinnacle he can look down to where Ivor Novello and Beverley Nichols gather samphire on a ledge, and to where, a pinpoint on the sands below, Mr Godfrey Winn is counting pebbles. But success is all there is, and even that is temporary. For one can't read any of Noël Coward's plays now . . . they are written in the most topical and perishable way imaginable, the cream in them turns sour overnight – they are even dead before they are turned into talkies, however engaging they may seem at the time. This book reveals a terrible predicament, that of a young man with the Midas touch, with a gift that does not creep and branch and flower, but which turns everything it touches into immediate gold. And the gold melts, too.

Few reviews of the Master's work were ever written with the intelligent care of Mr Connolly's, and few have ever been so totally disproven by time. Granted, the interest in Coward lies not only in what he was but also in what he might so easily have been; granted that Godfrey Winn never finished counting the pebbles, that both Novello and Nichols got stuck on the ledges, albeit at different heights; what then took Coward alone to the top of that particular pinnacle and, despite a few unnerving lurches, kept him there for half a century?

'Talent, dear boy, sheer talent': one hears the clipped reprimand, sees the index finger raised in admonition that the question should even have been mooted; but talent alone does not explain Coward's longevity. Other playwrights have been as funny, other songwriters as tuneful; none have contributed as much to light entertainment in the twentieth century. Adaptability is obviously one answer: to labour Mr Connolly's metaphor, once the gold had melted Coward knew how to recast the mould and use it again without appearing to repeat himself. Dedication is another – a fervent, religious belief in the virtues of hard and regular work at both typewriter and piano. A third answer is that Coward knew what he was up to: undeterred by Marie Tempest (who once wrote 'at Noël's birth two godmothers sat over his cradle, the benevolent one who gave him one superb gift – playwriting – and the malignant one who tossed in a handful of gifts almost as good') he bounced around the media with all the resilience of a jumping jack.

When the National Theatre under Laurence Olivier's directorship decided to revive *Hay Fever* in 1964 they were not paying tribute to a long-dead author: Sir Noël himself was there, ready to direct it and to make sure that its standards were kept up to those of his original production – if not actually higher. It is given to few artists to preside over their own renaissance, the minimum requirement for such a renaissance usually being death. Coward broke that rule as he broke many others in the theatre, not out of wilful vandalism but simply because it was incompatible with the way he always cherished and preserved his own image.

As a child of the twentieth century and one of its most elegant veterans, the writer of its blues, chronicler of its moods and provider of its escapism, Coward belonged to no single theatrical period. He stood apart, in John Osborne's phrase 'his own invention and his own contribution to the times through which he lived'. His career, whether viewed as a long procession through applauding parties or as a serious attempt to mirror the mingled gaiety and despair of those who grew to maturity through the First World War, is on public record and there is little more to add to what he and countless critics have already said about it. Except perhaps that during and long after the age of the matinée idol he remained true to the one talent he celebrated and nurtured above all others – the talent to amuse.

A Tea-tray in the Stalls

by *Philip Hope-Wallace*

CALL back yesterday is easily said and the conjuration is so potent that like the sorcerer's apprentice one is soon overwhelmed. I don't lay claim to any very special powers of recall though when I match the dates and the vividness with which I recollect events, sights and theatrical impressions with others of my own age I think I must have started remembering things at an earlier age than many people. The comparison is never very fruitful: like arguing that you dream more vividly than others, some of whom deny that they dream at all. In my dreams figures, long dead, not consciously given thought for year upon year, surface wearing exactly the right clothes, saying all the expected things in precisely the remembered accents. The brain is a mysterious computer and memory the trickiest part of it. I would like to think that remembering a long love-affair with the theatre going back into the first world war was something which could be drawn around me like a cloak. 'Oft in the stilly night, Ere slumber's chain has bound me, Fond memory brings the light Of other days around me.' Thomas Moore makes it sound simple and orderly. It is not so. I believe there is much wisdom in Proust's observation that a photograph of some loved person or place far from jogging your memory into activity gradually weakens the true ability to summon up the past. Disillusion often accompanies a physical return to a honeymoon resort. Even a rerun of a movie once admired can cause dismay and sorrow. Ask me to re-visit, re-read, analyse and attempt to re-create all my thousands of theatrical experiences and

I would refuse. fearing to disinherit myself, deaden a living spirit within me. These things must be allowed to float to the surface without too much stirring.

Am I, I wonder, in a special case in that my theatre going of today as an elderly grudging professional critic is so intensely unlike the theatre going of my childhood and adolescence? Even the visual angle is completely altered. In those far off days one looked down on actor's heads from galleries of terrifying giddiness. In these days of colour television and wide screen cinema where the eye is always drawn to the most telling angle of vision it seems scarcely credible that we in the upper circle or the distant pit could have picked up such strong impressions of stage events. Projection, we are told, was more powerful in those days, which may well be true. But it now seems odd to me that we put up with such oblique glimpses.

Then of course there was not really much alternative. Stalls were simply too dear. But why the compulsion to visit the theatre at all?

Compulsion is the only word. I thought it the most exciting of all prospects and cannot immediately understand why this should have been so. I did not come of a theatrical family: indeed one of my grandmothers would have said that the queue for the Pit was exactly what it said; an orderly progress to hell.

But my parents were keen theatre-goers and wonderful describers of what they had seen and heard. Nowadays when a touch of the television knob brings into your room the talking heads of the popular pundits it may be difficult to recall the excitement engendered by the talk-feasts of the plays of Bernard Shaw. That such things should be said at all let alone said in public and applauded made my parents eyes shine with the recollection: and this was communicated to the eagerly listening children.

I was the youngest of three children and much behind them in the skill of reading. While they frightened themselves into fits reading Walter Scott (sometimes by the light of bicycle lamps in the forbidden after-dark), I had to make do with second-hand accounts of these adventures. I think we often forgot that the theatre exercised its greatest popular appeal at a time when the only way most of the illiterate mob could pick up a good story was to *see* it enacted. I rather think that if I had not had the theatrical experience before I had learned to peel excitement off a printed page I might have succumbed to it less readily. I feel that today's children, who almost certainly get experience of dramatic excitement in the first instance from television or cinema screen might hardly ever acquire the taste of live theatre at all strongly.

Being slow to learn the pleasures of reading led to a taste for hearing books read aloud. All these years later I am not at all sure that the most intensely moving artistic experience I ever underwent was not my father reading aloud to us *The Tale of Two Cities*. Far into the night I shuddered and re-mouthed the words. (*The Only Way* proved a slight let-down later.) Father had a good, over-lordly but dramatising voice and he and my mother were pillars of the suburban Shakespeare Reading Society, which often met in our house, my parents the leading spirits. I think this was not entirely unconnected with the fact that they fancied the way they themselves spoke Shakespeare. For instance it cannot have been mere selfishness that when *Antony and Cleopatra* was the choice, mother of course read the Egyptian queen but father read not merely Antony but Enobarbus as well! There were mild protests about this. But as a loyal son I will at this date say that it was probably the best casting. I have heard much Shakespeare in the theatre, some of it wonderful: Ion Swinley as Hamlet, my favourite and first (that's the way it should be) Sybil rounding on Cardinal Wolsey in *Henry VIII*, Olivier as Mercutio: but I did not really think I heard it better spoken than in my home.

Hence I suppose a largely uncritical approach to Shakespeare even when we had to start acting it ourselves in the gym at boarding-school and I found to my amazement that the other boys didn't much care for it. Lysander, Lady Macbeth, Bottom the Weaver (and *like* him too) all parts were or should have been *mine*. It had been so in the nursery too: but then we just acted the substance of the plots, like scenes dramatised from Lamb's *Tales from Shakespeare*: Iachimo getting out of the trunk to seduce Imogen in *Cymbeline*. I think these preparations to a long infatuation with Shakespeare made me wholly uncritical and I wish I had remained that way. Today I cringe from much Shakespearean production: unfair to people who may have a quite different understanding of the man's sublime genius than I who simply took to him as I took to Verdi or Chopin as simply another treat, another sort of pudding.

This freedom to roam at will through Shakespeare, as through the equally uncensorable Bible, led in due course to Awkward Questions. 'Why is Parolles called a Cat?' one asked at lunch. Perhaps a catamite's it was suggested? One didn't know what it meant but duly looked it up. All good education for the boy, it was no doubt felt. But critical feeling did not come into the reaction to the plays when eventually collected at the Old Vic. There my first encounters were taken up as the stuff of the universe, unquestioned. There was not even any question of suspending belief. I knew of course that Mercutio was not really dead and would be appearing at the matinée next day. But my tears came without stint. I knew he had feigned death but to me the death was as real as that of any street accident I might have witnessed. Thus I acquired a total surrender to 'acting' which had to be very bad and obviously insincere to make me draw back a little. Though as a schoolboy I had acted myself and knew how many problems it posed I thought for many years of theatre-going that all acting was 'marvellous' as I believe many good people do today: pausing only to ponder how do they manage to memorise all those lines and organise the timing and the movement so perfectly? I must have been the most uncritical spectator any player could have hoped to lay under a spell.

I make it sound as if my playgoing had been entirely occupied by visits to performances of Shakespeare and though there was quite a lot of this (I can 'see' Ben Greet as Malvolio in *Twelfth Night* with the pristine brightness of a child's eye) there were many other and more varied theatrical experiences. All I am saying is that the approach was conditioned in this way. In fact if I sort through my experience in a historical way I find first a First World War *Peter Pan* which enthralled and ravished me as Barrie still has power to do, thank heaven. That was a production in which there must have been a very minimum of men of fighting age and many a lady pirate, for Lord Kitchener had called and there might be white feathers at the stage door. But there was *Chu Chin Chow* too, which induced a gasping delight in the glamour of a stage which has remained with me to this day, though perhaps *Bitter-Sweet*, when the curtains rose on the ball scene, was the last time I watched such a scene without a faint checking up as to whether it were as accurate an illusion as it might be. Sometime just after the First World War I sat with burning cheeks (too many ices or chocolates) watching Charles Hawtrey in *Ambrose Applejohn's Adventure* wherein I noticed, I believe for the first time, that there was something called 'acting' in which a person not even pretending to be a 'real' character manipulated his spectators in such a way that a flimsy situation and worthless words (or no words at all) snowballed to exert total fascination – prolonged for just as long as the actor desired. It was a kind of acting which you do not get on television: a kind of acting which was to lose favour and belonged of course wholly to the live audience, squirming and guffawing in communion.

I want it believed that we were not particularly naïve as audiences, even those who enjoyed seeing themselves, the upper middle classes, mirrored for the upper circle matinée patrons. Many plays, definitely aimed for exactly that public, were very far from vapid or shallow, unless they were frankly family farces, like *George and Margaret*, with french windows and a comic maid with halitosis. This king of thing was anyway pilloried in its own time. That wit Herbert Farjeon would pepper his Little Revues with such pieces in parody. But a play like Dodie Smith's *Dear Octopus* would seem to be catering for a very limited section of potential theatre-goers today. (Don't forget another *Family Reunion* – T. S. Eliot's.) In a less cynical time the ironies of a play about hidden resentments and failures in a well-to-do bourgeois family such as Somerset Maugham's *For Services Rendered* struck home quite alarmingly. Beautifully acted, with Flora Robson going mad as a sex-starved spinster, Ralph Richardson as an axed naval chap who had got into money difficulties, spurned the spinster's offer of help in exchange for a wedding ring, blew his brains out which sent the spinster round the bend and brought the curtain down with her singing 'God Save the King' in a cracked giggle – such things seemed quite strong meat. Also in a time when the supernatural meant more than perhaps it does today, the faintly spooky play such as Sutton Vane's *Outward Bound* (where the passengers on a cruise discover they are really all dead), plays juggling with reality and dream-like commercialised Pirandello, Barrie's *Mary Rose* and *Dear Brutus* or that waif's dream *A Kiss for Cinderella* had more chance of weaving a spell.

We had a taste of realism too, social realism: not all a post-Second World War importation by any means. *The Likes of Her* and *Love on the Dole* seemed very 'real' and I daresay still would. Crime and the lower orders were however generally still comic, as in Shaw. But don't forget Galsworthy: *Loyalties* and *The Silver Box*, society's victims and scapegoats. Besides we were getting plays by O'Neill already: I remember standing at the back of a full house to see Flora Robson and Paul Robeson teamed together in *All God's Chillun*: she a white schoolmistress married to an industrious black student, a situation which (once again) sent her out of her mind. She suddenly appeared with a carving knife and yelled 'Nigger!' with such a sudden and powerful punch that a woman standing next to me healed over in a dead faint. I seem to remember many moments of real anguish: Sara Allgood in the final threnody of *Juno and the Paycock*, the recantation scene in Sybil's *Saint Joan* and Masha (Carol Goodner) saying goodbye to Gielgud's Colonel Vershinin in *The Three Sisters* (the Saint Denis master production). But here we are talking of plays of lasting greatness, furthermore they are dotted across a span of my life when I passed from boyhood through adolescence to young manhood and would, I feel sure, hit me quite as hard today after years of rather wary *critical* play-going.

What I am feeling for as indicative of theatre accepted if not quite believed in, during the Twenties and Thirties, is a play such as *Cynara* by H. M. Harwood and R. Gore Brown. late 1930. The title from Dowson's poem pointed to the theme: fidelity. ('I have been faithful to thee Cynara, in my fashion.') But the hero, who was du Maurier and so handsome, gentlemanly and highly sympathetic wasn't *strictly* faithful: there was a 'not to-night Josephine' line which brought down the curtain of a bedroom scene and was received with something like a collective blush, I recall. Better still was a curtain where Doris Fordred came to upbraid our hero who had got a pretty shopgirl whom he'd met at a bathing belle competition 'into trouble', and she had died. As her friend Miss Fordred broke the news with venom, adding 'you *bloody gentleman*!', I assure you that even at that date quite a sense of shock swept the dress circle.

It is permissiveness I suppose which has taken the sting out of that kind of outspoken curtain line. Somehow one always sensed that illegitimate sexual unions were doomed to death in childbed or, worse, by what was called 'an illegal operation' – nonsensical to our aborting times. It would seem that dramatists of our day have a harder time to find subjects which will shock or even surprise a modern audience; when drug taking was a hideous secret (*The Vortex*), homosexuality totally taboo except in disguise (*The Green Bay Tree*), a certain dramatic power still clung to adultery or danger of incest. But who would not think the fuss concerning Paula Tanqueray's dilemma disportionate today?

This is adduced as a reason for the cult of foul language and sheer brute violence prevailing in the theatre of today. But how specious seems such reasoning if you give it a little thought. Has there not always been violence in our theatre – however romanticised for the kind of kingly historical quasi-Shakespearean costume drama (of which *Richard of Bordeaux* is a good example and a fine way for the youngsters to appreciate the rising John Gielgud)? Even 'outside Shakespeare' (and I have taken pains to establish that this was always the position I play-went from), even without Gloucester's eye ('Out, vile jelly! Where's thy lustre now?') I think of the anxious cruel question at Joan's trial ('Has she been shewn the instruments?' [of torture]). Can I pretend that *that* did not stir me as a twelve-year-old?

Robert Loraine could swashbuckle romantically and run a sword through many a walk-on (all good clean fun). But what about that lamp he threw at his wife as *The Father* by Strindberg? And here the door of memory swings wide onto scenes of the most appalling albeit triviallised cruelty: those seasons of *grand guignol*, with hospital nurses in attendance for those who felt faint. Did we not as children and at matinées too gloat over the scene of two deranged old ladies waiting till dusk fell to put out the eyes of a girl forced to share their ward in an institution? Or the one about the White Russian princess bribing a prostitute to take the girl's place at a private supper with a bolshevik general and get her revenge with her long white gloves knotted into a garrotte? Throttlings: was it not the superb protean glamorous star of *Cavalcade* and that sort of Madame Ranevsky of Rodney Ackland's lovely *After October*, Mary Clare, who in *Ladies in Retirement* whipped a cord round her batty sister's throat?

The more I gaze at the crowded scene the more does it seem to me that only the most bold historical labelling and categorization can make out a case for there being one dominant sort of drama. The same person would appear in so many guises. Emlyn Williams, now, would *he* be a matinée idol under some classifications? I think I would have considered him so and have gladly taken my aunts (ah! this is getting warmer!) to see him in *The Corn is Green*, the illegitimate baby being cancelled out by the joy of seeing him autobiographic-ally winning his Oxford scholarship. But also *Night Must Fall*, with the head

'. . . she possessed a dreamlike quality, yet personified a perfect English rose':
Lily Elsie in a 'Merry Widow' hat.

George Alexander and
Mrs Patrick Campbell in
The Second Mrs Tanqueray
by A. W. Pinero, 1893.

Charles Wyndham and Mary Moore
in *David Garrick*
by T. W. Robertson, 1886.

Lewis Waller as Henry V. 1900.

LEWIS WALLER
AS
"HARRY THE KING"

Marie Tempest in *Penelope* by
W. Somerset Maugham, 1909.

Doris Keane and Owen Nares in
Romance by Edward Sheldon, 1915.

Henry Ainley and Evelyn Millard in
Paolo and Francesca
by Stephen Phillips, 1902.

Gerald du Maurier
in *Brewster's Millions*
by McCutcheon,
Smith and Ongley,
1907.

Gerald du Maurier and Lawrence Irving in *Raffles* by Presbrey and Hornung, 1906.

Gladys Cooper: from the perfect
'Pear's Soap Beauty'
to a true matinée idol.

Gaby Deslys: among her 'victims' were
Jean Cocteau, James M. Barrie and the
King of Portugal.

Gertie Millar in
The Quaker Girl
by Lionel Monckton, 1910.

Jack Buchanan in
Mr Whittington, 1934:
'the word "debonair"
might have been invented
to describe him.'

Gertrude Lawrence photographed by Cecil Beaton:
'style, beauty, glamorous charm, gaiety, heart-throb'.

Bobby Howes and Cicely Courtneidge in *Hide and Seek*, 1937

Ivor Novello:
'He had merely to appear on the stage
or walk into a room
for that stage and that room
to glow with what seemed to be
the light of many lamps.'

Ivor Novello in *Perchance to Dream*, 1945.

Ivor Novello
and Gladys Cooper
in *Enter Kiki* by
Blow and Hoare,
1923.

José Collins
in *A Southern Maid*
by Fraser Simson,
1920.

Phyllis and
Zena Dare,
their parents
and brother Jack,
1906.

Evelyn Laye in *Bitter-Sweet*
by Noël Coward, New York, 1929.

Yvonne Printemps in *Mozart* by Sacha Guitry, 1929.

Anna Neagle, Cedric Hardwick and Jeanne De Casalis in *Nell Gwyn*, 1934.

Noël Coward:
'a child of the
twentieth century
and one of its more
elegant veterans,
the writer of its blues,
chronicler of its moods
and provider of
its escapism'
Portrait by
Cecil Beaton.

Coward,
the Master
by Cecil Beaton.

Laurette Taylor,
'wistful, quaint, beguiling'.

Alfred Lunt and Lynn Fontanne,
'the perfect stage combination',
in *The Taming of the Shrew*, New York, 1935.

John Barrymore as François Villon
in the film *The Beloved Rogue*:
'every inch the matinée idol'.

Lionel Barrymore:
not only a very fine character actor,
but a painter and a musician of ability.

Ethel Barrymore
numbered Winston Churchill
among her suitors
and was once engaged to
Gerald du Maurier.

Lillian Gish: when Hollywood decided that her days as an idol were numbered, she left without a backward glance to return to a career on the stage.

Louis Jouvet and
Madeleine Ozeray in
Tessa, Paris, 1934.

Jean-Louis Barrault,
Cécile Sorel
and Arletty in
Crions le sur les toits,
Paris, 1937

Maurice Chevalier: 'he *was* France'.

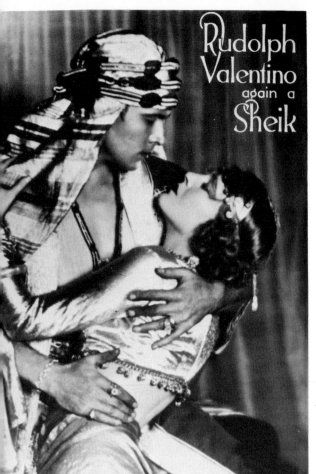

Rudolph
Valentino
again a
Sheik

Rudolph Valentino
and Vilma Banky in
Son of the Sheik,
1926.

Ramon Navarro and May McAvoy in *Ben Hur*, 1927.

Douglas Fairbanks Sr. and Mary Pickford in *The Taming of the Shrew*, 1929.

Clara Bow, 'the ''It'' Girl'.

Pola Negri in *Woman of the World*, 1926:
she represented a new kind of female exoticism.

Theda Bara, pre-World War I 'prototype exotic'
·of the screen.

Greta Garbo and Mervyn Douglas in *Ninotchka*, 1939.

Humphrey Bogart and Ingrid Bergman in *Casablanca*, 1942.

Marlene Dietrich in
The Scarlet Empress,
1934.

Clark Gable
and Jean Harlow
in *Red Dust*,
1933.

John Gielgud in
The Importance of Being Earnest,
1947.

above right:
Margaret Rutherford,
Kay Hammond and Fay·Compton
in Noël Coward's
Blithe Spirit,
1941.

Marilyn Monroe:
the idol of the Fifties.

Lawrence Olivier in *Richard III*, 1944.

John Neville as Iago
and Richard Burton as Othello
in *Othello*,
1956.

Richard Burton
as Iago
and John Neville
as Othello
in *Othello*,
1956.

in the hat box? Less certain. And what about Edith Evans for the sound of whose voice one would queue at any play whether she were miscast in it – this could happen, with a trifle or two which I suppose were dismissed as matinée plays – but pre-eminently, would might say eternally, as Millamant in *The Way of The World*? And Fay Compton, whose timing and comedy and eternally youthful voice made a play like *Autumn Crocus* seem as worthwhile also as *Mary Rose*? Gwen Ffrangcon-Davies who could be so wonderful in O'Neill or Chekhov (Olga of *The Three Sisters*) drew the town as Elizabeth Barrett in a skilful but hardly more than superficially searching play about a father-daughter relationship and a happy elopement ('Flush, if you bark now . . . '). Ought this to be rated a matinée play because it gives a leading lady the test of a long part on a couch? (Poor Sarah, after she lost a leg, actually had such a play written for her, in which she played an ailing young man tormented by debts, and played it in London at the Prince's Theatre.) Would a Frenchman – since my eye has strayed near Paris – have thought that Réjane playing *La Parisienne* by Henry Becque was involved in 'a matinée play' and making a matinée idol of herself? I think not. Marie Tempest, an English equivalent in some ways, was apt on the whole to despise matinée audiences, though I fancy the label might stick better on her career than some others, if we mean that she consistently played in roles which she could decorate her own way rather than meet the challenge of great acting parts. Still, perhaps just because of this, some of us can now still see her drawing off a pair of gloves (or some such gesture) and tilting her head preparatory to saying something trivial with a timing and sarcasm that set the audience off like a ten gun salute.

Lilian Braithwaite, Yvonne Arnaud? We *did* know, it is true, exactly what we wanted them to do and that may well be a rough and ready way of making up the category (not a task I am at all adept in). As for the gentlemen of the boards my thoughts stray (as it should not for purposes of this chapter) to the lyric stage: to dancers of the Russian ballet such as Massine, surely a matinée idol if ever there was one, or to Harry Welchman who was every rogue prince, royal student and gentleman pirate rolled into one, and then on to IvorNovello, of whom Lewis Casson said, when the young profile assayed Shakespeare, that, as Henry v, his prayer on the eve of Agincourt was the best he had ever heard!

It has been strange to stir so many ghosts and I should now feel that I can separate matinée idols and the matinée plays in which they flourished from all the other theatrical thrills of a long, pre-critical or largely pre-critical love affair with the glamour of the theatre. But I cannot truly do so. In self defence I do declare there ain't no such animal.

There is farce which we know: there is tragedy we recognise. But comedy intrinsically excellent or passable only as vehicles for players of strong, beautiful or notorious personality, will elude any simple definition. It was Queen Christina of Sweden who said 'A bad comedy is a great mortification.' The corollary is also true.

THE matinée idol was not confined to the West End of London, Both Broadway and the theatres of the boulevards saw the rise and rise of the same phenomenon. From the earliest days there was some to-ing and fro-ing of idols between each of these centres. An impresario such as Charles Frohman, friend of J. M. Barrie and Somerset Maugham, operated from both London and New York until his untimely death in 1915. He started the tradition of American involvement in the West End. In this section George Oppenheimer looks at the Broadway theatre in a long perspective of idols over which the Barrymore dynasty and the Lunts cast their regal shadows. The actor O. Z. Whitehead then gives us an intimate close-up of one silent movie idol, Lilian Gish, in her later years as a stage actress, and Roland Gant unrolls a proud Parisian pageant of monstres sacrés.

A.C.

The Great Days of Broadway

George Oppenheimer

WHEN I was a stripling well over half a century ago I was sent to a boys' camp in the Thousand Islands on the St Lawrence River. Much to my displeasure, since I was not an ardent sports fan, I was forced to play baseball. Since the other boys at camp were not notably good at the game, I elected to play in the outfield and could be found there on a sunny afternoon reading *Theater Magazine* in a rocking-chair. I was seldom disturbed except by an outraged councillor who thought I was being un-American.

Theater Magazine with its feature reviews, 'Mr Hornblow Goes to the Play', was my bible and since I had to be on an island instead of on an aisle, I made the best of it. In those days I had my own collection of matinée idols, male and female and have remained loyal to them until they either died or retired.

In 1955 I became drama critic of a flourishing newspaper, Long Island's *Newsday* and even that could not douse my enthusiasm for the theatre. The affair began when I was taken to my first plays, circa 1906 or 7. (My memory isn't what it used to be. In fact, I can't even recall what it used to be.)

When I started going to theatre, the play was less the thing than the player and those were idyllic days for the matinée idol. As early as 1912 George Jean Nathan wrote an article in *Theater Magazine* in which he said, 'The star system is falling gradually from grace.' He had a long time to wait before his prophecy came true. Today you can count on one hand the names that will fill a theatre and even they can no longer do so if their play is bad.

During the time that this book covers the star system flourished. There were some who were not very good actors but who, by the appeal of their personalities or good looks, overcame their histrionic lacks. Such a one was Maxine Elliott whom some considered 'the most beautiful woman in the world'. The financier J. Pierpont Morgan built a theatre for her, King Edward VII was rumoured to have built her a villa on the Mediterranean, and scores of famous men were supposed to be her lovers. She was a legend as a woman and a wash-out as an actress. There is an amusing photograph in *The Movies* by Richard Griffith and Arthur Mayer. Maxine had gone in 1918 to the Goldwyn studio to make *The Eternal Magdalene*. The picture was captioned 'Watching director Arthur Hopkins trying to knead Maxine Elliott's beautiful face into the semblance of an expression.' Fortunately she did not like acting and retired early.

Lou Tellegen, Sarah Bernhardt's leading man and for a short while the husband of the lovely opera singer Geraldine Farrar (I saw this idol being drawn through the streets when the young blades of the Opera Club pulled her car, with garlands of flowers, on the occasion of her farewell performance, for well over two miles) was another who depended more on his striking looks than his acting. His fame and popularity resulted from his reputation as a great lover. He led an adventuresome and romantic life and capped it with a book which he modestly called *Women Have Been Kind* and which Dorothy Parker summed up by adding 'of Stupid'.

In 1910 Broadway, 'the Great White Way', and its side streets housed over forty theatres, several of them on 42nd Street. Today it is infested by massage parlours, pornographic bookstores and peep-shows, and largely inhabited by drug-pushers, junkies, prostitutes and hoodlums. By the 1920s the number of theatres had doubled and according to the former dean of critics Brooks Atkinson, in his sterling book, *Broadway*: 'The annual number of productions had increased from 126 in 1917 to 208 in 1927 and to 264 in 1928 – the all-time peak of production.' A handful of these playhouses were in Greenwich Village and other parts of Manhattan in what we now call off-Broadway. By way of contrast, at the time of this writing and at the height of the season, there are no more than 20 plays on Broadway and only a few more off.

From 1910 until the advent of talking pictures in 1927, vaudeville was tre-mendously popular. Its showcase was the Palace Theatre, which opened in 1913. Many of the foremost stars, such as Sarah Bernhardt, Ethel Barrymore and Alla Nazimova, appeared at the Palace in sketches sandwiched in between trained seal acts and song and dance teams. It was an honour to play at the Palace – both for the idols and the seals.

After the play the 'stage-door Johnnies' would wait outside the Broadway theatres for the more glamorous actresses or for the most attractive showgirls, especially those who decorated Florenz Ziegfeld's lavish 'Follies'. On matinée days the ladies had their innings, munching chocolate creams and sighing volubly over their favourite male stars.

I remember a matinée of *Hamlet* when John Barrymore was in the midst of his 'To be or not to be' soliloquy. A lady behind me turned to her female companion and muttered, 'I hear he takes dope.' I hushed her so loudly that everyone in the vicinity hushed me.

On an opening night in those dear dead days the orchestra seats were filled with gentlemen, either in white ties and tails or tuxedoes, while their ladies were festooned with jewels and minks. I doubt greatly if the coatless, tieless, spotted dirndl set of today could have got past the outer lobby on an opening night or even thereafter.

The royal family of the theatre was the Drew-Barrymore clan. John Drew Senior, an actor, married Louisa Lane, who became one of the first actress-managers of the American stage. Their son, John Drew Junior, was a leading actor from the late nineteenth century well into the twentieth. He won the admiration of both men and women, not alone for his acting but for his court-liness and gentility. He was, in his day, one of the first gentlemen of the stage. Plays in which he exhibited his skill and personality were *Smith*, *Major Pendennis*, adapted from the Thackeray novel, Somerset Maugham's *The Circle* in which he co-starred with Mrs Leslie Carter, and many Shakespearean comedies.

He had a younger sister, Georgianna. Her father, Drew Senior, died at the age of 35 when she was only a child. She too went on the stage and met a young and handsome English actor, Maurice Barrymore. He had been the lightweight champion of England and, by all accounts, was a better boxer than an actor. They married and from this union came Ethel, Lionel and John, three of the most remarkable and popular actors of the century. Since their mother and father were constantly touring in various plays and places, the three youngsters were brought up mostly by their grandmother, Mrs Drew.

I fell in love with Ethel when I first saw her in *Déclassée* by Zoe Atkins. She had beauty, stature, a deep voice and a personality so commanding and attractive that you could hardly take your eyes off her to watch the other actors. Again and again she scored in a variety of plays – *Captain Jinks of the Horse Marines*, *Our Mrs MacChesney*, *The Second Mrs Tanqueray*, *The Lady of the Camellias* and so many more.

I remember a reception in Hollywood for Adlai Stevenson. I had the good fortune to sit next to Miss B. as we waited to be presented to Stevenson. She was as excited as a debutante at her first dance and I feel sure that Stevenson was equally excited at meeting her.

On her seventieth birthday in 1949 there was a radio tribute to her by President Truman, ex-President Hoover, Winston Churchill, Eleanor Roosevelt and many of the most prominent actors on stage and in films. She described the happy occasion in her book, *Memories*, the final lines of which read: 'Since I have finished this book Lionel has died. I like to think that he and Jack are together and that they will be glad to see me.' Who wouldn't?

When she was stricken with pneumonia during the Second World War, the news bulletin on the Times building announced in its travelling electric light strip, 'General MacArthur lands at Leyte. . . . Ethel Barrymore's temperature lower.' And Alexander Woollcott said of her, 'Do you know that practically all the staid gentlemen of London were about to jump out of windows for love of her?' Among her many English suitors was Winston Churchill who, it is said, proposed to her but was turned down because Ethel could not see herself as the wife of a politician; and for a while she was engaged to Gerald du Maurier.

She loved laughter and had a keen wit of her own. When she was playing in her last play, *Embezzled Heaven*, a doorman came into her dressing room and announced that a lady, who claimed to have been in school with her, was waiting outside. 'Wheel her in,' commanded Ethel. There were so many sides to her character and her interests were so diversified. Katharine Hepburn, a close friend, said of her, 'it's the world she's interested in – or rather a lot of different worlds – sports [she was an ardent baseball fan], history, music, politics, books.'

The greatest hit of her later years was *The Corn is Green* by that gifted actor and writer, Emlyn Williams. In it she played a school-teacher of a group of children of miners in a small Welsh town. One of these youngsters proved to be a pupil of great promise and the play revolved largely about their relationship. Although she was at first undecided about it being right for her, it became one of her best and most successful roles.

Ethel died in Hollywood, where she had made a number of pictures, in 1959 at the age of 79.

Lionel was never an idol to the same degree as his sister and brother. There are those, however, who considered him the best actor of the three in addition to being a remarkable man. 'Lionel Barrymore is not only one of the greatest character actors of his day,' said Arthur Hopkins in his book, *To a Lonely Boy* (a series of inspirational letters that he wrote to a friendless, invalided boy), 'but the most cultured and gifted man I have known. He has a deep knowledge of the arts, music, painting, sculpture, is himself a painter and musician of ability, does etchings that compare with the masters, and has absorbed more literature than seems possible.'

His start was not auspicious. In 1894 he appeared in his grandmother Mrs Drew's stock company and received a letter from her that read in part: 'You were somewhat inadequate and it is with the deepest regret that I convey the news that it is no longer necessary that you appear in the cast. I shall see you in the morning, dear boy. Until then, good night, and God bless you. Your affectionate grandmother, Louisa Drew.'

One of my most vivid memories is seeing Lionel and John in *The Jest*, a rich Italian Renaissance melodrama adapted from Sem Benelli. Lionel played Neri, a mercenary who was the sworn enemy of John, who succeeded in outwitting him. With Lionel as the brawn and John as the brain, they brought terror and wonder to their parts.

Even in his youth, Lionel cast himself as a character actor. In actual fact, he did not like acting and may have hidden himself behind beards and wigs to overcome self-consciousness.

One of his earliest roles was an organ-grinder in one of his uncle John Drew's starring comedies *The Mummy and the Hummingbird*. He came off so well in the part that his uncle used to complain, according to Mr Atkinson in *Broadway*, 'Every night I have to play second-fiddle to that preposterous nephew of mine.'

Probably Lionel's most famous role was in *The Copperhead*, a Civil War play by Augustus Thomas, in which he was suspected of being a traitor and had to conceal the fact that he was actually a spy for President Lincoln. Another great success was as the terrible-tempered Colonel Ibbetson with John as his son and Constance Collier as the Duchess of Towers, young Ibbetson's great love, in *Peter Ibbetson*, adapted from George du Maurier's popular novel.

Lionel never recovered from a disastrous production of *Macbeth*, one of his rare failures. They tell the story of Kelcey Allen, drama critic for *Women's Wear*, who was seated next to a theatre ticket agent by the name of McBride. In the last act, during the battle, Macbeth challenges MacDuff with the words, 'Lay on, MacDuff,' whereupon Allen added, 'Lay off, McBride.'

Under pressure he did one more play and then fled to Hollywood with his second wife, the actress Irene Fenwick. Here he would no longer be exposed to audiences.

In Hollywood he became one of Metro-Goldwyn-Mayer's brightest stars. He played with Lew Ayres in the *Doctor Kildare* series and it was sometimes difficult to recognize the gruff and grumpy old doctor with the heart of gold as the former bright star of Broadway. However, he succeeded in Hollywood, as he had back East, in acting character parts with consummate skill.

Lionel died there in 1954 at the age of 76, leaving behind him a book about himself and his family, *We Barrymores*.

John was the most highly publicized of the Barrymores, not always in a good light. His personal life was, to put it mildly, colourful. His marriages and divorces, his drinking bouts, his uninhibited wit were all grist for the mills of the newspapers, especially the tabloids. Yet he was a brilliant actor in both comedy and drama, in the frothy *The Fortune Hunter*, Tolstoy's tragic *The Living Corpse*, renamed *Redemption*, Shakespeare's taxing *Richard III* or the melodrama, *Kick In*.

His acting in Galsworthy's *Justice* still seems to me as great as anything I have seen since. As for his *Hamlet*, there has never been anything quite like it. It was a triumph both here and in England. One of the very few dissenting voices was that of George Bernard Shaw, whom he had invited to the opening night in London and who sat with John's wife, Michael Strange.

In John's book, *Confessions of an Actor*, he reprints Shaw's letter. Shaw admitted that 'Everyone felt that the occasion was one of extraordinary interest, and so far as your personality was concerned they were not disappointed.' Then he goes on to complain about the cuts that John had made, in the text and some of his divergencies from tradition. 'Now your success in this,' says Shaw, 'must depend on whether the play invented by Barrymore on the Shakespear [Shaw never allowed the Bard his final 'e'] foundation is as gripping as the Shakespear play.' Despite Shaw's objections that it was Barrymore's *Hamlet* rather than Shakespeare's, it was a great success, so much so that Lionel claimed Shakespeare had John in mind when he wrote *Hamlet*.

In appearance John was every inch the matinée idol with his piercing eyes (Lionel, when asked what colour they were, said 'bloodshot'), his grace and his virile figure. He seemed to me the embodiment of Shakespeare's Mercutio, a part he played to perfection on film in Metro's *Romeo and Juliet* with Norma Shearer and Leslie Howard. There was about him a quicksilver quality.

One of his greatest entrances was in *The Jest*. A banquet was taking place on stage when there was a knocking at the door. The back of the banqueting-room opened and there stood John, 'the Great Profile,' in tights and Renaissance garb, a dagger at his belt and a dwarf crouched at his feet, against a sky-blue background. Strong women fainted (and if they didn't, they should have).

Years later another actor, not nearly as attractive or as able as John, revived *The Jest*, claiming that he would outdo John in the part. On his first entrance he was dressed in tights with a wig like John's and all the other costume appurtenances. There was a pause. Then from the back of the house there could be heard a man's voice that said, 'My God, it's Ethel.'

John not only looked romantic, he was. In addition to his numerous affairs he was married four times – to Katherine Corri Harris of the *Social Register*, to Michael Strange, a poetess, to Dolores Costello of film fame and to Elaine Barrie.

Gene Fowler, John's close friend, wrote a highly readable biography of John, *Good Night, Sweet Prince*. He quotes the great lover on his marriage to Katherine Harris: 'This event was the first of my three and one-half marriages – all of them bus accidents.' Michael Strange, his second wife, wrote a play entitled *Clair de Lune*. Somehow she persuaded John, who persuaded Ethel, to act in it. It was a disaster. Fowler says of the second Mrs Barrymore, 'She had the face of a Romney portrait and the spirit of a U.S. Marine.'

Dolores Costello came of a family of film stars. The moment John saw her, he insisted that she should play opposite him in *The Sea Beast*, a film he was about to make. He wooed her, won her and lost her. The fourth or 'half-marriage' was to a would-be actress and a would-be Mrs Barrymore, Elaine Barrie, who made news by pursuing him cross-country. She finally caught him and their marriage was the stormiest of all. 'I never married any of my wives,' said John. 'They married me.' He appeared with Miss Barrie in a worthless comedy, *My Dear Children*, in which he misbehaved and improvised outrageously.

Ethel was constantly watching over Jack but it was not an easy task. His drinking increased by leaps and bounds. 'You can't drown yourself in drink,' he once said to Fowler, 'I've tried: you float.' Painter John Decker, another one of his good friends (he did an amazing line drawing of John on his death-bed) went to visit him in the hospital and advised his nurse, 'Never give him anything in a small glass unless you know it can be safely taken internally.'

John died in 1942 at the age of 60. Despite his drinking, his eccentricities (he once appeared at a curtain-call in *Hamlet* with a saxophone under his arm) and his highly publicized romances, he is to be remembered for his well-deserved theatre fame rather than his notoriety.

Although Ethel had acted with John, and John had acted with Lionel, the three of them did not appear together until the Metro film *Rasputin*. It was said to have been less a reunion than an up-staging contest.

Another idol whose life, in her later years, was spoiled by drink was Laurette Taylor. At the start of her career she acted in Seattle in a series of melodramas written by her husband Charles A. Taylor. Her second husband, an Englishman by the name of J. Hartley Manners, was also a playwright and Laurette acted in many of his plays.

The most successful of these was *Peg O' My Heart*, which opened in 1912, ran for 604 performances on Broadway, and won for her a crowd of adoring followers. Manners, in common with Taylor, was more prolific than profound and his plays, though they provided excellent roles for his wife, were mostly second-rate.

Despite the fact that Miss Taylor had a difficult time getting it produced and that it received mixed reviews, *Peg* turned out to be one of the best-loved comedies of its time, both here and in London. Queen Mary, wife of George v, called Laurette 'quite the most delightful actress America has ever sent us'. 'Delightful' was the word for Laurette. She was wistful, quaint, beguiling, not a beauty but so full of charm and spirit that she seemed beautiful. According to her daughter, Marguerite Courtney, in her excellent biography *Laurette*, her mother said of herself, 'I was born round. Everything. Eyes. Cheeks. Lips. Figure.'

In *Peg* she played an Irish waif who came into an English household and managed to creep into the hearts of its members. She had with her a dog called Michael ('he' was actually a 'she'), an ingratiating mongrel, who loved acting and did it to perfection.

One of her early successes was in *Alias Jimmy Valentine* in which she played opposite another idol, H. B. Warner, in the role of a safecracker. She also made a hit as an Hawaiian maiden in *The Bird of Paradise* opposite Lewis Stone, who years later went to Hollywood to become the father in the Andy Hardy series. Among the plays by her husband in which she appeared was *Out There*, revived during the war with an all-star company that added a considerable amount of money to the war chest. Its cast consisted of such popular names as George Arliss, Chauncey Olcott, James K. Hackett, George M. Cohan, idols all.

Other plays by Manners in which Laurette starred were *The Harp of Life*, *The Wooing of Eve*, and *Happiness*. She could also play glamorous roles as she proved in her husband's *The National Anthem* in which she impersonated the young wife of a wastrel on their Paris honeymoon. It was during the jazz era and Miss Taylor died beautifully to the faint strains of an orchestra that was playing 'The Sheik of Araby' in their hotel.

After the death of Manners, Miss Taylor became an alcoholic. Then in 1938 she came back in *Outward Bound* in a small but rewarding role. It was six years later that she made her great success and gave the finest performance of her career (and the best I have ever seen) as Amanda Wingfield, the Southern lady come on bad times and living in an imagined past, in Tennessee Williams' poignant *The Glass Menagerie*. She died shortly thereafter.

One of the actresses in Laurette's company was Lynn Fontanne, a rather scrawny young English girl whom she had met and befriended in London. Laurette believed in her and invited her to come to New York and join her acting company. Lynn consented and was with her in several Manners plays.

According to Maurice Zolotov in his biography of the Lunts, *Stagestruck*, it was in 1919 that Lynn first caught sight of a young man called Alfred Lunt. She asked to be introduced. 'Alfred, who was nervously poised on the iron staircase backstage, took a few steps forward to take her hand. He stumbled and tripped and fell on his face before her.

'Upon hearing of this, George S. Kaufman remarked: "Well, he certainly fell for her".'

Kaufman was prophetic. They played together in a stock company in Washington, DC and before long they were in love. Booth Tarkington, the popular novelist and playwright, had written a play especially for Alfred and now it was ready. It was called *Clarence* and Alfred played the title role (and a saxophone) with Helen Hayes, Glenn Hunter and Mary Boland. Alfred was an overnight success and so was the play.

However, the affair between Lynn and Alfred did not go smoothly. Hattie, Alfred's mother, being a possessive lady, objected to giving up her son. And producer George C. Tyler had separate plans for them. A young British actor-playwright-composer-lyricist with the odd name of Noël Coward (still an idol until his death in the Seventies) came to America and looked up Lynn, met Alfred and approved heartily.

However, further complications ensued with Alfred appearing with Billie Burke in another Tarkington opus *The Intimate Strangers* (a failure), and Lynn was still in *Dulcy*. Finally, on 20 May 1922 *Dulcy* closed and *Intimate Strangers* shuttered and Lynn and Alfred, again according to Zolotov, six days later 'went by subway to the Municipal Building. They entered the Marriage Bureau. They filled out the forms. Two witnesses were needed for the civil ceremony.' Alfred scrambled out into the corridors and managed to get two witnesses from whom they had to borrow the marriage fee of two dollars. Alfred having forgotten his wallet and Lynn her purse. Thus began the most successful, the happiest and most productive marriage in recent theatrical history.

For a while they acted apart. Then Theresa Helburn of the young and struggling Theater Guild had one of her many inspirations. The Lunts were made for the Ferenc Molnar comedy, *The Guardsman*. They agreed and the rest is history.

There followed such outstanding successes as Shaw's *Arms and the Man*. They did, in addition, the same author's *The Doctor's Dilemma* and *Pygmalion*. However, it was playwright Robert E. Sherwood who supplied them with three of their greatest triumphs – *Reunion in Vienna, Idiot's Delight* and *There Shall Be No Night*.

Sherwood in *Stage* magazine stated that 'from the point of view of the writer, to have a play produced by the Lunts is the highest possible privilege. More than that it is the best possible training in the art and craft of the theatre.' And he wrote in the same article: 'Yes – they are hams in all respects save one – and that happens to be an enormously important one; they are entirely unselfish.'

Probably no two actors were ever so in tune with each other. They formed the perfect stage combination. They lived and breathed the theatre. That fine critic, John Mason Brown, said of them in his book *Dramatis Personae*, 'Although I have no way of proving this, I suspect that they must have been married near the altar of Dionysos. Undoubtedly, had they trouped up the gangplank of the Ark, they would have turned it in no time into a showboat.'

In *Idiot's Delight* Alfred played Harry Van, a vaudevillian who has an act with six chorus girls, while Lynn acted Irene, posing as a Russian courtesan, whom Alfred swears he has slept with 'some years before'. To see Alfred tap-dancing with his six blondes was a revelation and Lynn's phony Russian was a delight.

Reunion in Vienna had to do with an Austrian archduke and his former mistress. In one scene Alfred was supposed to lift the skirt of a hotel proprietress (played by that superior character actress, Helen Westley) to reveal her red drawers. His line was, 'I see nothing has changed in Vienna.' One evening Miss Westley, who was notoriously careless, forgot her drawers. Always the complete professional, Alfred hoisted her skirt and unabashedly spoke the line.

There Shall Be No Night was a brilliant and moving anti-war drama which provided them with a change of pace and two of their greatest roles.

Proof of their perfect timing and their oneness, if such proof was needed, was contained in a scene from Friedrich Dürrenmatt's *The Visit*, their last play. Lynn was an enormously wealthy woman returning to her village to wreak vengeance on Alfred, who had seduced and then deserted her many years before. They met and, for a few moments, Lynn's plan was laid aside, while they reminisced. With every move and every speech and gesture attuned, it seemed like a lovely ballet.

S. N. Behrman, Noël Coward and Shaw provided them with other successful comedies. One of the most popular of these was *Design for Living*, which Coward wrote for the Lunts and himself, a comedy in which Lynn, Alfred and Noël lived together in semi-amity.

Lynn loves clothes and makes most of her own; Alfred's main hobby outside the theatre is cooking, which he does superlatively well. They live in Ten Chimneys, Genesee Depot, Wisconsin, and only a superior play with rewarding parts might lure them back to the stage. Since they started acting together, they have only been separated once (by the Theatre Guild), when Lynn starred in Eugene O'Neill's mammoth stream of consciousness, *Strange Interlude*, and Alfred was in the same author's *Marco's Million*.

As regards their roles, they are altogether selfless. Lynn, one season would play Maxwell Anderson's *Elizabeth the Queen* in which she had the major role; at another Alfred would have the far better part in Behrman's *Meteor*.

Not only on stage but off, they are immensely popular with a wide circle of friends and idolators. Even now, in their old age, they make a striking couple that commands all eyes, even those of the benighted few who have never seen them, when they enter a room. They happen to be my particular idols of all the actors and actresses that I have seen and been fortunate enough to know.

I think I have seen almost every one of their plays. I may have disliked a handful, but I could never dislike the Lunts, not even if I were put to the rack.

American audiences warm to husband-and-wife and other family teams. In this respect one of the most durable and versatile of idols was George M. Cohan, who was already a popular star in 1910. Not only did he write the books for his musical shows such as *Yankee Doodle Dandy, Forty-Five Minutes from*

Broadway, The Yankee Prince, Broadway Jones and *The Little Millionaire*, he was also responsible for the music and lyrics. For a long while he appeared with his father, mother and sister in a series of musical comedies, and in every one, he made a curtain speech that, together with the American flag which he was constantly waving, became his trademark – 'My mother thanks you, my father thanks you, my sister thanks you, and I thank you.'

He produced his own shows and was a theatrical industry in himself. He presented a series of 'Cohan Revues' which poked gentle fun at the Broadway scene. He also wrote popular and creditable straight comedies, notably *Seven Keys to Baldpate, Get-Rich-Quick Wallingford* and *The Tavern*. Only in his later years did he consent to appear under other managements than his own or in plays by other authors – Eugene O'Neill's *Ah, Wilderness!* and *I'd Rather Be Right*, the Richard Rodgers and Lorenz Hart musical with its book by George S. Kaufman and Moss Hart, in which he impersonated Franklin D. Roosevelt. Among his many songs was World War I's 'Over There' for which he received a Congressional Medal from F.D.R. There is a statue of him on Broadway, the avenue he helped to make famous. After Cohan's death James Cagney played him in a movie called *Yankee Doodle Dandy* and Joel Grey impersonated him in a stage musical, *George M.*

Cohan, on stage, was a dynamo. He danced and sang and waved the flag with an energy that bordered on the supernatural. Critic Ward Morehouse wrote a biography of this song-and-dance man, called *George M. Cohan. Prince of the American Theatre*. In it he describes him as 'a slender, jaunty, bounding young man with a straw hat and a bamboo cane, a nasal twang and a Yankee Doodle strut'. He was not a handsome man but his personality was so engaging and his grin so infectious that his popularity grew to great proportions.

Cohan's image was badly tarnished when in 1919 Actors' Equity called a strike in order to reform certain unfair practices. Cohan sided with the managers. (He was a manager himself, both alone and with Sam Harris, one of the best-loved men of the theatre.) Cohan helped form a rival union to Equity, known as The Actors Fidelity League or 'Fido', as it was called by the strikers. Such Equity members as Ethel Barrymore, Marie Dressler, Ed Wynn, Eddie Cantor and scores of others joined the strikers, and Cohan became one of their principal targets. Equity won and Cohan never quite recovered from the battle.

Nor in any survey of Broadway idols however incomplete should one forget the producers who were responsible to a great extent for cultivating these idols. One of the foremost was David Belasco, actor, playwright, impresario, director and eccentric with his rages and his clerical collar. Under his management were Mrs Leslie Carter, Blanche Bates, David Warfield, Jane Cowl, Frances Starr and Lenore Ulric, a sultry, sexy lady who scored highly in *Kiki* and *Lulu Belle*.

Perhaps the greatest maker of idols was Charles Frohman under whose management were the three Barrymores (they later went over to Arthur Hopkins), Maude Adams (it was rumoured that she was either secretly married to Frohman or was his common-law wife), Julia Marlowe who, for many years, co-starred with her husband, E. H. Sothern, in a series of Shakespearean productions, Otis Skinner, Marie Doro and for a while, Billie Burke. Frohman, unhappily, was one of those who went down with the Lusitania in 1915.

Then, of course, there was Flo Ziegfeld who, according to the subtitle of a recent biography, was *The Man Who Invented Women*. The loveliest show girls of all time – Kay Laurell, Marion Davies, Dolores, Olive Thomas, Lilyan Tashman, Justine Johnston and many more beauties appeared in his 'Follies'. Ziegfeld's first wife (there were some doubts about the legality of their marriage) was musical comedy queen Anna Held; his second was Billie Burke, who played to acclaim in many straight shows.

Another of his girls became the finest comedienne of her day. She was Ina Claire and she went on from musical comedies (such as *The Quaker Girl*) to star in several of Behrman's sophisticated and witty comedies, notably *Biography*. Not only was she (and probably still is) a great beauty, but she seemed the acme of sophistication. She was also one of the most beautifully dressed women on and off stage.

A stage couple that made history was Howard Lindsay and Dorothy Stickney, mainly by reason of *Life With Father* which broke all records for longevity. The play was written by Lindsey and Russell Crouse. The latter one night acted the part of the doctor to see, as he said, 'if there was a doctor in the Crouse'. And there were also Frederic March and Florence Eldridge, who worked together in several plays until March went to Hollywood to become a motion picture idol.

During the great period there were many actors who started on Broadway but whose principal popularity came after they were lured to Hollywood. Among them were Douglas Fairbanks Senior, John Garfield, Milton Sills, Barbara Stanwyck, Claudette Colbert, Clark Gable, Chester Morris, James Cagney, Melvyn Douglas, Herbert Marshall, Brian Aherne, Franchot Tone, Frank Morgan, Spencer Tracy, Francis Lederer, Miriam Hopkins, Katharine Hepburn, and Paulette Goddard. Some of them returned from time to time to the stage but their main fame was in films.

There were also the English actors, imports who chose to do a large portion of their acting in this country. Foremost among them was Noël Coward who wrote and acted his way to enduring fame. His comedy *Private Lives*, in which he originally starred with Gertrude Lawrence, is constantly and happily being revived. He wrote, directed, composed and acted, all with equal success. At the moment of writing this there are two successful shows celebrating his songs and lyrics, *Cowardy Custard* in London and *Oh, Coward* off-Broadway.

His was an infinite wit on and off stage. One of my favourite stories concerns the late Clifton Webb, the musical comedy and film star. Webb was constantly with his mother, Mabel. When she died at a ripe old age, he was plunged into gloom. Coward, an old friend of his, phoned him from England to Hollywood to condole. At the sound of Coward's voice, Webb burst into tears and continued to cry uninterruptedly while the telephone toll mounted. Finally Coward, who could not get a word in between sobs, lost patience and said, 'Clifton, it is not unusual for a man of seventy-three to be left an orphan.'

Coward wrote much of the material of *Charlot's Revue* which brought to this country the glamorous Gertrude Lawrence, one of the most courted ladies of the stage, and my favourite comedienne, Beatrice Lillie, who makes me laugh even when I think of one of her sketches. In it she played a famous French actress of the Nineties come to London to hear the reading of a play. The playwright was just completing the reading as the sketch started and he eagerly turned to Miss Lillie to get her impression. 'I have not understood one goddamn word you say,' said the inimitable Bea.

Before I close let me recall three actresses who all became idols of the first magnitude in the period between the wars. Tallulah Bankhead was not nearly as fine an actress as Katharine Cornell and Helen Hayes (John Brown wrote of Tallulah's Cleopatra, 'She barged down the Nile and sank.') but she had a host of fans. Tallulah, early in her career, went to England and became something of a sensation. She was forthright and outrageous, beautiful and utterly uninhibited. They tell a story of an assignation that she had with a young actor in her company. At the last moment, after the curtain fell, she discovered that she had to stay on for photographs. She apologized to the young man and handed him the key to her flat. 'Let yourself in,' she said, 'play the victrola, fix yourself a drink, get undressed and if I'm not there by then, start without me.'

Tallulah's finest performance was in Lillian Hellman's *The Little Foxes* in 1939. She acted in films, had her own show on radio and continued to attract men and women alike until her death. She took an old play of mine and toured it on an off for a year. With all her vagaries, she was wonderful to work with.

Helen Hayes for many years has been a first lady of the American stage. (She started her career when, at the age of nine, she appeared with comedian Lew Fields in *Old Dutch*.) She still holds that position although she does not appear as much as she used to. She is the complete opposite of Tallulah, soft, charming, lovable, restrained and a superb actress. She had great variety, acting in such dissimilar roles as Shakespeare's Portia and Mrs McThing, an endearing slavey; as Babs, a sub-debutante, and as Queen Victoria, one of her greatest roles, in *Victoria Regina*; as a tragic Southern girl in *Coquette* and as a spinster on a comic fling in *Happy Birthday*.

On the occasion of her having a Broadway theatre named after her, I did an interview with her and Charles MacArthur, her husband and co-author with Ben Hecht of the comedy, *The Front Page*. I particularly liked her reaction to the honour which had just been bestowed upon her. 'I called Charlie,' she told me, 'and asked him how he felt about being married to a building.' Miss Hayes not only acts, on the stage, in films and television; she writes books and good ones too.

The third of these stars is Katharine Cornell. I still recall the excited impression she made on me when she first appeared with the Washington Square Players, an organization that was eventually to develop into the Theater Guild. Her first great Broadway hit was in Clemence Dane's *A Bill of Divorcement*. Not only was she possessed of glamour but she was also a brilliant actress as she proved so tellingly as Iris March in *The Green Hat*, as Elizabeth Barrett Browning in *The Barretts of Wimpole Street*, as the dark lady of the sonnets in *Will Shakespeare*, in Shaw's *Saint Joan* and *Candida* and *The Doctor's Dilemma*, as Juliet and in so many other roles.

Since the death of her husband, director-producer Guthrie McClintock, she has not been active and now illness has forced her to retire.

I have chosen mostly those whom I have seen or heard so much about that I thought I had seen them. I have undoubtedly omitted names that will occur to me shortly after this book goes to press. However, there are certainly more than enough to prove to you or to remind you (if you are old enough) of a day in which we had our idols and the theatre was, in the words of Robert E. Sherwood, 'the dwelling-place of wonder'.

Life with Lillian

O. Z. Whitehead

During the fall of 1930 my first term at Harvard University, my cousin, George Greene, a senior student, came to see me at my rooms one night and said, 'I have two tickets in the first row of the balcony to see *Uncle Vanya.*' Fortunately, I was free to go with him. I had never seen or read a play by Anton Chekhov before.

This remarkable production by Jed Harris of *Uncle Vanya* had been a great success in New York the season before. His direction and everyone in the cast had received enormous praise. I can see Lillian Gish now as Helena, Sere-bryakov's young wife, looking radiantly beautiful, in her first entrance, as she walked silently with much grace from the garden into the house. I can re-member, too, the appealing manner in which, at the end of the second act, she said to her husband's daughter, 'Sonya, I have a longing for music; I should like to play something,' and then, with much disappointment, learns from Sonya that her father would object. Lillian played Helena with fine feeling and wonderful charm. I wondered why she was no longer in films.

In the fall of 1937, three years after I had gone on the stage myself, I went to see John Gielgud in *Hamlet* at the Empire Theater. Lillian was playing Ophelia. After having seen her in three silent films and in one play I did not expect to see the kind of performance that she gave in this part. In her scenes before her madness she was quiet and modest, but after that she lost all reticence. She even went so far as to roll on the ground. Lillian made the madness of Ophelia certainly disturbing. She gave a most striking performance.

After the play was over I went backstage to see John Cromwell, a friend of mine since the time when we went to the Buckley School in New York. He was playing Rosencrantz and under-studying John Gielgud. As I was on my way downstairs I saw Lillian standing outside her dressing-room. Wearing an attractive dressing-gown she was saying goodbye to an old lady who had been visiting her. She spoke to this lady in a kind, gentle tone, 'Be careful, honey, about going downstairs.' I looked at Lillian carefully; I could see that she noticed this. I did not expect to meet her again.

In fact I met Lillian for the first time at a small lunch party that Mrs Charles Lindley, a friend of my family's, gave at the Colony Club during the spring of 1939. At this first meeting she struck me as having unusual quiet charm. Becomingly dressed in pastel colours, she looked younger and even more attractive than she had when I had first seen her two years and a half before in the doorway of her dressing-room. I said to her, 'You know an old friend of mine, John Cromwell.' 'Oh! yes,' she said. 'He is a very sensitive actor. We were in *Hamlet* together. I would like to have seen his Marchbanks in *Candida* with Cornelia Otis Skinner.' I said to her 'I thought that he was very good.'

Although extremely intelligent and not lacking in artistic perception Mrs Lindley did not understand how actors approached their work or what they went through in between jobs. She described a little how Michael Chekhov taught acting at a school in Connecticut that her friend, Beatrice Straight, was financing. What Mrs Lindley said about his method was very strange and complicated. I do not think that anyone has ever taught like that. Holding her fingers together as if in an attitude of prayer Lillian listened calmly. At the end of Mrs Lindley's description Lillian smiled with amusement and said nothing. Mrs Lindley became more personal and asked her, 'Are you working now?' Lillian answered her with subtle humour. 'Oh! yes, I'm working very hard, I'm moving.'

Eventually, I became an actor myself. Early in January of 1940 about six weeks after I had finished playing a part in John Ford's now classic film *The Grapes of Wrath* from the book of the same name by John Steinbeck, Oscar Serlin, the producer, asked me to play Clarence Day Junior in a company of *Life with Father* that, after a week in Baltimore starting on 12 February, was to open in Chicago at the Blackstone Theatre for an unlimited engagement. The original company with Howard Lindsay as father and Dorothy Stickney as mother had already opened with enormous success almost three months before at the Empire Theater in New York. This play was adapted by Howard Lindsey and Russell Crouse from two books of sketches, *God and My Father* and *Life With Father*, written by Clarence Day about his childhood. Before making up two books all of the sketches had appeared in *The New Yorker*. Although I had never read any of the sketches I had certainly heard a great deal about them.

Four days before the first rehearsal Oscar Serlin gave me a script. I had been taking lessons from a great teacher, Boris Marshalov, for more than two years and a half. I began to work with him on my part without delay. Our first rehearsal took place on the stage of the Empire Theater on the set that the company in New York was using.

Lillian arrived at rehearsal just a little while after I did. She wore a becoming hat and an attractive sweatered dress. As always extremely beautiful, she still looked a little pale. Although I naturally felt nervous at the prospect of a first rehearsal, I could not believe that an actress of her vast experience felt the same way. She shook hands with me in such a manner as to make me think that she was glad that I was in the cast. Oscar Serlin asked Bretaigne Windhurst, the director, and the cast composed of sixteen, to sit around the dining-room table used in the play. Oscar had with him a copy of the current issue of *Life* magazine. He said to us 'This issue contains an article about *The Birth of a Nation*.' Lillian said with enthusiasm, 'Oh! yes, there's a story about it and many photographs.' Oscar said agreeably, 'That is very nice.'

On this first morning of rehearsal we read through the play. Our director did not believe in giving his cast much time for lunch. I think that Lillian's consisted of a chocolate ice cream soda. The first days of rehearsal went smoothly. Percy Waram, who had obviously done a great deal of work on his part beforehand, already seemed to be just right as my father, Clarence Day Senior. The rest of us were gradually trying to understand our parts and at the same time to learn our lines and positions.

One night after rehearsal as I was crossing Sixth Avenue on the way to Fifth I met Lillian walking up Sixth Avenue with Malcolm, her West Highland white terrier.

'Hello, John,' she said in a rather tired, absent-minded tone.

'You are thinking of my friend, John Cromwell,' I said.

'How is he?' she asked.

'He was very successful last year,' I said. 'Now he is looking for a part again. My name is Zebby,' I added.

'Oh! yes, dear,' she said.

When I came close to Lillian I could see large circles under her eyes. We walked cross town together and stopped every once in a while because of Malcolm.

'Were you out late last night?' I asked her.

'Yes, I went out dancing, but don't tell on me.'

As we continued walking down the street she became a little more lively.

'Are you looking forward to going to Chicago?' I asked her.

'In this play, yes.'

'When did you decide to do it?' I asked her.

'Oh, I went to see this play during the first week that it opened and I thought that it was the darlingest play that I had ever seen. I said to myself I could be in this play, and then I went to see it again to make sure that I was right. My second visit confirmed me in my opinion. I made an appointment to see Oscar Serlin and asked him to let me tour in this play. I met Mrs Clarence Day, Howard Lindsey, Russell Crouse and Bretaigne Windhurst. The next day Oscar Serlin telephoned me and offered me the part in the company going to Chicago, but I wasn't really sure that I was going to be in it until I went into rehearsal on Monday.' 'When I get home,' she added, 'I'll have to get hold of my sister and have her come over to mother's apartment and cue me.'

I left Lillian at the corner of Madison Avenue and 57th Street. She walked by herself to the apartment at 430 East 52nd Street that she and her sister, Dorothy, provided for her mother and where for the time being Lillian was also living.

On the afternoon of the third Monday after the company had started to rehearse, Bretaigne Windhurst said rather casually, 'I want you to run through the whole play today without stopping. Whatever goes wrong – just go ahead with it as if nothing was the matter.'

I do not think that much character, humour or real vitality emerged from this rough rehearsal. No one seemed certain of what they were doing. At the end, after a chilling silence, a man stood up in the back of the balcony. He walked forward to the front row and looked down at us. I heard someone say, 'It's Howard Lindsey.' Bretaigne Windhurst, seated in the front row of the orchestra, made no comment. The rest of us, with much concern, waited for Howard Lindsey to come up on the stage and say what he thought of us.

He criticized each member of the cast with dry humour and great severity. I feel sure that we all deserved his disapproval. After he had at last finished Lillian asked him gently, referring to his wife, Dorothy Stickney, 'Where is Dorothy? I want her to help me on make-up.' He replied, 'She is resting quietly at home in preparation for the evening's performance.'

During the last week of rehearsals in New York we gave a performance on two successive afternoons before invited audiences at the Empire Theater. Howard Lindsey, attending both of them, showed sincere satisfaction at our general improvement. Lillian said, 'I will have to get one day in which to do business before we leave for Baltimore.' I do not think that she managed to get more than half a day.

On Saturday morning, 10 February, two days before the opening in Baltimore, the company took the train for there. Dorothy Gish came along too. This was the first time that I had met her. She looked very tired as if she had been up late on the night before. Her bright, blonde hair made her face look like a masque. Lillian looked young and fresh beside her. Dorothy offered everyone chocolates out of a big, fine box. On Sunday night after the dress rehearsal I walked part of the way back to the hotel with Lillian and her dog. With no lack of confidence, but a little tensely, she said, 'Now that we've finished rehearsing we should be ready to play it.'

The audience as well as Oscar Serlin, Mrs Clarence Day, Russell Crouse and Bretaigne Windhurst, seemed pleased with the opening night's perform-ance. Ruth Gordon, a great friend of Lillian's came down from New York to see it. This enormously gifted actress, talented writer and extraordinary woman, said to Oscar Serlin, 'Thank you, it was a great treat.' With much enthusiasm she walked on to the stage and carefully examined the set with its interesting old Victorian furniture.

During the week in Baltimore the Gish sisters spent some time with their old friend, the distinguished journalist, H. L. Mencken, whose home was in that city.

The sisters and I were staying in the same hotel. After the Wednesday matinée Lillian knocked on my door and asked me to join them for dinner. Still suffering from a cold that I had caught on the day after Howard Lindsey had come unexpectedly to the unfortunate rehearsal I have already referred to, I was looking forward to taking a rest and having dinner alone in my room. Despite this I could not refrain from accepting her invitation. I had so far only talked to Lillian a little and to Dorothy not at all. What were they going to be like? I tried to forget my still tired feeling and stuffed up nose in happy antici-pation of finding out.

Their suite consisted of a sitting-room and two bedrooms. Lillian had not taken off her make-up. Rested by now, Dorothy looked very bright and attractive. After they had made sure that I was comfortable the sisters sat down opposite me, Lillian on a small sofa, and Dorothy on an easy chair.

What struck me most strongly at this my first meeting with them both, apart from their rare charm and feminine appeal, was their admiration and love for each other. There seemed to be no real conflict between them. Lillian obviously found whatever Dorothy said amusing and seemed content just to listen to her. Dorothy had come to Baltimore to help Lillian over what is always a trying period for an actor or actress, the opening week of a play. Enormously pleased with her sister's performance as Vinnie Day, Dorothy certainly showed no envy that she was not playing her, only happiness at what she now felt was going to be a great success for her sister in Chicago.

After Lillian had ordered dinner for us, Dorothy said to her, 'I wonder how mother is?' Lillian said, 'We can telephone to New York now and see.' While the operator was getting her number, Lillian explained to me, 'Mother came to the trenches in France during the First World War, while Dorothy and I were making propaganda films for the English War Department, to encourage the war effort of this country. She has been an invalid ever since.' Dorothy added, 'She has done so much for us that we can never do enough for her.' Their mother could only speak a few words, and never over the telephone.

Miss Fairborn who had been taking care of Mrs Gish for many years, assured the sisters that their mother was fine.

Much to my concern we started back to the theatre a little late. As we were getting out of the taxi at the stage door a middle aged woman came up to us and said to the sisters, 'You are Lillian and Dorothy Gish, aren't you?' They quickly admitted, 'We are.' She said with much enthusiasm, 'I have admired you both all my life.' The sisters acknowledged her remark politely.

On Saturday evening after the performance the cast and everyone connected with the production took the train to Chicago and arrived there late on Sunday afternoon. The Blackstone Hotel was situated at the corner of the impressive Michigan Avenue that faced the lake. Lillian had engaged a suite and Percy Waram a room at this hotel for as long as the play should run. Dorothy decided to live there for the two weeks that she planned to stay in Chicago. Because this hotel was very expensive I only took a room there temporarily. The Blackstone Theater where the play was going to open on the following evening was situated down a side street only a few doors from this hotel.

I did not see either of the sisters on Sunday evening. I think that they were resting like myself. A short rehearsal was called on Monday afternoon to which all the company came. Bretaigne Windhurst gave the cast a few notes.

Most actors are naturally nervous on opening nights. On this one Lillian appeared very calm. When I came downstairs ready to go on, she said brightly, 'How do you feel, dear?' I said, 'All right.' She then made some small suggestion to improve my make-up. I had plenty of time to fix it.

About five minutes before the rise of the curtain Lillian, most becomingly as Vinnie Day, a lady of New York in the 1880s, stood off stage on the landing waiting to go downstairs into the main room of the house belonging to her husband Clarence and herself. I, as their eldest son, meant to be seventeen years old, waited directly behind her and the three boys playing my younger brothers waited behind me.

As soon as the curtain had gone up on an empty stage, in a very dignified manner well suited to the character that she was playing, Lillian walked downstairs. The audience applauded her entrance with considerable enthusiasm. I could hear her first remarks in the play to Annie, the maid. Clear and distinct, her voice showed no signs of nervousness. When I followed her on the stage to greet my mother before breakfast I could quickly feel her complete assurance.

Perhaps because the distinguished actor, Percy Waram, who played Father spoke rather too loudly, which threw his performance somewhat off balance in relation to Lillian's and the rest of the company's, I do not think that the play went as well as it had in Baltimore. For this reason and because I was not satisfied with myself I did not feel happy after the play was over.

On my return to the hotel I saw Lillian standing in the lobby. She looked rather tired, and very serious.

'Hello, Zebby,' she said from a little distance. 'I am going to a party.'

Glad to be under no obligation for the evening I went by myself downstairs into the grill room and ordered scrambled eggs, toast and milk. Dorothy Gish was seated at a table nearby with a distinguished-looking gentleman with grey hair whom I did not know. Deeply engrossed in her conversation, Dorothy at first did not seem to notice me. After a while, however, when she saw that I was alone, she called my name and said, 'Come over here and sit with us.' After I had reached her table she said 'This is Mr H. L. Mencken.' He half stood up and said warmly as if he meant it, 'I saw your play again tonight. I thought that you were all very good.' He then spoke with much enthusiasm about Lillian's performance. 'I think that it will be a great success here.' he said. 'That will be a relief to me,' I said. 'I have acted in several failures.' I mentioned one that I had been in during the winter of nineteen thirty seven *Oh Evening Star* by Zoe Atkins, which lasted five performances at the Empire Theater.

He explained to Dorothy and me: 'Zoe Atkins was at one time a serious writer. She even wrote beautiful verse. She was very poor. The opening of her play *Déclassée*, starring Ethel Barrymore, was an obvious success. The evening afterwards when I was sitting in The Algonquin, Zoe walked in wearing a plumed hat and an expensive fur coat. I said to her "Zoe you look so different." She said, "Can't one dress up when one is opulent?" ' Mr Mencken did not want us to leave him until he had finished all that he had to tell us. I could have listened to him indefinitely.

The next morning I hastened to buy all the newspapers as they came out. Each critic, Robert Pollak, Lloyd Lewis, Claudia Cassidy, Ashton Stevens and Cecil Smith, gave the play most excellent notices and the performances too, with one reservation about Lillian's and two about Percy Waram's. Although happy and relieved to read the notices and pleased too at what the critics had said about me, I still felt that all of us could have been much better.

In the afternoon I met Dorothy walking with Malcolm on Michigan Avenue. 'How is Lillian today?' I said. 'Ah! fine. You should both be happy about the notices.' 'Do you want to go into Woods and have ice-cream?' I asked her. 'Certainly,' she said.

With no apparent sadness in her tone, Dorothy spoke about how little she had been working lately. Although people had offered her many plays she had felt compelled to turn them down either because she did not like the plays or because she did not think that the parts were right for her. During over six years and a half since my first appearance on the stage I had spent a great deal of time either in looking for parts or in waiting for one. Because of this I could well understand how Dorothy must be feeling.

Before the second night's performance Oscar Serlin, his face temporarily twisted from nervous tension, came backstage. Waving his hands in the air, he said to the cast, 'We're in all right. We're in.'

Shortly before it was time for the curtain to go up I walked out on the stage to join Lillian. Looking very relaxed and rested, she came up to me and said lightly, 'Where did you and Dorothy go?' She added, 'I had to do my mail all alone.'

Although Lillian would have liked her to stay longer, Dorothy returned to New York on the second Saturday after we had opened.

I often called for Lillian at her suite on Sundays. The first time that we went out together she was dressed most becomingly in a blue sweatered suit, hat and veil, both of the same colour, the last just slightly over her forehead. She looked very fresh and young, hardly old enough to be playing Vinnie Day, supposedly the mother of four children, the oldest being seventeen. As we walked down Michigan Avenue towards The Auditorium to attend a concert, she said, 'I want to see all of the United States in this play. Maybe we will run here for three months and then start to tour in June. Wouldn't you like that?'

I said, 'No, I don't want to stay in this play for too long. I want to act in films.'

'Ah!', she said, 'but one's work in a film is quickly over. A play like this is very hard to find. Films are not so hard to come by.'

'I should think that if one toured in a play for too long one would be almost forgotten.'

'To work in a successful play like this is a career in itself, dear. I've waited a long time to find it.'

She looked up at me for a moment. 'When we started to rehearse your colour was very bad, almost green,' she said. 'You're looking much better now since you have been working.'

'I have never been very strong,' I said.

'You must take care of yourself, dear, and become stronger,' she said warmly. 'Regular work will be good for you.'

One Sunday evening a few weeks after we had been in Chicago I took Lillian to see John Ford's *The Grapes of Wrath* in which, as I mentioned before I played. Lillian liked this film. She said, 'Mr Ford directed films in the silent days. He learned how to tell a story with plenty of movement and without the constant use of dialogue. Most of the directors nowadays make the actors talk all the time.'

After the film during dinner I asked her, 'Lillian, why don't you consider seriously going back into films?' A fiery expression came into her eyes. She said, 'I was the little pet out there once. Everyone did as I said. I did fine pictures that I liked and they always made money. I never did a story just because I thought that it would make money. The people out there now wouldn't understand that kind of thinking. I would have to do just what they said and I wouldn't want to do pictures that way.' I asked her, 'Couldn't you produce with your friend, Mary Pickford?'

'Oh! no, dear, Mary and I have very different ideas about doing films. She always did stories that she thought people would go to see, not necessarily what she liked. I am more selfish than that. Mary and I could never do pictures together. To try might end a life-long friendship.' I understood what Lillian meant. 'Couldn't you produce them alone?' I asked. 'Not any more. No one would listen to me. Everything that you do has to get past the exhibitors and their taste is not mine.' Despite my enthusiasm I could think of no further questions to ask on this subject.

During the first few weeks of the run in Chicago many people said that they thought our company was better than the one in New York. Although I am not sure how many members of our company agreed with this opinion still none of us failed to appreciate the compliments that most people gave us. Some said to Lillian, 'We like your Vinnie Day even better than Dorothy Stickney's.' Lillian said graciously, 'I should be better. I have been on the stage much longer than she has, thirty-five years since childhood.'

Because of quick changes that she often had to make during the play, Lillian used an improvised dressing-room hidden from the audience at the top of the set's staircase. During moments of waiting which she experienced once in a while, she often wrote letters. Sometimes she would just lie down, with her feet high up on a chair.

The anniversary performance of our show celebrating a year's run which took place on the evening of February 1941, was a great success. Many people who had seen the play before came again. Lillian seemed happy about it, like the rest of us.

One day, soon afterwards, I read in the newspaper that the Museum of Art was going to have a special showing of *Broken Blossoms* on the following afternoon. That evening at the theatre I suggested to Lillian that we go to see it. 'Well, I might,' she said, 'if it's the first time for you.'

D. W. Griffith had directed this remarkable film in 1918. I had seen it about three years later when I was around ten. Some of the scenes had stuck vividly in my memory. The next afternoon at four o'clock, Lillian and I arrived at the small auditorium of the Museum, mostly filled with women.

Lillian's performance as the twelve-year-old girl living in London's Chinatown with her brutal father was deeply moving. Richard Barthelmass played beautifully the pure-hearted Chinaman who tried to rescue her. Donald Crisp acted the father with much effectiveness. Lillian's death scene with Richard Barthelmass was unforgettable.

Simple, unpretentious, in no way sordid, without a trace of vulgarity, and obviously directed by a master, the film had a fine sense of tragedy. I thought that it was a masterpiece. At the end of the showing, after a moment's silence, the audience broke into applause. Someone asked Lillian to say a few words. She stood in front of the audience and said modestly,

'I hope that it moved you. It did me a little.'

Sacred Monsters Off and On the Boulevards

by *Roland Gant*

FRANCE too had its matinée idols but they were not so called by the Parisian public. During the last quarter of the nineteenth century and until 1914 there were actors and actresses who were idolised by that public and lived up to their reputations both on the stage and in private life. Among them were Sarah Bernhardt, Lucien Guitry, Eve Lavallière, Réjane, Mounet-Sully and Suzanne Reichenberg – all idols in a sense and all stars in the grand manner. Productions revolved around them. They were known as *monstres sacrés*. It was precisely to this system that Jacques Copeau objected to so strongly and proclaimed 'Let's have no more stars! Yesterday's queen is today's servant; everyone must be trained, educated and disciplined in a single-minded manner and completely united under the director.'

Jean Cocteau wrote a play called *Les Monstres Sacrés*, a comedy in Boulevard style about an ageing married couple in the theatre which, as he said, 'should give the idea of a prima donna, a *monstre sacré* in the style of Réjane or Bernhardt'. It was produced in 1940 and gave a brilliant and memorable idea of what such stars were like.

If there was someone who carried into the inter-war years something of the tradition of the *monstre sacré* it was Sacha Guitry. Sacha, son of Lucien and with an actress-mother, first stepped on the boards at the age of five and until his death at the age of seventy-two he lived and breathed the theatre. Even in marriage he did not step outside as his wives, Charlotte Lyses, Yvonne

Printemps, Jacqueline Delubac, Geneviève de Sèverol and Lana Marconi were all actresses. His first play, *Le Page*, was produced when he was seventeen and acting with his father. Lucien, furious with him because of some carelessness in rehearsal threw him out and for more than ten years they were not on speaking terms. During that time Sacha went on writing, acted in his own plays and then, when father and son had made up their quarrel he wrote for his father as well.

For over fifty years Paris was rarely without a Guitry entertainment, usually starring Guitry, whether in one of his one hundred and thirty odd plays or in something like thirty films. His Boulevard comedies were on the themes of the siege and conquest of a woman by a persuasive seducer who, usually idle in everything but dalliance, employs every kind of ruse to achieve his aims. Guitry also wrote and starred in plays and films based on historical characters – Mozart, Talleyrand, Louis xiv, Napoleon, Frans Hals, Napoleon iii. Whatever part he played was written for Sacha the entertainer by Sacha the playwright. And when he was not writing and performing, this darling of the Paris public relaxed in his favourite way – by going to the theatre. He was very fond of revue. Arletty told me that 'Sacha said that if he couldn't watch his father on the stage he would go to see Dranem or Montel.'

Sacha was one of the great princes of stage royalty and I have frequently been struck by something that would have amused him. Just off the Boulevard de Clichy at the end of the short Avenue Rachel is one of the entrances to the North Cemetery of Paris, usually known as the Montmartre Cemetery. A few yards inside the gate to the right lie Lucien and Sacha Guitry. Opposite, on the left, is the tomb of a Saxe-Coburg and Gotha Princess on which lies a dusty, faded spray of wax flowers. At all times of the year the Guitry resting place is covered with fresh bouquets like a first night stage . . .

To return to those wonderful performers Montel and Dranem. They both starred in many of the hundred or so revues written by Rip of whose work Colette wrote 'Among the trump cards of this *revuiste* I remember his caustic quality. To wound is also an art . . . '

Arletty appeared in her first Rip comedy, *Le Scandale de Deauville* in 1920 at the Capucines and with Dranem and Cheirel in 1921 in *Si que je serais roi*, with Montel in 1924 in *La Danseuse Eperdue*. The following year she appeared in *Mon Gosse de Père*, again with Montel. Arletty says 'Most of us played in revue at one time or another. Raimu was in revue for years before becoming an actor in the legitimate theatre. Fernandel used to tour as a singer, Jean Gabin was a dancer and was in the Folies Bergère. He had a sort of Chevalier routine and was a very good dancer. You can see that by the way he walks, just like James Cagney who was a vaudeville dancer before going into films.'

In her book *La Défense* (1971) Arletty evokes that period and its stars – Maud Loty, Dranem, Montel, Mistinguett, Chevalier and the rest – with a concise and vivid clarity. Frequently mocking in tone, her book is never more so than when writing of herself. She appeared in a Rip revue, *La Revue des Nouveautés*, in 1935, for the last time and only played in revue again some fifteen years later. In 1936 she starred in *L'Ecole des Veuves*, written for her by Cocteau and later in the same year in Edouard Bourdet's *Fric-Frac* with Michel Simon and Victor Boucher. This was made into a successful film in 1939 with Arletty, Simon and Fernandel.

Arletty and Simon worked well together and made a second film, *Circonstances Atténuantes* in 1939. Once when about to go on stage on their famous tandem in *Fric-Frac* a twinge of stage-fright overtook Arletty who said 'Say something nice.' Michel looked at her and said 'You look exactly like Zaza,' [his pet monkey who had died a few months before] and they pedalled on to the stage. In the interval Arletty asked 'In what way?' to which Michel replied 'The hair-style.' Arletty knew that he had been so devoted to Zaza that he had paid her the biggest compliment he could think of.

Bourdet and his friends were much amused at his slangy comedy about crooks becoming an instant Boulevard hit at the Michodière on 15 October 1936 followed by his appointment the following day as administrator of the Comédie Française. In this post, which he held until 1940, he initiated a broader policy and invited the work of such producers as Copeau, Pitoëff, Jouvet, Baty and Dullin.

With the intention of bringing literature closer to the theatre, to 'animate' it with ideas, Copeau, a dramatic critic and co-founder with Gide and Schlumberger of the *Nouvelle Revue Française* in 1909, had formed in 1913 the Théâtre du Vieux-Colombier in a small, shabby place in the Left Bank district of Saint-Sulpice, distant in every way from the elegant Boulevard houses. Sent by the French Government on a cultural mission to the USA in 1917 Copeau lectured and also presented at the old Garrick Theatre in New York French plays performed by his company which included many who later became famous idols such as Valentine Tessier, Lucienne Bogaërt, Jean Dullin and Jean Sarment. Playing small parts while doubling as stage-hand and then stage manager (*'valet de chambre de théâtre'* in his own words) was a young man who had been wounded and discharged from the army – Louis Jouvet. Reluctantly following the family tradition of medicine (he qualified as a pharmacist in 1913) Jouvet's passion for the stage was in no way diluted by his being turned down three times by the Conservatoire. But in his early days he spelt his name 'Jouvey' until he had made a name – his own – in the theatre.

Copeau's aim was to establish a 'non-theatrical theatre shorn of useless artifice, deformation, compromise and dishonesty'. He was much influenced by Gordon Craig: he presented his plays against scenery that was reduced to the bare minimum. In 1924 he retired to a Burgundy village and formed a drama school to teach those aspiring actors and actresses who remained 'un-contaminated by the usual climate of the theatre'. He handed over most of the effects and the repertory of the Vieux-Colombier to Louis Jouvet who, in 1926, joined Georges Pitoëff, Charles Dullin and Gaston Baty in the *Cartel des Quatre*, dedicated to continuing Copeau's reforming movement.

Georges Pitoëff, born in Tiflis, and his wife Ludmilla, who was also Georgian, were one of those royal couples of the stage like Lunt and Fontanne in America. But with their two children Sacha and Svetlana carrying on the tradition one is almost reminded of the Redgrave family. After working in Russia and then for eight years in Switzerland the Pitoëffs brought their company to Paris. This troupe of twenty was comprised of seventeen Swiss, a Russian, a Dutchwoman (Marie Kalff, wife of the playwright Lenormand) and a single French actress, Héléna Manson! One of the Swiss actors was Michel Simon, formerly a Geneva photographer.

Georges spoke with a thick Russian accent but his gaunt, hollow-cheeked face and burning eyes made him a commanding figure on stage. His know-ledge of world theatre and his extensive repertory were extraordinary: Ibsen, Shaw, Synge, Wilde, Shakespeare, Gorki, Buchner, Tolstoy, Calderón, O'Neill, Gide and Anouilh who was utterly devoted to him.

Ludmilla, a tiny woman with beautiful diction and an angelic face, was a brilliant and moving actress in whatever role she played. She is best remem-bered for her Saint Joan. Under her husband's direction, she played the part with a saintly purity and no concession to Shaw's irony.

In 1939 Georges literally drove himself to death while playing Stockmann in Ibsen's *An Enemy of the People*. Ludmilla survived him until 1951, playing in the United States and Canada during the Second World War. Claudel had become her favourite dramatist, possibly because of the spiritual effect her long years spent in portrayal of Joan of Arc had had on her. Returning to France after the war she played in Claudel's *L'Echange*, Ibsen's *A Doll's House* and in a play written for her by René Arnaud and her husband, *Le Vray Procès de Jeanne d'Arc* which was based on contemporary reports of the trial.

While working in a wide variety of jobs Charles Dullin followed Conserva-toire courses and then joined the theatre. Copeau cast him as Smerdiakov in *The Brothers Karamazov* and he won a great personal acclaim. Following Copeau to the Vieux-Colombier with Jouvet and others, he accompanied the troupe to the USA during the First World War. Like Copeau, Dullin wanted to form his own theatre and his own school of drama. In 1922 he turned the old Théâtre Montmartre, a home of melodrama, into L'Atelier. Like both Copeau and Pitoëff, Dullin was beset by financial difficulties but he did manage to establish his school. This ardent *animateur*, a small, thin and delicate man, gave his best performances in such parts as Volpone and Richard III. Among younger actors who profited from his tuition were Marcel Herrand and Jean-Louis Barrault. Herrand is familiar to filmgoers as Arletty's co-star in

Les Visiteurs du Soir and for his portrayal of Lacenaire in *Les Enfants du Paradis*, again with Arletty and with Jean-Louis Barrault. Others taught by Dullin were Jean Vilar, Jean Marchat, Raymond Rouleau and Michel Vitold – all of whom made their mark in the French theatre. Dullin himself appeared in a number of films, the most memorable being *Volpone* in which Jouvet played Mosca.

Dullin considered theatre to be a complete art in itself and everything was grist to his mill. In 1923 he raised a storm by presenting *Atelier Music-Hall*. He later explained why he made use of music hall, the *commedia dell'arte* and the *café-concert*. These were real, he maintained, unlike those productions in the commercial theatre put on by 'grocers'. Dullin never wavered from that point of view and he never hesitated to take a chance on something he considered of real quality, however much the public and the 'grocers' might object. It was Dullin who produced and played in Sartre's first play, *Les Mouches*, in German-occupied Paris in 1943.

The only member of the Cartel who was not an actor was Gaston Baty. He was dedicated to the idea of 'total drama' and his frequently-uttered opinion was that the text of a play was not everything and that beyond the text lay a 'zone of mystery and silence which one calls atmosphere, ambiance or climate as you will. We perform the text and everything which the text can say but we also want to extend it into that area which words alone cannot express.' He put forward this point of view with an almost reckless violence in *Sire le Mot* (*His Majesty the Word*) and was equally violently attacked for it by dramatists, but not by those whose works he presented.

In 1923 Baty formed his company *Les Compagnons de la Chimère* and presented plays by Amiel, Lenormand, Bernard and others but his greatest success two years earlier was Gantillon's *Maya* in which he launched a brilliant actress, Marguerite Jamois. Her comprehension and rendering of the poetry, colour and mystery to which he attached such importance made her the ideal interpreter of parts like Hedda Gabler, Mary Stuart and the Madame Bovary in Baty's own adaptation. In 1947 Baty handed over the direction of the Théâtre Montparnasse to Marguerite Jamois who then concentrated on playing O'Neill's Electra and Cassandra in Barrault's Agamemnon and always in the individualistic manner which continued the ideals and influence of Baty.

Louis Jouvet, whose début has been mentioned in connection with Copeau, in 1923 formed his own company, which included a number of his Vieux-Colombier colleagues, at the Comédie des Champs-Elysées, presenting and acting in works by Romains, Achard, Sarment, Cocteau and others. Then, in 1928, taking a risk with a Franco-German theme he put on the first play by Jean Giraudoux, *Siegfried*, made from the author's novel. It was an instant triumph and was followed by many original plays including *Amphitryon 38* and *Intermezzo*. From then on Jouvet concentrated more and more on Giraudoux's work. Moving to the Athénée in 1934 he had a first-class company that included Valentine Tessier who, like Jouvet, had been refused three times by the Conservatoire, Lucienne Bogaërt, Madeleine Ozeray, Romain Bouquet, Pierre Renoir, son of the painter and brother of Jean the film director, Michel Simon and another actor who later became well known in films, Jean-Pierre Aumont. In addition to producing, directing and acting Jouvet also taught at the Conservatoire and attracted many disciples. In the Second World War Jouvet and his company toured South America and Mexico for four years. During his self-imposed exile Jouvet became increasingly concerned with spiritual questions. He wanted to play the priest in Pierre Bost's adaptation of Graham Greene's *The Power and the Glory* and it was while rehearsing the part in 1951 that he collapsed and died on the stage just as Molière had done.

One of the features of the French theatre for which there is no parallel in England or the USA is the relatively high number of non-French actors and actresses who have made their names in the Paris theatre and become great idols and/or sacred monsters. Besides those from French-speaking countries like Belgium and Switzerland and the Russian Pitoëffs already mentioned, from the beginning of the century there was always a large group of Rumanians. Among them were Alice Cocéa who began her Paris career in 1910 at seventeen in the Boulevard comedy *Phi-Phi* and went on to play Nora in *A Doll's House* and Lucie in Salacrou's *Une Femme Libre* in which she played opposite Claude Dauphin, one of the most popular *jeunes premiers* of the inter-war period. Other illustrious Rumanians were Edouard de Max, Marie Ventura, Jean Yonnel, Samson Fainsilber and Elvire Popesco.

Popesco has always made the greatest use of her accent for comic effect. This, combined with her petulance and infectious laugh, made her a darling of the French public. One of her greatest successes was in Jacques Deval's *Tovaritch* in 1933 and she played the same role in the 1948 production. This play was adapted as a musical and Vivien Leigh played the lead in New York in 1963. Since the war Elvire Popesco has continued her successful career, notably in parts written for her by André Roussin.

Pierre Fresnay has been one of the most versatile as well as one of the most popular matinée idols since his début at the Comédie Française in 1915. Three years later he had established his reputation in Racine's *Britannicus* and then, in 1927, he joined Guitry at the Variétés and became a popular Boulevard actor. From 1931 when he starred in the film version of Marcel Pagnol's *Marius* he became a film star as well. He did not desert the theatre however and André Roussin has written and continues to write for him.

Fernand Gravey, a debonair and gay leading man in pre-war years later made a considerable name for himself in Hollywood, and he too did not desert the stage.

An interesting case of a brilliant actor being influenced in his subsequent work by a part he played in a film is Pierre Brasseur. He started in the theatre when very young and it was his playing at the age of twenty-four in Bourdet's *Le Sexe Faible* in 1929 (the play ran for three years) that brought him many similar roles as an attractive, smart and cynical young man. He remained type-cast until the war and also gave some powerful film interpretations, notably in *Quai des Brumes*. In 1944 he played the actor Frederick Lemaître in *Les Enfants du Paradis*. Bewitched by the part and by the legend of Lemaître, Brasseur's style and even his physique took on something of a *monstre sacré* grand manner which achieved its highest point in 1958 in the title role in *Kean* adapted for him by Sartre.

A playwright adept at moulding his pieces for the matinée idol public was Henry Bernstein, a dramatist whose early work was performed at the turn of the century and whose last plays appeared in the early 1950s. In many of Bernstein's Boulevard successes the star was Gaby Morlay. She always played with convincing emotion and gave the impression that the personality of the character and that of the actress were completely fused into one. For about thirteen years in Bernstein plays she attracted a large and admiring audience. The *Stage Yearbook* (1928), reviewing Paris theatre productions of 1927 selected Bernstein's *Le Venin* as the best-acted play, both as ensemble and as individual performances by Yvonne de Bray, Gaby Morlay and Charles Boyer'.

The Boulevard was rarely without a Bernstein play and glittering perform-ances by the players. Some, like Boyer, moved away from the theatre to the cinema and, in his case, to Hollywood. Gaby Morlay had a successful film career that ran parallel with her stage work and Yvonne de Bray also played in films but only towards the end of her career, giving unforgetable performances in *Gigi* and *Les Parents Terribles*.

There is no space to discuss in detail all the popular actors and actresses of that period but among those who made their mark (and some became known through the cinema as well) were Harry Bauer, Marie Bell, Fernand Ledoux, Marguerite Moréno, Jules Berry, Pierre Blanchar, Gabrielle Dorziat and Louis Salou.

Three younger actors, of disparate abilities, who earned public acclaim were Jean Marais, François Périer and Gérard Philipe. Marais' physical per-fection brought him twenty years' adulation by women of all ages. Cocteau wrote for him *Les Chevaliers de la Table Ronde*, *Les Parents Terribles*, *La Machine à Ecrire* and *l'Aigle à Deux Têtes* (in which Edwige Feuillère was his co-star). He was the epitome of the French matinée idol, an enduring Prince Charming. François Périer, who was at the Théâtre Français in 1938–9 before attracting attention in *Jours Heureux* by Claude-André Puget, never lost his youthful charm nor his ability to portray nice young men in muddles over the years, and neither has his enormous popularity waned. Perhaps the best example of the intellectual and romantic *jeune premier* is Gérard Philipe who was at the Conservatoire at the outbreak of war and then in Claude Dauphin's company in Cannes in 1942. His enormous success in plays and films did not begin until after the war and was ended with his tragically early death at thirty-seven.

There was between the wars, as I have shown, a constant osmosis between the various categories of theatre. Playwrights wrote for the experimental theatre and for the Boulevard, players appeared in classics and in revue, and music hall routines were used by serious playwrights. What of those entertainers whose main careers lay outside the regular theatre and who became idols of the public?

Inevitably the first to come to mind is Maurice Chevalier, perhaps the greatest matinée idol of all time, a tireless consummate artist who worked and reworked his timing, delivery, gestures and material (he polished '*Ma Pomme*' for some thirty years), international solo performer and film star who influenced cabaret style and inspired more imitators and mimics than anyone has ever done.

Born into a working-class family in Paris in 1888 he earned his living at a variety of trades including those of carpenter and electrician. At twelve he was singing '*V'la les croquants*' at the Casino des Tourelles and working in *cafés-concerts*. At seventeen he was billed as '*Le petit Jésus d'Asnières*' (!) and in 1907 he followed Dranem at the Eldorado – the great 'Eldo' – where the stars of music hall all appeared. Two years later he partnered Mistinguett, Gaby Deslys and Polaire at the Folies-Bergère. During the First War he was wounded and taken prisoner and on repatriation in 1916 he sang at the Casino de Paris and at the Bouffes-Parisiens. In 1929 he made *Innocents of Paris* in Hollywood and began a cinema career that entertained the world through nearly four decades from the early features with Jeanette Macdonald (*The Love Parade*, 1930, was the first) to his performances in the late 1960s. In all he appeared in forty-four films (nine of them silent) and still managed to tour the world many times with his one-man show.

Maurice personified for his public in France or elsewhere the gaiety and charm of Paris, the Frenchman's appreciation of pretty girls and the determination to turn all to laughter. His oft-imitated voice was as inimitable as his grin, the expression in his eyes, his dance steps and the jauntiness of that boater and bow-tie.

Several years had elapsed since I had last seen him when we met late at night at a mammoth party in the house of a Hollywood movie mogul. As we were talking he looked round quickly and, switching to French, said: 'These midnight cocktail parties don't mean much to me at my age but I am obliged to attend for the sake of France.' From anyone else such an ambassadorial statement would have been the height of pompous vanity but from Maurice it wasn't. I knew exactly what he meant and it was true. He *was* France.

IV

*T*HE *coming of the cinema put the idol at the disposal of the masses. But if the audience increased a thousand-fold so did the tiny area at the top of the plinth become ever more slippery and treacherous. Many clambered up there only to topple into oblivion after a picture or two. However from the earliest days there were those who by a peculiar combination of talent, grace, luck, capacity for work and steely determination made a permanent niche for themselves. This section divides into two halves, before and after the moment when the introduction of sound faced the silent idols with the great problem of whether to utter or to quit. David Robinson describes the real personalities as well as the screen images of such legendary figures as Rudolph Valentino, Douglas Fairbanks Senior, Mary Pickford, Pola Negri, Gloria Swanson. Then Dilys Powell takes up the story at the point when the news 'Garbo Talks!' was flashed around the world and reviews the subsequent career of that great lady and other goddesses of the pre-war era. To end this section I asked George Axelrod for his views on the idol phenomenon in the cinema as it is today.*

A.C.

The Mute Idols

by David Robinson

THE idols were never enshrined in such splendour, or worshipped with such devotion as in the movie theatres of the 1920s. Hollywood set itself to manufacture dream and romance for the whole world. The people who made (and were made by) the movies, saw their role as being, as they often said 'to make the truckdriver and his wife feel like a king and queen'. The movie palaces that rose up in America, in pursuance of this admirable aim, between the First World War and the Depression were palaces in much more than name. To reach their seats in a vast auditorium, seating perhaps five thousand people, the truckdriver and his wife trod, as of right, deep-piled oriental carpets, passed through salons, and mounted *grands escaliers* that might have dwarfed Versailles, glittering with rich crystal, decorated with antique furniture and statues and paintings and tapestries brought at un-counted cost from Europe. They were shown to their seats by members of an impeccably drilled army of ushers with pill-box hats, white gloves and swagger sticks; and if they went to the lavatory, even there all was marble and Louis Quinze mantels.

All this was only the frame for the pictures on the screen; only the temple for the idols who appeared in them. Their silence, far from seeming a depriva-tion in them, elevated them to another sphere, remote from ordinary mortals. In their Valhalla of beauty it seemed normal that all thought and feeling found expression in expansive mime and mobile features. Eyes were for flashing and rolling and hooding with langorous lids; lips were for curling or primping into seductive bee-sting *moues*. 'We didn't need voices then,' said Norma Desmond, in *Sunset Boulevard*, remembering with the idol of silent days who personated her: 'We had *faces* then.' It made no difference that this new race of beings had not so long before been manicurists and electricians and hair-dressers and that in private life they were often confused and carried away by fame and adulation and salaries that far exceeded those of presidents and princes. To their audiences they were more than princes; objects of worship indeed.

The two among them who more than all the others gave the Twenties their taste of high romance, Rudolph Valentino and Douglas Fairbanks, were as it happened, poles apart. Valentino, a poor immigrant from Italy, was exotic, effete to his detractors, the ladies' man supreme, an object of fear and jealousy and unease to the American male. Fairbanks, aggressively home-grown, was all man's man, hearty, frank, extrovert, as American as hominy grits even if he was playing Robin Hood or Ahmed, the Thief of Bagdad.

Fairbanks was somewhat exceptional among the silent film stars as coming from a reasonably comfortable middle-class background, albeit an unsettled one. His father, Charles H. Ulman was a successful but somewhat footloose Jewish lawyer who abandoned his wife when Douglas Elton Thomas was five; whereupon Mrs Ulman reverted to the name of the first of her three husbands, John Fairbanks. The young Fairbanks inherited his father's restlessness and tried military academy, dramatic school, a bit of law, three months at Harvard, a cattle-boat trip to Europe, marriage and a job in his father-in-law's firm; but always he came back to acting.

No one seems to have regarded him as a very good actor, but the critics admired his attack, his athleticism, his ebullience – and a certain charm. By 1914 he was a Broadway star, and consequently propositioned by the films, at that moment determinedly buying up stage talent from the East. Fairbanks was always game for something new, and accepted. The then master of American cinema, D. W. Griffith, was quite bewildered by this irrepressibly buoyant personality; but rapidly, working with the director John Emerson and a teenage scenarist, Anita Loos, Fairbanks discovered his true screen persona. Though history has credited Emerson and Loos with the 'creation' of Fairbanks there is a consistency throughout his entire work which shows that this screen image was a completely spontaneous expression of his own personality.

It was, as it happened, a personality which exactly chimed with the nation's preferred self-image in those self-confident days between America's entry into the War, and the Depression. The titles alone of many of his films from 1915 to 1920 are revealing: *Reaching for the Moon, Mr Fix-It, His Majesty the American, The Habit of Happiness, He Comes Up Smiling, The Knickerbocker Buckaroo*. The habitual form of the films of the first stage of his career was to cast Fairbanks as an ordinary young man in some situation where he was restricted by circumstances, more often than not through enslavement to some current fad or foible – fake psychology (*When the Clouds Roll By*), hypochondria (*Down to Earth*), dreams of an aristocratic lineage (*Reaching for the Moon*), nostalgia for the values of the old West (*The Mollycoddle*), yearning for romance (*A Modern Musketeer*) or, in 1916, pacifism (*In Again, Out Again*). Somehow or other he was landed in adventures which called out his better self, and forced him to extricate himself by marvellous feats of agility and physical resources. In his neat city clothes, he would scale walls, leap from rooftop to rooftop, slide down drainpipes or dive head first through windows. For Fairbanks, wrote Alistair Cooke, a room was 'a machine for escape'. Invariably he emerged from his adventures a better man and a better American, cleansed and cured of whatever quirk had first beset him.

Evidently this resolution of all problems through instant action and individual physical effort appealed hugely to the American temperament in those First World War days. Within a very short time Fairbanks was a folk hero. In 1917 a mountain peak was named after him. The myth became complete when he married America's Sweetheart, Mary Pickford: so intensely did the public respond to romance that it quite overlooked the previous marriage and divorce of each partner in this idyll.

After the war Hollywood's prosperity demanded even greater opulence and display. Fairbanks abandoned the day clothes and workaday settings of the early films to embark on a series of costume spectacles; but the personality remained unaltered. The hero of the first of the series, *The Mark of Zorro* (1920), a kind of early Californian Scarlet Pimpernel – an effete young dandy who gradually reveals his secret self as gallant avenger – was only another aspect of the characters he had been playing. Next came *The Three Musketeers*; and it was clear that Fairbanks had always seen himself as D'Artagnan. After this he was *Robin Hood, The Thief of Bagdad, Don Q, Son of Zorro, The Black Pirate, The Gaucho* – in every role outsmarting his enemies, fighting off armies single-handed, astounding with his agility and the grace which imposed its own rhythms on any film he appeared in. He seemed able to defy gravity with his standing leaps. He ran up trees or slid down mainsails, supported only by the point of his dagger as it sheared down the canvas. Always, of course, he carried off the girl at the end.

Whatever the character, Doug – with his peppy, get-up-and-go optimism and extravagant ebullience, the broad grin never long extinguished by the dramatics – was youth, life, success, America. The nation's young were inspired by books published under his name, with titles like *Laugh and Live* or *Making Life Worthwhile*.

Talking pictures hit him when he was well past forty. Ominously, in *The Iron Mask* (1929), his last silent film, D'Artagnan was silver-haired, and died in the final reel – the first Fairbanks character to admit mortality. *The*

Taming of the Shrew (1929), in which he played opposite Mary Pickford for the first and last time, showed that he was more than equal to speaking roles; but he suspected the talkies, recognising that his proper medium had been the mime film, and that it was now defunct. Restlessness took hold again, and he wandered from country to country. His marriage broke up. He made four more sound films, without recapturing his audience. He died, alone and in his sleep, just after the outbreak of the Second World War.

Valentino had the greater good fortune perhaps to die at the very peak of his career, before his fanatical fans had noticed that their Sheik was putting on weight and losing his hair. His stardom had lasted little more than five years; but in that time the publicists wove such a web of myth about his beginnings that even his true name is no longer quite certain. They claimed that he was born Rodolpho Alfonzo Raffaelo Pierre Filibert Guglielmio di Valentina d'Antonguolla; though he was probably just plain Rodolpho Guglielmi, the son of a vet in the little southern Italian town of Castellaneto. His father died when Rodolpho was eleven, in 1906.

A military academy and an agricultural college figure vaguely in the sparse accounts of his education. At eighteen he emigrated to New York, worked as a gardener, among other odd jobs, and ended up as a taxi driver. His dancing was graceful enough for him to turn professional and partner Bonnie Glass, Joan Sawyer and Mae Murray. After trouble with the police on a charge of misdemeanour related to White Slavery, he left New York, dancing his way to the West Coast in the chorus of musical stage shows. Around 1918 he had reached Hollywood. Whatever magic the public was ultimately to find in his personality, it was evidently not immediately apparent. For two or three years he hung around the moving picture business, making friends, borrowing money, getting the odd supporting role, even on one occasion playing an Irishman. Mostly he was cast as the villain, though the best part he had, opposite Clara Kimball Young in *The Eyes of Youth*, permitted him to masquerade as romantic hero until his unmasking in the final reel.

The best scenarists in silent Hollywood were all women. One of them, June Mathis, saw *The Eyes of Youth*; and with the eyes – and intuition – of a woman, perceived the quality in the young 'heavy'. Despite the resistance of the Irish director, Rex Ingram, she insisted on putting Valentino into the main role of *The Four Horsemen of the Apocalypse*, which she was producing as well as adapting from Vicente Blasco Ibañez's portentous marathon about the First World War. The role of Julio, the playboy who finds himself and becomes a war hero, was built up. Despite the current reaction against war subjects, the morning after the film's première there were queues round the block; and *The Four Horsemen of the Apocalypse* went on to become one of the most profitable films of the decade. The reason was not merely that it was Art (with a capital A and trick photography), but that Valentino – whose overnight stardom took the studio so much by surprise that they had to call back the prints of the film and alter his billing – did the Tango.

Even before the film was released however Valentino had been put into *Camille* opposite Alla Nazimova, the celebrated Russian actress, into a tepid adventure, *Uncharted Seas*, and a version of *Eugénie Grandet*, renamed *The Conquering Power*. But the Metro studio could neither select suitable material for their star's talents, nor would raise his salary to match his drawing power. In consequence Paramount captured him, and gave Valentino his second triumph in *The Sheik*, an appalling bit of rubbish by an English lady, Miss E. M. Hull, which had thrilled readers throughout the English-speaking world. It was a lurid tale about how an English maiden, alone in the desert, is swept off to the tent of a passionate sheik. Naturally the miscegenation implied was only a thrilling illusion: at the end the Arab reveals that all along he has been the blue-blooded Earl of Glengarryl in disguise.

The Sheik confirmed Valentino as the supreme symbol of unrestrained, illicit, exotic passion. 'Shriek for the Sheik Will Seek You Too!' exhorted the publicity for the film, frankly inviting the American woman to identify with the lady swept off and ravished in the barbarian's tent. America and a good deal of the rest of the world went Sheik-mad. While the Arabian influence infiltrated interior decoration and clothes design, and young men cultivated the Sheik look, a pop song 'The Sheik of Araby' helped boost the vast commercial takings of the film. Valentino's next big success, three films later, was again from Blasco Ibañez, *Blood and Sand*, which proved that Valentino's success was more than a fluke. In real life he might have a cauliflower ear and slight squint; but he was uniquely photogenic. His myopia only gave his eyes a depth of mystery. He was possessed, on screen, of a highly charged sexual magnetism. While an inherent deficiency of humour enabled him to play pathos and drama with total lack of inhibition (his death scene in *Blood and Sand* still retains all its original power) there was a grace and charm which gave conviction to his treatment of light comedy. The lithe elegance of a dancer seemed often transmitted to the movement of the films in which he appeared.

Yet if on screen he was the very essence of eroticism, the undisputed master of the weaker sex, his private life had no such clarity. Everyone who knew him personally said that he was just an amiable, simple peasant boy, delighted by pretty and extravagant clothes and possessions, fond of tinkering with the expensive sports cars in his garage. His sexual life was equivocal. He seemed always easier in the company of his close men friends. He married twice, each time rather unsuitably choosing girls from the harem of beauties which the actress Nazimova maintained about her. His first wife locked the door on him once and for all on the wedding night. The second, the heiress of Richard Hudnut, the cosmetics manufacturer, was a pushy and pretentious designer who called herself Natacha Rambova. Dominating the admiring Valentino and wearing him like a jewel, she converted him from a modest and cooperative actor into a difficult and demanding temperament. She contrived to thrust him into a series of overblown and arty dramas, the most successful of which was an adaptation of Booth Tarkington's *Monsieur Beaucaire*, though even this was only a moderate success with the public, who thought Valentino's get-up rather sissy.

A contract with United Artists specifically prohibited the interference of the intolerable Rambova, who thereupon soon drifted away from her husband. His career revived at once. With a good director, Clarence Brown, *The Eagle*, adapted from Pushkin's *Dubrovsky*, wittily guyed the romantic convention. Against all expectations the sequel to *The Sheik*, *Son of the Sheik* – with Valentino in a dual role as father and son – was converted by another of Hollywood's star lady writers, Frances Marion, into a passably coherent story, and won another huge success with the public.

At which point, in 1926, Valentino died suddenly from a perforated ulcer. Not even *The Four Horsemen* had called out such public excitement as did his passing. The New York lying-in-state was the signal for unprecedented crowds and demonstrations, which continued as the body was taken by rail to its final rest in Los Angeles. In his death Valentino seemed to become an even greater object of adoration for the women of the whole world than in his lifetime. Girls tried to leap into his casket, and tore the chapel of rest apart to carry off souvenirs. There was a spate of suicides. The flamboyant Pola Negri, a star recently imported from Germany to Hollywood, announced that she was to have been his bride, and staged a coast-to-coast display of hysterical and spectacular mourning. Her floral tribute of 4,000 blood-red roses with POLA picked out in the middle in white blooms, measured eleven feet by six.

Valentino's appeal outlived him by more than his own lifetime. There are still Valentino fan clubs, and obsessive collectors of films, photographs and relics of the star. When his pictures are reissued audiences are divided between titters at his Latin extravagance and the silent rapture of renewed passion for the shadow of a young man dead nearly half a century.

The kind of fantasies he fulfilled had been a staple of popular female literature for decades before him; but he topped them with new fantasies and daydreams. He was, said *Life*, a quarter of a century after his death, 'the symbol of everything wild and wonderful and illicit in nature'. He offered a dream of escape, of impossible erotic adventure, to all the quiet, grey-lifed women from Manchester to the Mid-West. This was the role of a matinée idol.

After Valentino's death and canonisation in the heart of the mourning public, the Hollywood studios desperately sought a successor. His own brother was brought from Castellaneto and renamed Alberto Valentino; but despite agonising plastic surgery to amend his bulbous nose, all he achieved in films was a couple of dismal flops. The nearest heir was Ramon Novarro. Mexican-born, he had been playing bit parts for years under his actual name of Ramon Samaniegos, when Rex Ingram decided to do the same for him as he had done for Valentino. While Valentino was filming *The Sheik*, Novarro made his debut as Rupert of Hentzau in *The Prisoner of Zenda*. Later he made his own answer to *The Sheik*, *The Arab*. As it happened the peak of his career came when he starred as the galley slave, *Ben Hur*, in the year of Valentino's death.

Novarro was beautiful and exotic and a capable enough actor; but he offered none of the sexual challenge that was so potent in Valentino. Partly it was that he lacked the special gift of humourlessness, which permitted Valentino to take himself so seriously. Again, his somewhat less virile charms were more inclined to inspire maternal than erotic responses. Novarro's career declined with the passing of the vogue for Latin lovers and the more sophisticated tastes of the talkie era.

The Valentino *furore* launched new stars: the Viennese Jacob Krantz became Ricardo Cortes – one of the most appealing and intelligent of the Latin lovers; and the Mexican Luis Antonio Damaso de Alonso modified his name to Gilbert Roland. Other careers were revived. Antonio Moreno, who had been working modestly in films since 1912 was turned into a temporary idol. But Hollywood's most romantic hero after Valentino was as homegrown as his name John Pringle. As Jack, and later John, Gilbert, he too had conscientiously been working his way up from rung to rung, acting, writing a bit, toying with offers to direct, when his flashing black eyes and bronzed Italian looks suddenly brought him into demand. Inevitably he made his *Sheik*, in *Arabian Love*; but he was too good to be typed in romance. He played the profligate Count Danilo in Erich Von Stroheim's *The Merry Widow*, then achieved the peak of his career with his ranging and dramatic performance in King Vidor's First World War drama, *The Big Parade*. He swashbuckled in *Bardelys the Magnificent* and *The Cossacks*, and was Garbo's best leading man in silent films, most notably in *Anna Karenina*, retitled *Love*, and *A Woman of Affairs*, a passionate if purified adaptation of *The Green Hat*.

At the close of the silent period, Gilbert was Hollywood's supreme masculine idol. With the coming of talkies his career was ended. His only successful sound film was *Queen Christina*, for which Garbo herself had insisted on him as leading man. Yet even in this film it was clear what had struck Gilbert. He is always instanced as the classic case of a career ruined by sound. It was not however that his voice was especially light for a romantic hero, or that sound technicians could not have coped with it. Rather he was one of those mythical figures of the silent screen, like Fairbanks, for whom a voice was no gift, but a liability, clawing them down to ordinary mortality, back from the extra-human world of the mute drama where all was in the play of bright eyes and fine bodies. In Gilbert's case the diminution seems actual, physical. The actor who plays in *Queen Christina* seems somehow smaller and slighter than the joyous lad in *The Cossacks* or in the soldier hero of *The Big Parade*.

At the end of the Twenties Gilbert had jockeyed for place at the top of the popularity polls with Ronald Colman, an English actor from Richmond, Surrey, who combined a romantically handsome physique with immense versatility, so that he could turn from costume swashbucklers to drawing-room comedy, from Westerns to Wilde. The same versatility and grounding as an actor enabled him to survive sound and to hold his place as a star until the late 1940s, years after the death of his one-time rival at the age of 39.

Mary Pickford who, in terms of popularity in her own era, must be rated the greatest – indeed the prototype – of movie idols, remained a child star, on stage and screen, for more than a quarter of a century. She was born in Toronto in 1893; and after her father died when she was four became the family's princpal breadwinner, touring in stock companies as 'Baby Gladys Smith'. In 1907 she achieved Broadway under the management of David Belasco, who renamed her Mary Pickford. In 1909 work was short, and shamefacedly she went into pictures. D. W. Griffith, at Biograph, thought she was too fat, but then perceived in her the ideal Cinderella waif. Audiences thrilled to her even at a time when screen players were not identified by names and fan letters had to be addressed to 'The Girl With the Curls'.

Even in the early years a keen commercial spirit and sense of her drawing value sent her bargaining from company to company. When she returned to Belasco and Broadway in 1912 in *A Good Little Devil*, it was the first time that the personal appearance of a film star had resulted in the mobbing of a legitimate theatre by eager fans. After this the artful Adolph Zukor, designer of Hollywood economics (who in 1973 became the movies' first centenarian), produced her films until even he was unnerved by Mary's insatiable salary demands – always spurred by a competitive desire to keep abreast of Chaplin's million-dollar earnings. Finally, with Fairbanks, D. W. Griffith and Chaplin, she formed the United Artists Corporation to distribute their own films and ensure that the leading creators of the industry took their rightful share of the vast fortunes they attracted to the box office.

Perhaps it was the memory of her own lost childhood and premature responsibilities which gave the special poignancy to the child portrayals which made Mary Pickford America's – and the World's – Sweetheart as she was variously styled. She was *Cinderella*, *A Poor Little Rich Girl*, *Rebecca of Sunnybrook Farm*, *Pollyanna*, *Little Lord Fauntleroy*, *Little Annie Rooney*. As she grew older and the actress within the character roles showed more and more evidence of maturity, her typing as eternal child became a nightmare. Every effort to break out of the mould and play mature roles was resolutely rejected by the public; when she cut off her curls (not till after her mother's death) it seemed a betrayal; and the shorn locks were accusingly preserved like saintly relics in the museums of San Diego and Los Angeles.

Pickford was a trouper and did her best to please her audience. Her child roles were varied and skillful. Reared though she was in Victorian melodrama her characterisations were realistic and meticulously observed, too full of humour and spirit even to fall for long into sentimentality. Ending her career definitively when she did perhaps saved her from a worse fate. For her first talkie, *Coquette*, she won an Oscar; but she made a shrill and limited Shrew for Doug's Taming; and her subsequent and last two films were costly failures. She retired in 1933, having invested well the tribute of her adoring public.

Pickford was only one of a whole generation of girls discovered and developed by D. W. Griffith, a convinced Victorian, whose power over the audience was such that he prolonged beyond its natural lifetime the public's enthusiasm for an innocent, virginal, Tennysonian ideal of girlhood. Even the names he found for them were significant – Blanche Sweet and Bessie Love, for instance, two girls who, as it turned out, had fun and verve enough to break out of the image of frail romantic beauties created for them. Lillian Gish, with her fragile, altogether individual beauty, was by any standards a great actress; so that when the studios – if not the public – decided that her days as an idol were numbered, she left Hollywood without a backward look to return to a career on the stage, as O. Z. Whitehead has shown.

Other studios produced other styles of the home-grown, All-American girl. The star of Mack Sennett's Keystone comedies was Mabel Normand, beautiful and irrepressible, at least until the advent of sickness, tragedy and early death), one of the first screen stars to delight her fans as much by her off-screen pranks as by her performances. The Pathé Studios offered Pearl White, the undisputed queen of the weekly serial, who grappled with gangsters, gamblers, rustlers, smugglers and every other sort of bad lot through episode after episode between 1914 and 1922.

Post-war America, however, with its New Morality, New Woman and the New Riches of booming business, wanted more exotic thrills than Griffith heroines and spunky girls-next-door. Cecil B. De Mille, with an infallible intuition for anticipating public taste, turned out a cycle of sophisticated socio-sexual comedies which embodied the dreams and fantasy self-image of the Twenties, depicted the new manners, moral freedom and marital infidelities, but invariably provided reassuring dénouements which reasserted fidelity and older moral ideals. For these films De Mille found an ideal sophisticated heroine in Gloria Swanson, who had worked her way from Mack Sennett's Keystone troupe through two-reel farces. De Mille exploited her vitality and fun, but at the same time created in her a symbol of American female *chic*. What Swanson wore and did helped create the clothes and the etiquette of

American women in the Twenties. Her fans were somewhat disillusioned when she descended so close to the workaday world as to have a baby; but elated as never before when she arrived from Europe with a real marquis as a husband. The off-screen image never compromised her work on screen: to the end of the silent days she was still game to play slapstick if the need arose; and in 1950 she came back to the screen to pay a bizarre tribute to silent days and silent idols in *Sunset Boulevard*. But Norma Desmond, the aging and egocentric star, still inhabiting her own forgotten legend, still declaring, 'I still am big. It's the pictures that got small!' was not in any respect an expression of the real-life Swanson, a beautiful and intelligent woman who had moved without any regret for the cinema into new fields of enthusiastic activity.

The studio publicists fabricated stories of ferocious rivary between Swanson and Pola Negri, though Swanson had far too much humour to go along very far with such theatricals; and probably was not seriously disturbed even when Negri outdid her in marriage, graduating from baron to count and finally to prince. Aside from these marriages Negri did not discourage rumours of a romantic liaison with Chaplin; and thrust herself into the role of Valentino's chief mourner. Humour was at no time her strong point.

Negri satisfied the public's desire for a new kind of female exoticism equivalent to the Latin lovers. The screen's prototype exotic, Theda Bara (in real life a quiet girl from Cincinnatti called Theodosia Goodman) belonged to a type of *femme fatale* which had already gone out of fashion by the end of the War. Another predecessor, Alla Nazimova had become almost an American institution since she first came from Russia in 1905; and in any case, though she played opposite Valentino in *Camille*, she preferred classic roles to the sort of romantic *kitsch*, the stuff of which the greatest matinée idols were ideally made.

Negri seems to have been trained in Russia, though she returned to her native Poland to become a leading film star in the early part of the First World War. Moving to Berlin, she enjoyed her greatest triumphs in the costume spectacles directed by Ernst Lubitsch. These films preceded her to the United States and established her great following there. Oddly enough the public were never captured to the same extent by her American films, though she ranged gamely from 'vamp' roles to the dramatic subtleties of Stiller's *Hotel Imperial* and the deft comedy of Mal St Clair's *Woman of the World*. In later years her career was largely sustained by colourful publicity, as other exotics like Vilma Banky (from Budapest) and Nita Naldi, 'Queen of the Vampires' (from Washington) arrived to dispute her eminence.

As the Twenties went on the American audience rediscovered interest in a new kind of home-bred girl. 'Joan Crawford,' wrote Scott Fitzgerald, 'is doubtless the best example of the flapper, the girl you see at smart night clubs, gowned to the apex of sophistication, toying with iced glasses, with a remote, faintly bitter expression, dancing deliciously, laughing a good deal, with wide, hurt eyes. Young Things with a talent for living.' There was no mystery or assumed innocence about the flappers – Colleen Moore, Marion Davies, Clara Bow, Crawford herself. They were tough, pretty and saucy, with inexhaustible resourcefulness and strength and wit. They breathed the spirit of emancipation. They could admire good-looking men without embarrassment; and sock any fellow who got fresh. They could dance till dawn, and then Charleston all the way home. As Wild Diana in *Our Dancing Daughters*, Crawford hugs herself and exclaims 'Oh! – it feels so good – just to be alive!' and their celebration of youth and beauty and the joy of living still calls out as vitally and as poignantly as anything from that lost world between the Armistice and the Wall Street crash.

Among them all Clara Bow – The 'It Girl', after Elinor Glyn saw in her fellow-redhead the ideal star for the screen version of her novel *It* – has a unique place. Her nervous vitality seemed to sum up the whole restlessness of the Twenties (in later years it was to torment her and turn to sickness and chronic insomnia). She was dazzlingly attractive, with her wide, magnificent eyes, her mass of red hair that photographed dark, the slight, childlike yet quintessentially sexual figure, the pout that was anticipation of kisses. Her intentions were never veiled. Setting eyes on an interesting male, she would narrow her eyes, give a slight, thoughtful pucker to her brows and then go into action with some such suitable, brief, admiring exclamation as 'Hot Socks!' Finding herself in proximity to an eligible man she would let her hips sag forward in a gesture of invitation which, conscious or not, was unequivocal.

Clara's was the Hollywood success story of a girl who made it to stardom from a childhood of poverty via a beauty contest at 17; and in many of her films she seemed to be constantly reliving the story, letting audiences vicariously enjoy the triumph of the little manicurist or shopgirl whose dreams of riches and a romantic marriage are fulfilled. Perhaps it was this, for a brief time, that they loved in her. She was a capable and charming actress; and remained so in her few talking pictures. But audiences it seemed preferred her silent image – or perhaps they resented the scandals that dogged poor impetuous Clara. After 1933 when she was twenty-eight, she vanished from the screen to obscurity in which she survived another thirty-two years.

Towards the end of the silent era a new shadow flitted across the screen, fragile and elusive, yet eclipsing all at once the flappers and the vamps, the Latin lovers, the child actors and the performing horses. But Garbo was a goddess, not an idol; and when the posters signalled 'Garbo Talks!' it proved that the enchanted age of the mute idols was over, for ever.

Time of the Talkies

by Dilys Powell

YEARS ago in some airless Oxford cinema I heard an undergraduate audience demonstrating in a cause of a kind no longer fashionable. 'We want Laura!' they chanted. 'We want Laura!' They were not making a political protest. They were waiting for a film which I am pretty sure was called *Thanks for the Buggy Ride*; and the star was Laura la Plante. The other day I looked Laura la Plante up in the handbooks. I had a job to find her anywhere. It is not just that like Congreve's Millamant she dwindled into a wife (she married her director, William A. Seiter). As a star she was not durable. In name at any rate a matinée idol must live on.

The title rings awkwardly in the cinema. Except at Christmas, except with their children, people don't queue for films in the afternoon. Provincial families used, at any rate mine used, to set off in a ragged troop to watch Harold Lloyd, and it is true we came home long before dinner (I mean supper; I must not elevate our modest domestic arrangements). But we did not see ourselves as going to a matinée. Today the word so far as the cinema is concerned means a performance exclusively for the tots – and with etymological correctness it is a morning affair. I know one must not take the words matinée idol literally. Nevertheless one associates them with the rattle of tea-trays in the auditorium, with a romantic personality – and with a kind of changelessness. Matinée idols shouldn't change.

And that is where the talkies come in.

When the cinema began to talk its players – and tea-trays or not there were matinée idols among them – began to act. Not that the players of the silent screen were incapable of acting. There was the language of gesture and look; Chaplin in *The Pilgrim* needed no words to tell the story of David and Goliath. All the same with speech and changing techniques the stars had more to manage. Not all of them stood the test. Producers and directors as well as audiences wanted a different style of performance; sound as much as the passage of the years obscured, at any rate temporarily, such idols as Pola Negri and Gloria Swanson. John Gilbert faded early, as David Robinson has shown. During a decade and more the great Buster Keaton seemed annihilated. Chaplin hesitated for years before risking coherent talk on the screen. Most significant of all, the moths ate into immutability. Players who act need to change their skins. The talkies, in fact, began to undermine the idols of the cinema – the smooth-cheeked intrepid heroes of prairie, ocean and Roman arena, the big-eyed heroines with their nimbuses of hair lit from the back.

All the same there were survivors. There were newcomers who, born to the realistic style presently demanded by speech and, later, colour, managed to preserve the appearance of a changeless seductive personality.

In a way it was her voice which made Greta Garbo the most celebrated of all the idols. Of course she was beautiful. The bone structure of the face with the strong mouth and the deep-caverned eyes gave her an air which was ageless, almost sexless. Silent – and already adored – she was the romantic star. But when at last she spoke – and I am not thinking of the 'Garbo Talks!' ballyhoo over *Anna Christie* and that first startling demand for whisky – the personality took on a new dimension. The slow husky tones caressed; passion was there. At first one might have said there was not much range in the voice. But as with its enigmatic accent it growled and purred and wept, it began to animate the most banal script.

The scripts were indeed banal, many of them. The subjects often came from the trash-bucket of their times. Unlikely that anybody today would put his money on *Susan Lenox: Her Fall and Rise*. The story of the girl hunted by a savage father, driven away from the man she loves (Clark Gable in this case) into not one but two pairs of alien arms – looked at today it seems to defeat even Garbo, and it was in fact one of the silliest of the roles she was called on to play. But the theme was typical of the novelettish stuff on which her gifts were spent. The cinema was still mesmerised by the idea of the noble-hearted prostitute, courtesan or at any rate kept woman, that figure of a forgotten age. The word mistress is rapidly becoming unfashionable, but in the 1930s Garbo was always being cast as somebody's mistress, always being called on to sacrifice a lover or perhaps herself. The feminine idol was no longer the innocent madcap or the pure wife, mother or sister; she was the woman with a past.

There was something cryptic in the nature, or at any rate the public nature of Greta Garbo, She really did, it seems, want to be alone or at least private. Gossip writers naturally enough seized on the qualities which separated her from the generality of Hollywood players. And the actress did more than fit the role; she magnified it. She avoided, except when working, the intrusive camera; wore flat-heeled shoes; went about in something not unlike a Hitler raincoat. In a decade when stars asked nothing so much as to be seen, she hid; she kept glamour for the screen. Her very secrecy was a gift to the publicity department. Perhaps they sometimes exaggerated her idiosyncrasies. But there is no legend without a kernel of truth, and her whole life lent itself to the legend of seclusion, solitude, inviolability. She was her own legend. Eagerly the public, noting her mannerisms, memorising scraps of her dialogue, enlarged the mysterious image.

The critics were sometimes less enthusiastic. To the sardonic she was La Garbo. The cinema had not yet become intellectually fashionable, and the films in which she appeared were scarcely of a kind to excite the highbrow. The general public was cheerfully indifferent to the critics. For an audience, Raymond Durgnat has said, the beauty of Garbo possessed 'the spiritual meaning that beauty carried for the Greeks', and to attack her performance was to question a divinity.

The men were less devoted than the women. She was a creature of lofty romance, not sexuality; I doubt whether many husbands dreamed of a week-end at Brighton with Greta Garbo. The women felt safe with her; a goddess is not to be competed with. And from the black-and-white rectangle at the far end of the cinema she exercised a magic which transcended sex, which transmuted the flaws persistent even in that beauty. For she was not, if you come to think of it, naturally graceful, the famous dance in *Mata Hari* was less than seductive. Heartbreaking though she was in *Grand Hotel* one found difficulty in believing in her as a ballerina, even a fading ballerina. The body was that of an athletic rather than a romantic divinity; those shoulders might have swum the Channel.

But who cared then, who cares now? She was loved: best loved, probably, in *Queen Christina*. It was a film which afforded her the severity of dress which she appeared to favour; and she was indeed splendid in the stylised masculine clothes, a Rosalind's, a Viola's, which a woman in revolt against the position of women might affect. But the image we all carry away, the most famous image of all, is of Garbo marble in grief at the prow of the ship bearing her dead lover. She wears a flowing cloak; the long folds frame and exalt her austerity. I think she was most exquisite in the most feminine costume. In *Marie Walewska* as the Polish beauty abandoned by the Napoleon of Charles Boyer; in *Camille* as Marguerite Gautier – about her Dame aux Camélias there was a kind of radiance; in the floating white dress of her country happiness she was all joy. And as the victim of love in *Anna Karenina* – I am speaking of the second, the talking version – she was allowed for once the dignity of tragedy. It is still difficult without tears to listen to her passage with the child she is forbidden to visit or to watch her last despairing walk in the railway station.

In the end she was destroyed by the legend she had herself done so much to create. At the beginning of the 1939–45 war *Ninotchka*, in spite of the new ballyhoo – 'Garbo Laughs!' as if she had never laughed in *Camille* or *Queen Christina* – preserves the intensity which was part of her spell. She tries on an absurd hat and is a bit flattered by the effect, she grows helplessly elated on champagne; the gravity is dissolved, but she is still playing within the framework of the character – passionate, self-immolatory – which her public adored. Two years later she was called on to assume a role against her temperament and the image so carefully established. *Two-Faced Woman* was a smart comedy. With George Cukor directing it was far from bad. As the woman posing as her own twin sister in an attempt to win back an errant husband Garbo herself was far from bad. With another actress the film could have been a respectable success. But it was not what people expected of Garbo. It was not what she had for more than a decade mesmerised them into expecting.

Another star might have been willing to accept if not defeat at least a kind of relegation. Of the famous names who appeared with her one or two, idols in their own right – Clark Gable, Charles Boyer – went to on drop the grand romantic mask and play second fiddle. Sometimes a regal figure from the silent screen – the incomparable Lillian Gish, for instance – would reappear not as a star but as a character player. Not Garbo. Perhaps public taste was changing. One might even say she got out in time. Anyhow she withdrew from the screen in 1941. There would be many rumours of a reappearance. Nothing has ever happened; only the fame goes on. She has found the best way of remaining an idol. Over thirty years after the release of *Two-Faced Woman* a season of her films can still make a stir. The reminiscences of her friends – Cecil Beaton among them – are news; she herself is news. Silent, private, in the eyes of her public she is changeless.

In the age of the talkies Garbo's position remains unique. The silent cinema produced names as lasting: Valentino, Fairbanks, Keaton, Pickford. But when one thinks of the darlings of the Thirties and Forties none, not Ingrid Bergman, not Norma Shearer or Bette Davis, or, among the men, Gary Cooper or Ronald Colman or Errol Flynn has an equal celebrity. Not even Marlene Dietrich, though to be honest there was a time when I thought her arrogant beauty outshone Garbo's romantic halo. But then Marlene Dietrich has never retired, and to be an indestructible legend a star needs to disappear. In one way she has made herself into more not of an idol but of a matinée idol. In later years she became a cabaret star and a solo performer in the theatre; the rattle perhaps not of tea-trays but of coffee-cups and the nip of whisky so painfully obtained at theatre bars may have punctuated her famous London evenings. Since the early sixties she has scarcely been seen in the cinema. But the siren voice is still heard. Her recordings of 'Lilli Marlene' and 'Where Have All the Flowers Gone?' see to that.

Again the voice is important. Recalling *The Blue Angel* one thinks as much of Dietrich singing 'Falling in Love Again' as of Dietrich in top hat, clasping a knee and sitting among the gross monsters of Joseph von Sternberg's night-club scene. The figure she presented there was so famous that in *The Damned* nearly forty years later Visconti could ironically re-create it and be sure that his audience would understand the reference.

The Blue Angel, made in Germany with an English as well as a German version, was not her first film. It was, though, the first in which Joseph von Sternberg directed her. The story of the high school professor (Emil Jannings was expert in communicating abasement) destroyed almost as a joke by a heartless bitch – the emphasis on humiliation made it typical of the German cinema between the wars. But in the excitement of the young actress's performance nobody bothered much about a touch of decadence. Sternberg (the 'von', by the way, was a Hollywood invention) has described how by accident he found his Lola for *The Blue Angel* in a theatre, leaning against the wings 'with a cold disdain'. There is no doubt that he was the creator of the exotic star we know. Dietrich herself has insisted on her debt. Other directors, for example Fritz Lang, have spoken of it. Sternberg, of course, could not stop talking about it. But he was not ungenerous; he paid tribute also to the intelligence, the patience and the teachability of his pupil, who with absolute obedience suffered the 'torments' of his direction.

Reuben Mamoulian, with whom she made *Song of Songs*, said that her face had to be carefully lit. Sternberg showed the world how to light it, how to refine its contours, how to touch with shadow the hollowed cheeks, how with veils and furs and spangles to set off the lovely mask. She worked for him for five years: walked barefoot over the desert in *Morocco*: was shot as a spy in *Dishonoured*; was held by bandits in *Shanghai Express*; refused to act for anybody else in *Blonde Venus* (a film in which Cary Grant was involved). At last after *The Scarlet Empress*, which was about Catherine the Great, and *The Devil is a Woman*, which was based on a book by Pierre Louÿs, the partnership was broken. But her implacable mentor had formed her. Or rather he would say that he had exposed qualities and talents which she possessed but had no idea how to employ and display. She had the confidence now to go on without him.

For a quarter of a century and more she rarely broke completely out of the mould which he had given her. When she did, as in *Golden Earrings*, where she appeared in walnut juice and Hungarian gipsy skirts, one felt a sense of outrage. Even her performance as the saloon singer, an ageing, brawling, self-sacrificing tigress in the famous and admired *Destry Rides Again* could be disconcerting to those who counted on her as eternally flawless. While Garbo had been the unattainable romantic Dietrich became the untouchable sex symbol. Her image was not called on to suffer the humiliations of a Garbo. If she played a harlot it was a victorious harlot; nobody wept for Dietrich.

As war came, as peace succeeded it she worked with the great directors. She acted the European adventuress in *The Flame of New Orleans* for René Clair, who in 1941 when France was Nazi-controlled was directing in the United States. She appeared for Billy Wilder as the dubiously-connected Berlin nightclub entertainer in *A Foreign Affair*; she submitted herself to false suspicions in Hitchcock's *Stage Fright*. In the company of John Wayne she was tough in the South Seas (*Seven Sinners*) and the West (*The Spoilers*); by the early nineteen-sixties she was conducting an intellectual argument with Spencer Tracy in *Judgment at Nuremberg*, an argument about the ethics of life under Hitler. The character varied; she moved from comedy to thriller to political drama. But the face – the cool insolent eyes, the exquisite lines of cheek and mouth and chin – that did not alter. The body, so elegant in the semblance of a man's clothes. the distinguished legs – there was no change there. Dietrich, then, did everything an idol should do except withdraw.

Voluntary or involuntary, disappearance has preserved, indeed embalmed, certain reputations. Beside the grand romantic or exotic symbols, beside Garbo and Dietrich the smaller fry of seduction flourished; after Clara Bow, endearing man-trap of the 1920s, came Jean Harlow, vamp of the Thirties. She was not the langorous Circe of silent screen vamps; her invitation was a good deal more vigorous. In *Hell's Angels* (directed, you may remember, by Howard Hughes) she played the glamour-puss who changed (the remark is famous) into 'something more comfortable'. She was the original Platinum Blonde, the girl whose bleached waves set a fashion said to be so dangerous that the gossip-writers began to warn; not only did it require the accompaniment of furs, velvets and teeth with not a trace of yellow, it could ruin a natural curl and break off the hair. What it did to Jean Harlow's hair one cannot say; she died, sad victim of the cinema, when she was twenty-six.

Possibly, like one or two stars of a later age, she was a victim of her own nature as well; she may have burned herself out. The suicide of her second husband no more than a few weeks after the wedding smudged her reputation but did not interrupt a career in films such as *Blonde Bombshell* which were designed to sharpen the image Hollywood had invented for her. She acted for Capra and Wellman, she played in gangster films and comedies, she worked with Spencer Tracy, Myrna Loy, William Powell. In her short life the platinum hair darkened to red and the vamp turned good-hearted. But somehow one still thinks of her in backless evening dress and marabout.

To be honest one does not often remember her except as a name in the histories of the cinema, a symbol of the variations in sexual taste of the nineteen-thirties. In the Sixties, however, the screen took to looking back, and from its past resurrected the story of the platinum blonde. An exercise in high-temperature biography appeared; it was called simply *Harlow*. Its attempt to recapture the frenzies of the Harlow of the 1930s was faintly distressing. But at least it was a reminder that the name was once dynamite. At her funeral Hollywood made extravagant demonstrations of grief, Nelson Eddy sang 'Ah, Sweet Mystery of Life' and Jeanette MacDonald obliged with the Indian Love Call from *Rose Marie*; one can imagine no more macabre farewell. Today one looks at a famous Harlow film, *Red Dust*, and wonders how the shrill, rather pathetic little figure can have cast such a spell.

One should bear in mind, though, that the performance in *Red Dust* of another player, a star often counted among the great ones, looks today as flat as poor Jean Harlow's. In 1932 to cast Clark Gable opposite Harlow was thought a master-stroke. Together the two unsentimental figures were a hit, and the partnership continued through several films now forgotten. But then Gable – the King, he was nicknamed; in Hollywood it was a mark of rank to have a public nickname – soon showed with or without Harlow that he had something more than the pale smooth personality of many romantic stars. True that he had played with Garbo, most romantic of them all. But he was never really the romantic hero. He was the adventurer, the fighter, the go-getter. Other tough fighters might present also an essentially romantic image. A John Wayne might have fine passages of pathos; not Gable, not until the very last of his films, when the actor took over from the star and in *The Misfits* presented a character in defeat.

Perhaps John Huston, directing, drew from him a quality which had always been there but kept hidden. Perhaps with the passage of time Gable – he was nearly sixty when he appeared in the film – was ready to yield to his own gifts. He had been an idol all right. 'Dear Mr Gable' – the song in the revue was addressed by a worshipper. To the end he conserved his talent for comedy; one remembers *The Hucksters* and *Teacher's Pet*. But it was his air of masculine command rather than his talent which captivated his admirers. He was the masterful one, a rough, sophisticated, up-to-date counterpart of Valentino's Sheik. The women in his audience dreamed of subjugation; the men, perhaps, respected the show of virility. And yet, sardonic though the face he presented to the world there was often something wry in his amusement. The hat tipped back above the broad cheekbones and the wide ears, the impudent eyes and the ironic lines round the mouth – he was made for the role of the journalist in Capra's *It Happened One Night*. And the film was made for him; he could go confidently on to *Mutiny on the Bounty*, he could go on to the Rhett Butler of *Gone With the Wind* and there create a sex symbol all the more popular because ultimately unattainable. In the end, you remember, Rhett turns down Scarlett O'Hara.

Gable vanished at the right moment. He had proved himself as an actor, he was not driven by age or fashion to climb down from his throne. Difficult to think of other men who not only achieved but held the same kind of position. The heyday of Hollywood between the wars and on into the 1940s produced players of greater adaptability, talent and, come to that, charm. Gary Cooper, for instance, the lean handsome horseman, master of the throwaway line, cool hero, cool joker, gallant partner of Jean Arthur and Barbara Stanwyck, Claudette Colbert, Grace Kelly, Ingrid Bergman, Audrey Hepburn and yes, Marlene Dietrich – give me Gary Cooper any day. He was loved; but he was not, I think, an idol in the sense in which Clark Gable was an idol.

Spencer Tracy was the greatest actor of them all, a man to set beside the best that the theatre as well as the cinema of his day could offer. But nobody, so far as I know, ever sang for Dear Mr Tracy. Possibly he was too fine an actor, an artist too deep in his work to endure the management of an image; one could say the same about Katharine Hepburn, brilliant on her own, brilliant as his partner in the series of comedies – *Woman of the Year*, *Adam's Rib*, *Pat and Mike* – which ended only with his death in the late 1960s. Miss Hepburn has never been a matinée idol; nor, I think, has Ingrid Bergman, already making her first delicate appearance before the Nazi war; though later she was the heroine of a film, *Casablanca*, with Humphrey Bogart, which has itself been idolised. And Bette Davis with her flouncing walk and her precise consonantal diction – a grand-scale performer from *The Petrified Forest* and *Jezebel* and *Marked Woman* in the Thirties, through the woman's magazine material of *Now Voyager* and *The Old Maid* and the acidities of *The Little Foxes* and *All About Eve*, down to the macabre extravagance of the Sixties, *Whatever Happened to Baby Jane* and the rest – it is magnificent, but it is not the stuff of romantic idolatry.

For romance of a special sort is the essential: not heroism, not sacrifice, not the love-clinch in the old homestead but romance allied with glamour, the dream of a sexuality far out of reach. Charles Boyer in his middle period had it; I think it has been denied to such flawless stars as Henry Fonda, James Stewart and Cary Grant or, among the women Jean Arthur and Claudette Colbert, Irene Dunne, Myrna Loy, Carole Lombard, even Joan Crawford. One or two of the famous partnerships of the 1930s might have claimed it. Nelson Eddy and Jeanette MacDonald, for example, popular stars of many a sugared musical; Fred Astaire and Ginger Rogers, most elegant and winning of dancers; or such soloists as Maurice Chevalier and Deanna Durbin; but their spell depended first on song or dance; deprive them of that, and sometimes (though not always) there was not much left.

Again, the high-powered, the electric personality of James Cagney never exercised the extraordinary spell. And genius has nothing to do with it. Orson Welles has genius, but nobody would call him a matinée idol. The title goes rather to the arrogant physical prowess of an Errol Flynn, who had lived a life of adventure before he came to fake it – though faking is not a wholly accurate word for the work of an actor who insisted on performing stunts for which most players would have needed a double. Like Gable he was the creation of the 1930s. At his best in the costume of the belligerent or the piratical past, he made his name in *Captain Blood* and *The Sea-Hawk*, in *The Charge of the Light Brigade* and, following the famous silent version by Douglas Fairbanks, *The Adventures of Robin Hood*; went on to play opposite Bette Davis in *The Private Lives of Elizabeth and Essex*; and caused what now seems an absurd stir in *Objective Burma*, a bit of war nonsense which gaily suggested that a party of American paratroops were responsible for the Japanese defeat. Probably the rumour of his private life did as much as his good looks and his confident impudence on the screen did to make him a masculine sex symbol.

Then towards the end of his life he was something else; in *The Roots of Heaven* he was an actor. Or perhaps it was not a metamorphosis. Perhaps one misjudges him and as with Clark Gable the actor had always been there, embedded in the idol. Charles Boyer, when, still in France, he played with Danielle Darrieux in *Mayerling*, was an actor as well as a romantic ideal. He was an actor with Garbo in *Marie Walewska* and with Irene Dunne in *Love Affair*. But to the yearning public he meant romance. The face, unheroically oval with smooth regular features, was not in itself remarkable. The voice, though, liquid and with deep reverberations, was a winner. Moreover it had a foreign accent, soothing, almost reverent; a good foreign accent can be no end of a help in the cinema. The figure had a protective, slightly courtly manner which suggested not just love but *l'amour*, and in the 1930s there was a feeling that for the real McCoy you needed a Frenchman. For a decade Charles Boyer was 'the great lover'. Then he began to slide out of the role. He began to settle for the safety of a good character actor.

Wisely. Younger stars were appearing, public notions of romance were changing. War brought a change, and not only in virility styles. The ideal woman was no longer some remote divinity. The soldier dreamed of the agreeably padded torso and the come-hither look. He wanted the pin-up girl; he wanted Betty Grable. Even before that, idols in new moulds were winning the day. Heavies and gangsters were moving up and ousting the accepted heroes. Hearts began to beat for John Wayne, Humphrey Bogart converted murder into sex appeal. And at any rate one of the young players of the pre-war decade would join the darlings of the Forties and Fifties.

By the end of the 1930s Judy Garland had already made a name as the girl in Andy Hardy's life and the heroine of *The Wizard of Oz*. She could dance, she could sing, she acted startlingly well. The singing voice was clear and true. She was not conventionally pretty. But the face, violet-shaped, was too much alive to be overlooked. From the brightness and bounce of the Andy Hardy series she advanced to join Gene Kelly (making in 1942 his first appearance on the screen) in *For Me and My Gal*. Two years later under the direction of Vincente Minnelli (whom she later married) she was the incomparable girl-next-door of *Meet Me in St Louis* with its warm, gay, affectionate family feeling. And she never lost that beguiling freshness of emotion. The voice took on a note of heartbreak; sometimes it seemed that there was a quality of desperation in her personality. Or perhaps that is recognisable only in retrospect; for now one knows that like one or two who followed her, like Marilyn Monroe, like James Dean, she was a desperate figure. She too would never be forced by time to change her role. Death, after all, is the great preserver.

Sometimes one is tempted to think of Judy Garland as the last of a dwindling band of idols. Then one remembers a spell-binder more recent, one remembers Elizabeth Taylor. And something else. Humphrey Bogart was hailed in the late 1930s; in the Forties and Fifties he was known as one of the unfailing stars. A few years after he died his image was being recalled in the films of France's New Wave; Godard would repeatedly refer to him, Belmondo would imitate him. In the 1970s his mannerisms, the faint lisp of his voice with its grating sexual undertones, his stance, even the tilt of his hat are being devotedly mimicked. Passages from his work are cited. He himself in his fictional guise turns up in other people's films. Humphrey Bogart has become a cult.

For the cinema is no longer ephemeral. Its idols can have a second life.

'A Pantheon of Gods'

a conversation between George Axelrod and Anthony Curtis

I went to see George Axelrod when he was living in Belgravia, London, writing the book for the musical version of his play *The Seven Year Itch*. I asked him first whether he thought the term matinée idol had a relevance to the American theatre.

AXELROD: Oh sure, we in America don't really use the same term although we mean the same thing by it when we say it. What we mean is a pantheon of gods. We want people who dare, on the stage or the screen, to do the sort of wickedness or the sort of kindness that we don't have the guts to do ourselves.

CURTIS: We have defined the matinée idol in this book as someone to whom an audience will flock irrespective of the work they're in . . .

AXELROD: . . . which makes it nifty for a writer. But you're absolutely right. Certainly there are certain plays in New York for example, I do believe indeed in London, in which, if a certain name is announced as the star or, if you will, matinée idol, you're sold out for a year. We just had an interesting example here in London. There is an American matinée idol, Lauren Bacall, whose play *Applause* isn't terribly good indeed but she's a sensation in it because people suddenly relate to her image. I think relating to the image of somebody larger than yourself, whether he be more wicked or more kind, is the thing that excites people.

CURTIS: Is there always an element of sexual attraction in any matinée idol? Can one be a matinée idol without having sexual magic?

AXELROD: There's no possibility of anybody, man, woman, child, or even Lassie, the dog, being a matinée idol without some sort of sexual excitement. That's our basic excitement as Mr Freud has told us. Maybe there are other things, but I've been making a living in this trade for a long time and I don't know what other. Now, the tragedy of this matter is, and there *is* a tragedy involved in it, fine splendid, wonderful actors, technically versed actors, trained actors, sometimes don't have it. The stupidest person in the world can wander on the stage yet has this particular – what Billy Wilder calls 'celluloid magic' – or what you call the matinée idol thing. And if they've got it, they've got it. You can't teach it, you can't take it away from them. Marilyn was dying and she still had it. If you got it, you got it.

CURTIS: On the other hand, it doesn't *preclude* great acting gifts does it? Marilyn Monroe, whom you worked with closely, wasn't she someone who both had the sexual charisma and the acting ability?

AXELROD: Marilyn had – and I loved her dearly, respect her deeply with all my heart and soul – absolutely no acting ability whatsoever. Had she had any it would have destroyed her. I loathe the word charisma, but it would have destroyed it. She was simply herself. I tell you how I really would define a matinée idol: a man or woman with tremendous style, tremendous over-confidence, who was covering up a huge sense of vulnerability. All matinée idols, if you examine them, are deeply, deeply – as human beings – vulnerable, and the only time they become alive is when they are in front of an audience. I mean, I can walk into my bedroom at night and my wife is angry at me, and there's no music behind me, but if I were a matinée idol or a star I would walk on to the stage and suddenly the audience would love me. The need for love, the need to be loved by masses of people because you are unable to deal with the love of one person is what makes you a matinée idol. Most matinée idols, I don't say this irreverently, are frightened people who can only find a realisation of themselves when they are acting out other people's fantasies in a non-real situation such as the stage or the screen, even if they have some kind of very, very special quality, even if they are a serious sex image, even if they are very, very fine actors. But damn few fine actors have made it, although in England you have more than we have in America. But the main thing is to take the flaws in your personality, the ones that destroy you as a human being and reverse them and project them on the stage.

CURTIS: Now when you write a script, a play or a movie, do you consciously tailor it to such qualities?

AXELROD: Oh yes, of course, all the people, they're hardly matinée idols but the protagonists, who have, for reasons not to my knowledge, come to be called Axelrod Heroes in American movies, always of course anti-heroes, Walter Matthau, Jack Lemon, people like that, for whom I almost always write, they are deeply, seriously vulnerable people who suddenly become alive and usually in the course of the plays that I write for them, win the girl, the million dollars, whatever it is, and the audience, who itself collectively is scared to death, suddenly sees someone who is in their image, actually winning.

CURTIS: This vulnerability is an essentially comic quality, isn't it? It's always the comic hero who is vulnerable. Not all matinée idols are comic figures. I mean Rudolph Valentino – to name a matinée idol of the silent period – was not a comic figure . . .

AXELROD: Rudolph Valentino was a matinée idol of the silent period for one reason only. Because pictures were silent. Had they had sound he would have talked like your local Italian grocer, I mean he had an Italiana accenta. He could hardly speak. He was . . . he was a *schmuck*! But on the screen he looked beautiful. Beauty is not against a matinée idol . . . beauty, even quite sick beauty, or perhaps, even better irregular or that kind of ugly beauty that Belmondo has. But usually you will find I think, sir, that the person who captures the imagination of the public is, if you were to plough deep enough in a nasty Freudian way, which I wouldn't dream of doing, you would find that what he or she is doing is covering his own sense of inadequacy.

CURTIS: A lot of the contributors to this book have felt in a nostalgic way that the age of the matinée idol is irrevocably over. I suppose it started around 1900 . . .

AXELROD: My friend, it started during the caveman period in pre-history when the boys were out there killing dinosaurs and chopping them up. One guy, one guy alone, scared to death of dinosaurs he was, stayed home and played around with the ladies a little bit while they were cooking last night's dinosaur meat, leftovers they called them I suppose, and when the guys came home they would gather around . . . I suppose they had invented fire by then . . . around the fire, which is sort of your television, anything that flickers, it doesn't matter what it says, it's something you look at, then he would get up and tell a story. People love to be told stories, they love to hear stories. The man or woman who can tell a story well was the base beginning of your matinée idol.

CURTIS: Yes, but don't you think that in the world of movies there has been
a great change, since about 1950? The matinée idol period has been
replaced by a period where the star, though he still exists, is much
less important than the director and the script?

AXELROD: We are going through a period in the movies now, in which the
director *is* the matinée idol or so it seems. When Antonioni or somebody makes a film he suddenly is the matinée idol. His players are
puppets, he moves them around. There's a lady in Sweden whom I
had the privilege of taking to dinner once at the Plaza, who didn't
know how to order dinner unless Bergman was there to point to the
menu. He was the matinée idol there and certainly we're going
through a period where the director, in the movies at least, is the
matinée idol, but actually not at all. Marlon Brando is the real
matinée idol at the end of the day.

CURTIS: Do you think he has this quality of vulnerability that you were
talking about earlier?

AXELROD: Of course.

CURTIS: And do you think that this period of the director being the matinée
idol will pass, that it is only a temporary period?

AXELROD: One hopes; one likes to believe that the matinée idol will return to
the writer. Shakespeare, were he alive today, would be a matinée
idol. Well, yeah, Shelley *was* a matinée idol. I like to believe I shall
be a matinée idol when my new show opens!

CURTIS: Ten years ago, *The Seven Year Itch* was on and writers like Arthur
Miller and Tennessee Williams were drawing vast audiences in
Broadway and London, just on their names. That period for the
moment seems to be over too. We don't have authors who are
matinée idols in that sense in the theatre today, do we?

AXELROD: Not in the theatre perhaps, but a new thing has happened perhaps
in hardback publishing. I can't think of a larger matinée idol than
Norman Mailer for example, who has combined journalism with
fiction and becomes his own hero in all his books – *The Armies of the
Night*, etc. The writer who injects himself. The kids in New York
call it 'the new journalism'. Mark Twain was a new journalist. Mark
Twain was a matinée idol. An actor has made a living for some years
just doing an *Evening with Mark Twain*, playing Mark Twain and
reading his works. Emlyn Williams crashes around now all over the
world, the Commonwealth at least, playing Charles Dickens. I think
the writer is the real matinée idol.

CURTIS: But to you think he can still have magic *in the theatre*? The young
people who follow Norman Mailer and who read his books and have
a feeling of relating to him, I have the sense that they don't relate
to theatre, they relate to movies, they relate to both stars and

directors in movies but they don't form an audience like the matinée idol audience of the pre-war and post-war period.

AXELROD: Well now sir, you are beginning to confuse very, very like things which are easily confusible. You are confusing, for example, celebrity, one, politics, two, and the theatre, three, they're all showbiz. I think Jack Kennedy was one of the great matinée idols of all times. I think Jack was . . . or go back even further, I mean Jesus Christ was your first matinée idol.

CURTIS: And of course *Jesus Christ Superstar* is doing very well at the moment.

AXELROD: I regard that as a *Jesus Christ Bit Player*. They messed up the book there.

CURTIS: Would you like to say who you think the greatest matinée idols you have ever encountered professionally in the theatre were?

AXELROD: Of course my theatre career is limited. I'm only fifty, a young boy. Marilyn Monroe for one. The camera loved her and she made love to that camera. Frank Sinatra makes love to a microphone and audiences love him. He makes a sound, he makes a noise that he understands the lyrics, he has never read a lyric in his life, can't even remember them, but some magic happens. We are talking really about magic, aren't we, in the end.

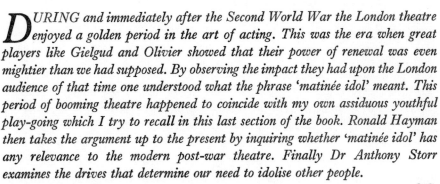

*D*URING *and immediately after the Second World War the London theatre enjoyed a golden period in the art of acting. This was the era when great players like Gielgud and Olivier showed that their power of renewal was even mightier than we had supposed. By observing the impact they had upon the London audience of that time one understood what the phrase 'matinée idol' meant. This period of booming theatre happened to coincide with my own assiduous youthful play-going which I try to recall in this last section of the book. Ronald Hayman then takes the argument up to the present by inquiring whether 'matinée idol' has any relevance to the modern post-war theatre. Finally Dr Anthony Storr examines the drives that determine our need to idolise other people.*

A.C.

Cutting My Teeth

by *Anthony Curtis*

B Y the summer of 1941 the German blitz on London had spent its fury.
The ack-ack guns on Primrose Hill were silent, the barrage balloons
remained like innocuous silver mobiles swaying gently overhead; beneath the
nightly curfew of the blackout the West End theatres burst into brilliant life
after a time of closure at the start of the war. There were plenty of matinées
now and lots of people on leave to go to them. As a stage-struck sixth-form
schoolboy I remember taking myself one afternoon in the summer holidays of
that year to see *Blithe Spirit* which had recently opened at the Piccadilly
Theatre. I was enchanted by the irruption of Kay Hammond from beyond the
grave as the sylph-like first wife Elvira, a grey-green ghost. Her astonishing
trapeze work with the basic vowel sounds of English delighted my callow ears
by its extravagance. I can see her still as she pronounced judgment on the
taste in drawing-room decoration of her successor, flashing her blazingly
lovely eyes over the furniture: ' . . . its thoroughly a-a-artsy-craftsy . . . she's
roooo-ined this room . . . ' (But you would need some system of musical
notation to pin down the swoops and leaps of that remarkable sound with any
degree of precision.) That indelible smear 'artsy-craftsy' epitomised a life-
style of the 1930s in England. Noël Coward's comedy showed us some fairly
typical members of its spoiled upper-middle class indulging in one of their
frivolous after-dinner pastimes of table-tapping under the authority of a stout
medium (Margaret Rutherford), a reincarnation of Nanny.

Miss Hammond's comic triumphs continued in other plays in partnership with John Clements who was soon to become her husband. He is an actor who has *par excellence* the style, the looks, the physique, the commanding presence of the classic matinée idol and he has survived as such into our own time during his reign at the Chichester Festival Theatre in Sussex. The revival of *Private Lives* in which he and Miss Hammond appeared in 1944 in London was in its graceful, langorous rhythms another nostalgic echo of life before the war. Perhaps the greatest achievement of the partnership came in 1949 in their revival of *The Beaux' Stratagem* at the Phoenix Theatre which ran for a record 500 performances, a landmark in rehabilitation of Restoration comedy.

But to go back to 1941 another great comedy hit of that year was an American import by George S. Kaufman and Moss Hart, *The Man Who Came to Dinner*, to which I duly made a matinée pilgrimage to see Robert Morley. As in my innocence I knew nothing of Alexander Woollcott and his wiles on which it was all so wickedly based a lot of the in-jokery passed straight over my head. Even so it provided a refreshing haven from the concerns of war and school the main situation of the aggressively adhesive guest was funny enough in itself to keep me hooked while relishing Mr Morley's performance. Later in 1947 he had another triumph in *Edward My Son*, a play he wrote, with Noël Langley for himself. The Morley aggression coccooned in charm struck home more readily here in that it was all channelled into a father's pride in a scapegrace son. I suppose I should have identified with the boy or at least – since he never appears – with the father but in fact it was with characters like the old schoolmaster browbeaten into submission with whom I found myself sympathising; not even a great talent like Mr Morley's could overcome my loathing of the bully. Yet it is his function as a matinée idol to personify lovable bullies as he did playing the Prince Regent in *The First Gentleman*, his other major role on the stage during the war.

Mr Morley was always larger than life, somewhat unsuited to the cunningly packaged product on offer from the naturalistic playwrights. Coward, Priestley, Ackland, Dodie Smith – I enjoyed them all but it was Van Druten who gave me most of all a pleasurable sense of eaves-dropping (as J. C. Trewin puts it) on what I should not be hearing. Nowadays his work has made itself air into which it has vanished. If he survives at all it is a name among the antecedents on the credit titles of the movie *Cabaret* on account of the play *I am a Camera* he made out of Isherwood's *Goodbye to Berlin*. (Apparently Dodie Smith lured him into doing it by saying firmly that there was no play there. A demon for work, he set about the task immediately and by the time they next met had blocked out the first act.) Before he went to Hollywood he lived in Hampstead where he was brought up and, after his first sensational success in the Twenties with *Young Woodley*, he made some delicate dramatic etchings of English family life full of strong maternal roles and worried ingénues in *After All*, *The*

Distaff Side and *There's Always Juliet.* It is his *Old Acquaintance,* tailored neatly to the requirements of a female matinée idol, that comes to mind from the *annus mirabilis* of 1941 with Edith Evans and Marian Spencer. I can still hear Miss Evans (as she then was) telling Muriel Pavlow, the Juvenile, in world-weary tones: 'Darling, if you start having affairs with every man who wants to, you know what you'll end up as, don't you? Are you in love with him?' As long ago as 1927, Maugham had made one of his stage heroines say that she was fed up with being 'a prostitute who doesn't deliver the goods'. This calling a spade a spade had not gone down at all well with the London audience even as uttered by the divine Fay Compton and the play, *The Constant Wife,* to Maugham's chagrin, rapidly came off. Since then purveyors of domestic comedy had practised a discreet evasiveness with the nomenclature of sex.

If the matinée idol of those days in the non-musical play had had to rely on contemporary dramatists he would have been in some difficulty. John Gielgud had at this time never appeared in anything by Rattigan or Van Druten and in Coward's *Blithe Spirit* only on tour among the troops in Burma during which he also revived *Hamlet.* It was in revivals of the classics that he challenged comparison with his illustrious predecessors. By the time I saw his Hamlet in 1944 – during the legendary Haymarket repertory season – it had created a style of Shakespearean acting for a whole generation and subsequent interpretations were so many efforts to break out of the Gielgud mould. It is a performance that inspired the critics of the period, Agate, Ivor Brown and others, to some of their most eloquent writings. I would only wish to add a couple of footnotes. The first is that as true idolators we went to see Gielgud play the role in the way that previous generations had gone to see Irving or Forbes Robertson and not as nowadays for someone's re-thinking of the text. There was a producer to be sure, George Rylands, but his role was mainly to keep a sharp eye on the verse and to see that its subtleties were preserved. Like all great Hamlets this one was a supreme expression of the period; it was Freudian, dream-obsessed, mother-ridden, intellectually speculative. All this came through in many magical ways but primarily – and this is my second point – through the fantastic care with which the lines were spoken. I want to suggest the same reason for Gielgud's becoming a matinée idol that Dilys Powell adduces in the case of Garbo, that it was essentially a question of voice. Gielgud is a complete actor if ever there was one – the smouldering presence, the elegance of movement and fineness of gesture, the impassioned depth of characterisation he can put into a glance or a toss of the head but what tops it all is that astonishing vocal instrument. His Hamlet was orchestrated rather than spoken. The words were boosted in such a way that we idolators felt raised to a higher power as we listened to them. The monosyllables, in 'O what a rogue and peasant slave am I', crashed out like chords working up to the climax of 'What's he to Hecuba or Hecuba to him that he should weeeeeep for her?' Sometimes quite ordinary lines, or lines that look ordinary on the printed page, were given an extraordinary incandescence. After Hamlet's first sight of the ghost – and Gielgud's encounter with the ghost was a terrifying experience – he says just before he exits with Horatio and Marcellus: 'Nay, Come, let's go together.' The way Gielgud delivered this commonplace line was quite stunning. It was spoken very softly and humbly but with a special emphasis on 'together' as he reached with outstretched arms for his friends to shepherd them through the exit. Somehow he managed to suggest the re-forming of a heart-whole community after the vision of betrayal that had just been vouchsafed.

Earlier I had gone to the Piccadilly to see Gielgud in *Macbeth*. I was at the same time 'doing' the play at school. I read Stephen Spender's article in *Penguin New Writing* on 'Time, History and Evil in *Macbeth*'. When Banquo said 'Alas poor country', we all thought not of Scotland but of France. Gielgud, marvellous at suggesting the permanent state of resentment in an insanely ambitious man, was partnered by Gwen Ffrangcon-Davies whose voice sounded like slow, steady drops of vitriol. 'You see,' said one's headmaster in a long disquisition on the play, 'we are all Macbeths.' I understand what he meant now, but at the time we all wanted to be Gielguds. To further this transformation we bought a set of records called (I think) 'The Voice of Poetry' on which Gielgud recited T. S. Eliot's 'Preludes' and 'The Journey of the Magi', Donne's sonnet on Death, 'Break, break, break' and 'When all the world was young, lad' and we played them again and again. But it wasn't any good. We remained inescapably ourselves.

It would be misleading to give the impression that Gielgud's impact upon his young wartime idolator was solely in the heroic and tragic vein since I rapidly became aware of what a great comedian he is during these years. *Love for Love*, in which he played Valentine, was a landmark in the re-discovery of Restoration comedy, and his John Worthing in the legendary revival of *The Importance of Being Earnest* including the ultimate Lady Bracknell of Edith Evans makes almost any other comedy performance seem feeble by comparison. Gielgud's reply to Miss Prism's inquiry about his brother: 'DEAD!!!' hissed emphatically with the sound of an express going in and out of a tunnel while gentle fingers unfolded a huge black-bordered handkerchief into which his face snivellingly disappeared, raised the roof. I only wish that his later attempt to revive the work of that very neglected playwright St John Hankin – Gielgud as Eustace in a pale-grey suit and a pink tie calmly blackmailing his family – had had the success it deserved and we might have seen him in more plays of this period with which he has such a delicious rapport.

Gielgud was not the only leading actor putting on Shakespeare and other classical revivals in London during the war. The Old Vic Company had for the moment been banished from the capital but Donald Wolfit came in from time to time with his Shakespearean troupe, providing me with my first opportunity for seeing *King Lear* in which he took the title role. Now Wolfit was never a matinée idol. He was a barn-stormer of an old-fashioned kind, a throwback to the nineteenth century. As a boy he used to brood over a mid-Victorian illustrated edition of Shakespeare with engravings of Macready and others and dream of himself in the roles. No one ever went specially to see Wolfit. One went for the play. This particular production was quite appallingly badly acted in many of the minor roles, yet the sound and fury of it has lingered strangely in my mind over the years when the subtleties of incomparably finer productions have evaporated. In 1942 the Old Vic returned briefly to the New Theatre with a production of *Othello* in which the Moor was played by a massive Czech actor, Frederick Valk, highly lauded by Kenneth Tynan in one of his earliest critiques. I couldn't take Valk in this part, or rather I couldn't, with my fixation on Gielgud, take the guttural noises that came out of his mouth, but the incomprehensibility of the Moor was compensated for by the lucid, super-sly, mischieviously malevolent Iago of Bernard Miles, giving surely his greatest ever performance.

It was, though, not in St Martin's Lane but a stone's throw away at the Arts Theatre in Great Newport Street, that one saw on a repertory basis a huge range of revivals from the English theatrical heritage during the Forties. In 1942 a tall thirty-year-old raven-haired actor of striking looks, Alec Clunes, founded the Arts Theatre Group of Actors at the Arts Theatre Club. Clunes had done his stint at the Old Vic and then had been in one or two pre-war commercial successes like *George and Margaret* and *I Killed the Count*, then he appeared at Malvern and Stratford Festivals and back again at the Vic; now he wanted to do the kind of plays which the big West End managements such as H. M. Tennent fought shy of. He was his own literary manager, director and leading man and he combined this versatility with a theatrical historian's knowledge of the English comic tradition. I soon joined the Club and my theatrical education proceeded apace. Over the years I saw *The Constant Couple*, *The Recruiting Officer*, *The Critic*, *The Magistrate*, *The Watched Pot*, *The Mollusc*, *Hobson's Choice*. Some of the productions left a lot to be desired by contemporary standards but the range of works performed was one of which no National Theatre would need to be ashamed.

But was Clunes a matinée idol? Once again the short answer must be 'no'. He certainly had the physique for the role and the grace upon the stage – he made a fine Hamlet in the Gielgud tradition – but in the last analysis there was something too aloof about him to capture the popular imagination; one might be interested or even awed by his work but one was never quite delirious. It was somehow appropriate that his favourite role should be Shaw's Don Juan in

Hell. He was a proud intellectual hero who relished the long verbal arias and recited them with fastidious aplomb. It you want a prefect illustration of the difference between a matinée idol and merely a very fine actor, consider this piece of history. Clunes discovered – or at any rate was the first person in the theatre to put on – *The Lady's Not For Burning* by Christopher Fry. That was at the Arts in 1948 with himself in the lead. Fry was then virtually unknown to the general public as a playwright. It was a modest *succès d'estime* creating no more stir than several other adventurous new plays performed at the Arts. A year later John Gielgud took up the play and appeared in it at the Globe Theatre in the part of Thomas Medwin. It was a sensation and Fry's reputation was made nationwide. Yet there are those, and I am among them, who consider the Clunes production to have been the finer of the two.

Certainly Clunes had a pretty keen nose for new plays. He gave Peter Ustinov his first break as a playwright with a production of his Chekhovian *The House of Regrets*; and through a new play competition he discovered John Whiting, whose *Saint's Day* saw the light at the Arts. On top of that you must put the first ever production of a Sartre play in London. This was *Huis Clos* in 1946 directed by a young man called Peter Brook. The atmosphere at the first night was one of intense expectancy, much more so that at the first night of *Waiting For Godot*, also first performed at the Arts ten years later (Donald Albery having failed to interest Robert Morley in it). After France had been liberated everyone wanted to know what had been going on intellectually in occupied Europe. A. J. Ayer wrote an article expounding Existentialism in Cyril Connolly's *Horizon* and by lunchtime on the day in which it appeared there were very few copies left on the bookstalls. The *Horizon* set were at the theatre, which they normally despised, to see this play. Sartre's inferno which presented a real, live Lesbian on the stage, screaming with rage as she watched a young girl she coveted rolling about on the floor with a lecherous journalist, seemed terribly daring in those days. What made it so memorable for me was the brilliance of the conception and of the performances: Beatrix Lehmann, Bette Ann Davis, Donald Pleasence as the lift-boy (he made a mark in it) and, the bankrupt journalist who discovers that 'hell is other people', an actor of marvellous concentration I had not seen before, Alec Guinness.

At this time when everyone was coming out of the forces to resume their civilian life again I was going in. In 1944 I left school to join the RAF. I was sent for the first six months on a 'short course' to Oxford in which a part of the week was spent playing at being an undergraduate and the rest as an air squadron cadet. The Oxford Playhouse was going through a rather good phase at this time under Peter Ashmore who liked to present plays of the great matinée idol period by Pinero and Maugham. I was thus able to collect *The*

Second Mrs Tanqueray, *The Gay Lord Quex* with Yvonne Mitchell, the company's leading lady, as Sophie Fullgarney, and *Sheppey* in which the role of Bessie Le Gros, the prostitute who becomes Death, was played magnificently by Jane Henderson, a kind of English Arletty and a great matinée idol among the undergraduates of those years. She had, I seem to remember, a witheringly sharp tongue off-stage. There was not much doing in the undergraduate theatre with people passing through so rapidly. The place was full of civil servants operating from several of the colleges, and the quadrangles of static water tanks, for putting out incendiary bomb fires which mercifully never came. The only fatal nocturnal casualty was H. W. Garrod's dog, Mud, whose sight was failing and who walked into a full tank and drowned himself. Some of the older dons in the English School like J. R. R. Tolkien and C. S. Lewis who had been in the First War continued to give lectures in a desultory way. I remember Lewis expounding Milton's doctrine of Limbo to a few of us: 'It s a place for those whose death was untimely. You'd better listen. It's probably where you'll all go.' In the event he was proved wrong. The war was practically over by the time we left the university and we went into the by then enormous bottleneck of aircrew training. This meant in my case, eventually, a London posting to Air Ministry, a 'billet' at home and ample opportunity to resume going to the theatre at a time when it was being given a wonderful new lease of life by the return from the forces of Laurence Olivier and Ralph Richardson.

'To my mind,' wrote W. A. Darlington in *Six Thousand and One Nights*, 'the post-war period began in our theatre while the war itself was still in full blast, on the day in June 1944 – which must have coincided almost exactly with D-Day – on which it was decided to bring the Old Vic Company back permanently to London and house it at the New Theatre under the joint direction of Laurence Olivier, Ralph Richardson and John Burell. That venture opened on the last day of August 1944, and for something like three years did work the best of which has not, I think, been surpassed upon our stage within living memory.' Olivier returned at full strength in a splendidly diverse succession of roles: Oedipus, Mr Puff, Hotspur, Shallow, the Button Moulder, Sir Peter Teazle, King Lear. Here was a force of destiny the polar opposite of Gielgud's. It was the difference between the feline grace of the tiger and the proud roar of the lion, formidable beasts both and riveting to watch.

One must guard against the danger of over-idealising this *belle époque*. If now, in middle age, one could see it all again, would it seem as good? The peculiar combination of circumstances meant that if a great matinée idol had not emerged we should have had to invent one. We had idolised a national leader whom we were about to discard. Now that the danger was past the theatre could take over. The sense of national identity that he had so eloquently aroused had found a poetic analogue in the plays of Shakespeare. *Henry V* was a film of which rightly we felt proud. Chests swelled as we listened to Olivier utter the mighty lines. Here and in his *Richard III*, later also filmed, did he emerge as the post-war matinée idol *par excellence*. In the two parts of *Henry IV* Olivier took the secondary role but such is the impact of an idol within an ensemble that he turned them into major ones. His Shallow joyfully summed up all the rheumy-eyed irresponsible unput-downable self-importance of old age. To find it unexpectedly in the same production as the Falstaff of Ralph Richardson was a combination the like of which we surely shall not see again. Richardson's work at this period included Peer Gynt, Cyrano and the title role in *An Inspector Calls*. But he was never an idol for all his marvellous pathos.

If Olivier inspired idolatry when observed even in minor roles, so to my mind, during those years, did Alec Guinness. I had seen him first, as I said, as Garcin, a part and a play whose philosophy was deeply inimical to his own; yet put across with that absolute conviction, down to a nervous tic around the chin, that is the hallmark of everything he does. Dilys Powell has singled out changelessness as the characteristic of the matinée idol and Ronald Hayman denies Guinness the title because of his passion for disguising himself. All very true, yet the fact remains that, for many people even now, Alec Guinness *is* a matinée idol. After each role the slate of his face is wiped clean and he starts again, but it is his protean power of renewal that is so spell-binding. Like Shiva he has an infinite number of ways of manifesting himself and through all of them we recognise the true god.

Such plasticity was not a characteristic of another matinée idol in these years, that of Michael Redgrave. He was not in the Old Vic at this time and his career on the stage was constantly being interrupted by spells of filming. He had one of his greatest successes in Robert Ardrey's play *Thunder Rock*. It concerns an American writer who retreats from the modern world into a lighthouse peopled by ghosts from the past from whom he learns an optimistic lesson for the present. Richard Findlater in his book on *Michael Redgrave – Actor* tell us that 'he won a new *moral* prestige from the role of Charleston, and the production was for him the turning-point in material success'. I only saw the film but the brooding introspective presence of Redgrave's Charleston, puffing away at his pipe, has stayed with me over the years, an icon in my private mythology; in the same way I seem to possess for ever his terrifying vision of split-minded paranoia as the ventriloquist who murders his doll in the film *Dead of Night*. His Macbeth appeared in 1947 and his Hamlet in 1950 with the Old Vic Company at the New; in the meantime he had appeared in unpopular plays by Henry Becque and Patrick Hamilton and in one smash-hit psycho-thriller *Uncle Harry*. As a champion of difficult roles in plays not at all obviously suited to English taste Redgrave's record for an idol is a highly honourable one. His career came in this aspect to a climax with his superlatively intelligent account of Hector in *Tiger at the Gates* (*La Guerre de Troie n'aura pas lieu*), one of the very few occasions when Giraudoux has really succeeded in the London theatre.

When I was eventually released from the RAF in 1948 and returned to

Oxford, the next war, the Korean one, was well on the way; the bottleneck had moved to the University, bulging with returned warriors and others as a grateful British Government doled out money with a liberal hand to anyone who wished to resume undergraduate work after his national service. At least half the undergraduates seemed theatre-obsessed. This was the period of Kenneth Tynan, Tony Richardson and a dozen others whose names are now part of the history of the post-war theatre. At the time the focus was on both Paris and on the renascence in England of verse drama, as a source of plays to serve a West End stage famished of new work. Two kinds of balloons were ascending rapidly, both being full of hot air: Anglican ones marked Eliot and Fry and Gallic ones, bearing such names as Anouilh, Sartre, Camus, Montherlant and Cocteau. He was creating in the cinema, for his own matinée idol Jean Marais, films like *L'Eternel Retour*, *Orphée* and *La Belle et la Bête*. For a while the intellectually novel and the commercially profitable combined forces.

But Cocteau in particular aroused some pretty extreme reactions. He was revered as a technician and we marvelled at the fluency of his surrealistic invention especially in *Orphée*, with its cryptic 'zone' and its wandering vendor of plate-glass. Gavin Lambert later wrote a persuasive article about him in *Sight and Sound*, And yet and yet? Was *L'Eternel Retour* so far removed from Ivor Novello? This unease rapidly spread to the whole cult of the matinée idol which seemed to us to epitomise all that was wrong with the pre-war theatre. We were highly ambivalent. Gertrude Lawrence was fêted when she appeared at the New Theatre, Oxford, on one of her last public appearances in Daphne du Maurier's *September Tide*. We sat at the feet of Gielgud, Guinness and Peter Ustinov when they came to talk of the Oxford University Dramatic Society. The ambivalence has shown in the work of Kenneth Tynan. In those days he was a great praiser of individual heroic acting and regularly went to Stratford to discover new idols like Paul Scofield, about whom he wrote rapturously in *Cherwell*. Tynan produced plays with idol-type roles at their centre: *Samson Agonistes*, *Winterset*, *Hamlet*. But what emerged from these productions was not the strength of the idol but the genius – or perverseness, however you viewed it – of the director's interpretation. *Hamlet* for instance was done from the 'bad' Quarto text in eighteenth-century costumes, with teutonic accents for the characters from Wittenburg University: John Schlesinger as Horatio and the present writer as Rosencraft (as he is called in this maddening version). When we brought the play to the Rudolph Steiner Hall in St John's Wood, London, this subtlety of diction was lost on half the audience who took it as quite normal.

The director as the overall architect of a production subordinating everything and everyone to his creative will had well and truly emerged as the prime force in the post-war theatre. In retrospect I can see the end of the cult of the matinée idol in Tony Richardson's undergraduate production of *Peer Gynt* at the Playhouse by comparing it with the Guthrie/Ralph Richardson one at the

Vic a few years earlier. Here in Oxford was that functional all-purpose set consisting mainly of boxes, ramps and hanging ropes; here were those uniform boiler-suit costumes for the entire company and those manic ensemble routines, the kind of director's field-night that is now such a familiar feature of work in dozens of arts complexes with their thrust stages all over the country.

For the moment in the London theatre itself in the early Fifties the idol enjoyed an Indian Summer. The wildfire acceptance of Anouilh's work, *Ring Round the Moon* with Scofield, *Colombe* with Yvonne Arnaud, kept him on his plinth. But the time bomb that was to destroy him had already started ticking on a long fuse. We all left Oxford. Tynan discovered Brecht. Richardson discovered George Devine (or should that be the other way round?) and the Royal Court. Before that I met him again at a party in Hampstead. 'I've found the best play to be written since the war,' he told me. 'It's called *Look Back in Anger*'. A new period was dawning with a new kind of idol, a new cult, a new audience. But this is the subject of the next article.

The Last Idols?

by *Ronald Hayman*

WE hardly ever use the phrase matinée idol today except when people are talking about the past. John Gielgud, a great matinée idol in the Thirties and Forties, still has a name which draws willing ticket-buyers to the box office, but they no longer crowd to see him unless they also want to see the play. Alan Bennett's *Forty Years On* could not survive for very long when another actor took over from Gielgud, but Gielgud's name alone was not enough to make Peter Shaffer's *The Battle of Shrivings* into a success. What is more, no actor nowadays can expect to be idolised in his sixties as he was when young, and the more he plays unattractive character parts, the more he alienates his worshippers. Only romantic actors can become idols: the performance is, among other things, a ritual at which the congregation's faith in romance is encouraged and reaffirmed. The aging actor who wants to keep as much as he can of his old relationship with his public must choose his parts very carefully. Each time he appears on stage he should look as much like his former self as possible – as young and as glamorous, as buoyant and as likeable. He should never play a character who is ugly, bald, shabby, untidy, immoral or even unsuccessful. Even if he is wearing heavy make-up and a toupee, it does not matter so long as the magic of the performance enables the fans to forget the facts. Few productions since the war have antagonised the audience at the Theatre Royal, Brighton, more than Charles Wood's *Veterans*, which, besides the swearing and the talk of flashing, had John Gielgud wearing a toupee that came off in Act II. Later on, worst of all, his character (an actor patently modelled on himself) was made to look ridiculous while sitting on a box so as to give the impression he was on horseback during a sequence that was being filmed.

The pleasure Gielgud himself takes in self-irony and self parody has been evident in a great many of his recent parts. In the film *The Charge of the Light Brigade* – which was scripted by Charles Wood and inspired him to write the play about the making of the film – and on the stage in *The Battle of Shrivings*, *Forty Years On* and *Home*, Gielgud has played characters at varying removes from himself with evident enjoyment. The performances have been warmly acclaimed by critics and by audiences, but letters he has received make it clear that many of his earlier admirers are bitterly disappointed with him. The actors they have most admired have come to represent their vanished youth. If only the actors could still look almost exactly the same, it would prove that time had almost completely stood still. To expose the wrinkles and the absurdities of an aging man is to force aging spectators to be realistic about their own age.

The matinée idols of the Twenties were nearly all stars who shone in light comedies and musicals but orbited away from the classics and tragedy. Gielgud, Olivier and Redgrave, who were all born during the first decade of the century, were serious actors who became idols in the Thirties and Forties, but who are the idols of today? Do we have any? The three outstanding British actors to be born in the period 1910–25 were Alec Guinness, Paul Scofield and Richard Burton. Burton was the only one of these who could have become a matinée idol. Guinness was too protean and Scofield not exuberant enough. The romantic idol's personality must seem talismanic. Crowds must wait for him at the stage-door in the hope of laying their fingers on his camel-hair coat. Guinness was evidently running away from his own personality, disappearing behind wigs and crepe hair and nose putty, pouring himself like liquid into costumes that made his gait unrecognisable. Even as Hamlet he sported a beard at first.

Scofield's talent for disguising himself is almost equally formidable. Perhaps the common factors between his characterisations are not quite so difficult to uncover, but he shies scrupulously away from any form of romanticism. Not for him the cult of beauty or elegance for its own sake. He insists on coming honestly to grips with all the gritty complexity of a character, all the unglamorous tensions and silly inconsistencies. If he simplifies or broadens, it is for the sake of comedy, not of heroics. A self-critical acid seeps corrosively into his voice, flattening its tones, pitching it constantly into a minor key. He is capable of panache, but even as he blows up a rhetorical balloon, the pin that will puncture it is visible in his hand.

Burton is a less fastidious actor, and his voice lends itself more readily to rhetorical inflation than ironic deflation. With his Wagnerian good looks, his vigour and his virility, he has all the natural endowments a matinée idol needs.

He could hardly have failed to become one had he embarked on a theatrical career twenty years earlier, whether he had devoted his time to the classics or to commercial comedy, whether he had launched his fine Welsh voice on a tide of blank verse or a stream of melodramatic sentiment. Like Guinness and Scofield, he is highly intelligent; unlike them he has nothing in his temperament to hold him back from a full-throated commitment to rhetoric and romanticism. He was nineteen when he made his West End debut and twenty-seven when he played his first Hamlet – with the Old Vic. But though he worked for two seasons with the company (1953–4 and 1956–7) and though by then he could have played virtually any part he wanted in the commercial theatre and attracted long queues to the box-office, he enjoyed his success as a film star so much that during the next ten years he played only four parts in the theatre, one of which was in the musical *Camelot* in the USA and another of which was in an Oxford University Dramatic Society production of *Doctor Faustus*.

The other actor of this generation who could have become a matinée idol was John Neville, who was born in the same year as Burton and grew up not only to bear a striking resemblance to the young Gielgud but to score successes in many of the same parts – Romeo, Richard II and Hamlet. He joined the Old Vic for the 1953–4 season, and in 1956 alternated Othello and Iago with Burton, as Gielgud had once alternated Romeo and Mercutio with Olivier. Unlike Burton, Neville stayed on with the Old Vic for the next two seasons, building up a very considerable following of fans who came to see him in every part he played, many of them returning – and more than once – to the same production.

In 1956–7 he played with the Old Vic on an American tour which started with a season in New York, rejoined the London company for 1957–8 and he took part in another American tour in 1958–9, voluntarily delaying his West End debut till 1959, when he was thirty-four, though he looked younger. But the instinct which had kept him away from Shaftesbury Avenue for so long was soon to take him away from it again. Of the parts he played in the West End, the only one to give him a relationship with the audience as satisfying as he had enjoyed at the Old Vic was in Bill Naughton's *Alfie*, one of the few contemporary plays that lets the leading actor talk straight out front. Neville needs to feel that through his relationship with the audience he is working towards a relationship with a coherent community. He had something of this feeling at the Old Vic, where there was more stability and a greater preponderance of local residents in the audience than in Shaftesbury Avenue. But he found more satisfaction still in Nottingham, where he worked at the new Playhouse from 1963–7, first as one of a triumvirate, later as sole Artistic Director, and he succeeded in building up a lively, reciprocal relationship with a large new audience, more or less representative of the city's population. He played leading parts himself, but even locally he was not worshipped as an idol. It seemed too much as if he were working with his audience, inviting its support, not its adoration.

Idols must seem idle but the word *work* is given more stress in the contemporary theatre than it ever used to have. During the run of Willis Hall's and Keith Waterhouse's *Billy Liar* (1961–2) Albert Finney silenced a man who was talking in the stalls by reminding him 'I'm working up here.' The old idols of the theatre had never seemed to be doing anything so down-to-earth as working.

It was first seriously suggested early in the century that actors ought to have an Association to look after their collective interests, but only eleven years had gone by since Henry Irving had been the first actor to receive a knighthood, and the profession was apprehensive of losing its new-found respectability. It was not until 1929 that Equity was formed and not until 1940 did it become affiliated to the TUC, when Godfrey Tearle, the former matinée idol who had been president for ten years, resigned in protest. Today, in a theatre that has become in many ways industrialised, Equity is a powerful factor, and work has become more of a negotiable commodity. At one time the actor's main professional relationships were with his management, his fellow-actors and his audience. Today, when he seldom has a continuous relationship with the same employer, the same fellow-actors or the same audience, his main professional relationship is usually with his agent or personal manager, while the only solidarity he can feel with the rest of the profession is through Equity. Even playwrights are liable to claim – as John Arden and Margaretta d'Arcy did during the row over the Royal Shakespeare Company's production of *The Island of the Mighty* – that they are workers before they are artists and that they can protect their own interests by withdrawing their 'labour'.

Is idolatry still possible in this climate? Of course there are still performers – and Danny La Rue is one of them – whose name outside a theatre guarantees a huge and continuing demand for tickets. Probably there are more musical stars and comedians in this category today than straight actors, but it is almost inconceivable that any play, however uninviting, could flop completely at the box office if Peter O'Toole, Albert Finney or Vanessa Redgrave were in it. But while their charisma is not totally dissimilar to that of the old matinée idols, their physical presence is not reassuring in the same way. Paradoxically, it is as if popularity no longer depends on being liked.

Consider Nicol Williamson's Hamlet. He played it without any concern for winning sympathy. Introverted, irasible and self-pitying, he crouched and snarled his way through the part, reacting so violently against the traditional way of representing nobility in the theatre that he often seemed more like a bricklayer with a grievance than a prince driven to revenge the death of his father. 'Rest, rest, perturbed spirit,' he snapped, impatient with the old King's ghost for being such a nuisance. Not that we know how a medieval Danish prince would have behaved, and some kind of reaction against the Victorian habit of refining rough-hewn Shakespearean heroes into decent English gentlemen was long overdue. David Warner's 1965 Hamlet at Stratford-upon-Avon was never bad-tempered, but hardly less anti-heroic or anti-aristocratic in conception. 'So far as I'm concerned,' he has since said, 'there's no such thing as a king. King is just a title given by other people. How the hell do I know what being princely is? You can be a prince and you can pick your nose, because the prince has the freedom to do what he wants.' But you cannot be a matinée idol and pick your nose.

While heroic theatre may tend to exaggerate the difference between the hero and the man in the street, the tendency prevalent in the English theatre since 1956 has been to focus on the common factors between them. There are two reasons for taking 1956 as the watershed of the reaction against hero-worship. It was the year in which the English Stage Company took over at the Royal Court and exploded John Osborne's *Look Back in Anger* in the face of a public which had no idea that this was what it had been waiting for. The two journalistic catchphrases 'angry young men' and 'kitchen sink' were both inaccurate as descriptions of the heroes and the settings that became theatrically fashionable, but clearly something had changed. It is always difficult to remember quite what one's preconceptions were twenty years ago, but the word *actor* has obviously acquired a somewhat different meaning. In the early Fifties, when people said 'He's rather like an actor,' it would convey an impression of someone rather good-looking, with regular features, an erect carriage, loud extrovert charm, clear enunciation and an educated accent. But then, before we realised what was happening, we were faced with a fresh generation of actors who were not at all like that – Nicol Williamson, Albert Finney, Peter O'Toole, Tom Courtenay, Robert Stephens, Alan Bates, Ian Holm, David Warner, Kenneth Haigh, Colin Blakely and Frank Finlay. Suddenly the fashionable faces had working-class features, and gritty provincial accents displaced standard English. Even Shakespearean noblemen began to speak with North Country accents, and Finney made Martin Luther sound as if he hailed from somewhere much nearer to the actor's native Salford than to Worms.

The expression on the face of the English theatre had changed totally, and the underlying reasons are to be found in social and economic history. Theatre is always a reflection of society, and working-class elements had been admitted only rarely and perfunctorily into a middle-class theatre, in much the same fashion as they had into other cultural and educational institutions of a nation dominated by its middle-class. But if the second major theatrical event of 1956 – the first visit to England of Brecht's Berliner Ensemble – was not the cause of the ensuing changes it was at least a powerful catalyst. There had already been reports from Kenneth Tynan and other visitors to East Berlin about this extraordinary company which was then at the apex of its development. They had marvelled at the quality of its teamwork, the willingness of leading actors to play inglorious supporting parts, the subordination of individual egos to collective effort, the immaculate precision of its productions, the subfusc brilliance of its costume and set designs, which showed up clearly in the un-coloured lighting. What no one who hadn't been to Berlin quite realised until now was that the actors did not look like actors at all in our sense of the word. They looked like workmen, not gentlemen, and when they played aristocrats in period costume, they looked more Hogarth than Reynolds.

We have grown accustomed to taking Brecht for granted. In many ways it is extremely odd that the theatrical trend-setter of the Sixties should be a didactic German Marxist who used the conventions of the Shakespearean theatre as a basis for theories which he worked out in the Twenties when he was reacting against the overblown rhetorical acting and the sentimental melodramatic writing which were current in the German theatre. His theories had scarcely any influence until he himself was given a chance to try them out when a puppet Communist government, with more interest in propaganda and pres-tige than in art, gave him a theatre in East Berlin and subsidised him to run his own company. Seventeen years after his death he is still one of the most powerful forces in European theatre, and in England his influence has worked violently against the tradition of the matinée idol.

Brecht was not interested in star personalities or in plays about personal relationships. Drama, he maintained, was valid only as contemporary social history, and useful only if it contributed to progressive social change. One of the main functions of his 'alienation effect' was to stop the audience from lapp-ing up the performance as if real life were being lived out on the stage. Instead of dreamily identifying with the actors, the spectator was intended to stay emotionally detached, critically aloof. Instead of admiring the good looks and commanding personalities of the leading men and the unattainable beauty, the generalised sexiness of the leading ladies, he should be concentrating on what the play reveals about the structure of the society it depicts and gauging its relevance to the society in which the performance is taking place. While senti-mental melodrama implicitly denies the existence of unhappiness except for villains who deserve it, comedy distracts from it and heroic tragedy makes it seem inevitable, Brechtian 'epic' theatre makes it seem unneccessary. The only evils are remediable social evils. For the audience that worships the matinée idol, nothing much can be wrong with the status quo. The glamorous star personifies its attractiveness. But the ideal Brechtian actor would be working towards making rebellious hackles rise on the back of every neck in the audi-ence. Not that we have any ideal Brechtian actors in England. The theatre has its own ironic dialectic and the virile young men who play angry young rebels – like the radical young playwrights who create them – are soon sedated by their own success. Whatever their misgivings about the Establishment and its theatre, the rewards it offers are so appetising that it would be a pity to subvert the whole structure.

Sometimes a star is also a good actor, but whereas good acting seems all the better for being seen at close quarters, stars do not seem to shine except when the observer is at a good distance. If our Victorian and Edwardian ancestors had gone in for theatre-in-the-round or thrust stages, the phrase matinée idol might never have been coined. Just as no man is a hero to his valet, no actor can be hero-worshipped unless he is on a different level from the audience, literally and metaphorically. Proscenium theatres isolate the actor by making him part of the picture created by the brightly illuminated scenery, while the audience sits in the outer darkness, invisible to itself. The footlights, which used to fortify the barrier between stage and auditorium, also flattered the actor's face with their upward beams of gold and pink light. The actor may not have been made quite into a two-dimensional image, but the face under the greasepaint belonged to the same perspective as the painted scenery.

Without aiming deliberately to undermine the tradition of the matinée idol, modern theatre design is tending not only to remove the barriers and diminish the distance between actor and audience but to make the actor into a more three-dimensional figure, as he had been in the Shakespearean theatre, declaiming at the prow of a projecting stage, surrounded on three sides by the audience, working without scenery and creating all the necessary pictures through words, groupings and movements. Today it is not only environmental theatre that aims to enclose the spectators in the same world as the actions of the play. While some dramatists (like Peter Handke in *Offending the Audience*) hit explicitly out at the traditional relationship between audience and actor, and some directors (like Peter Brook) mock it by having the actors clap at the curtain-call (as he did in the *Marat-Sade*) or try to alter it by dotting actors all over the auditorium (as he did in Seneca's *Oedipus* at the National Theatre) both stage designers and theatre architects are gravitating in the same direction. The abolition of footlights was only one step in a progression which is pulling actor and audience into a shared perspective. Meanwhile greasepaint had become old-fashioned, and even Max Factor pancake make-up is used less and less. Much as Gielgud's fans would have preferred to see him in make-up, he has made all his recent appearances on stage without it – in *Oedipus*, in *Forty Years On*, in *The Battle of Shrivings*, in *Home* and in *Veterans*. At the same time more and more of our lighting designers are belatedly adopting the technique of the Berliner Ensemble: only open white' light – no coloured gelatines in the spotlights and floodlights.

All this might seem to be leading towards the conclusion that the tradition of the matinée idol is dead, but how can it be when it is still the physical presence of the star rather than the work of the playwright, the director or the company that draws the audience to the theatre? Commercial managements recognise this when they budget their productions, allocating ten or even twelve and a half per cent of the gross takings to the star, if his name is magnetic enough. Often the decision about whether or not to go ahead with a project depends on whether or not a big enough star says yes. Without Ingrid Bergman, H. M. Tennants could not have afforded the 1971 West End production of a play like Shaw's *Captain Brassbound's Conversion*, which has a large cast and three sets. Without Deborah Kerr the dramatisation of Thomas Hardy's short story *The Day After the Fair* could not have succeeded as it did in 1972. Both productions had a fairly unfavourable press, but the public flocked to see them because of the physical presence of these two famous film stars. Lauren Bacall's presence in the musical *Applause* had a very similar effect. It is not something that can be explained in terms of beauty or sex appeal or good acting. Nor do words like 'charisma' really help to explain the phenomenon. One is reluctant to reach for a word like *love*, but there is little doubt of its relevance to the pleasure to be had from sitting in the dark, staring at an attractive woman with an attractive personality and a famous name, who is performing for us – talking to us while pretending to be talking to someone else, or singing and dancing without pretending that it isn't for us. The pleasure is quite different from that of meeting her. Nothing is expected of us. There is no question of whether she will like us. Whatever we contribute – applause, laughter, concentration, warmth – is contributed collectively, anonymously and almost involuntarily.

The phrase matinée idol may be discarded and the habit of hero-worship may be discouraged by changes in political ideology, social structure, theatre architecture and playwriting. But while our mythology changes, our need for myth does not.

The Loved Ones

by *Anthony Storr*

A N idol is – to quote the dictionary – 'any thing or person that is the object of excessive or supreme devotion. The use of the word 'excessive' is particularly apt, since it indicates that a person who becomes an idol does not in reality, deserve the whole of the devotion which is accorded him or her. Idols of screen or stage are human beings; and, although they may be exceptionally gifted in one way or another, they remain no more and no less than human beings. Yet, as the word idol implies, the devotees of idols treat them, not as human beings, but more like gods and goddesses.

This is an odd and interesting phenomenon. Although some worshippers of idols certainly realise that their devotion is 'excessive', their consciousness of excess does not necessarily dim their desire to idolise. Others, especially when young, seem genuinely to believe that their idols are as perfect as they would like them to be; and, even when clay feet of gigantic proportions appear from beneath skirt or trouser, will tolerate no doubt or criticism which might interfere with the luxury of total devotion to their personified ideal.

Idolatry is, of course, closely similar to being 'in love'; or rather, one should say that being 'in love' is one form of idolatry. For idolatry is not merely directed at some glamorous member of the opposite sex, but may be applied to 'stars' of any variety; to political leaders, to spiritual leaders, or even to such humble figures as psychiatrists, who are familiar with the phenomenon in the guise of what is known as 'transference . It seems, as this book has abundantly shown, that human beings have an insatiable desire to make certain persons into myths; to raise them, that is, above the mundane and the commonplace, and to transmute them into the magical and the miraculous. Although the political arena and, in the past, the Church, have been close competitors, it is the theatre and the cinema which, for most people, provide the setting where this transformation can most easily take place. As world-weary sophisticates, we may poke fun at the young and the simple who do not 'see through' their idols; but we should beware of ridicule. For the tendency to idolatry is universal; a part of the human condition which none of us entirely escape. If we look back through the mists of middle age to childhood and adolescence, we shall perceive that idolatry takes origin from our earliest years, and that the tendency to idolise never completely leaves us, however sophisticated and rational we may think we have become. Indeed, if it did so, we should thereby be emotionally impoverished; for the capacity to idolise, undesirable as it can be when misdirected, is so closely bound up with the whole life of the imagination that one cannot conceive that the former should disappear without some impairment of the latter. I suspect that the person who is so 'mature' that he refuses to have any heroes or heroines may be unable to fall in love, or to experience the ecstatic in any form, perhaps not even in the less obviously personal forms of painting, or literature, or music.

Idolatry begins in babyhood. The human infant is so constituted that, compared with the young of most other species, he is unusually helpless for an unusually protracted period. No wonder that the adults who care for him appear not only much more powerful than he, which they are in reality, but omnipotent or superhumanly powerful, which they certainly are not. The infant's first perceptions of other people are distorted; seen in a subjective mirror which exaggerates every perceived characteristic. The effect of this subjectivity is to prevent the infant seeing people as whole persons, since what he requires is not whole persons but only those facets of persons which meet his needs at the time. Thus, the mother who provides nourishment, or warmth, or comfort, is seen as 'good' when she is in process of purveying these necessities. There may also be a mother who leaves the infant cold, or hungry, or wet and uncomfortable. This is the 'bad' mother; and so intensely opposite is the infant's feeling towards her from that which he experiences towards the good mother that it does not at first occur to him that these opposing figures are one and the same person. In the all-or-nothing world of passion which he inhabits there is one 'star' who is the perfect, divine, provider; another who is nothing but poison and malice. The first inspires smiles and cooing; the second screaming and rage. The stage is set for 'good' and 'evil'; and, in the morality play which seems to be enacted within the infant psyche, good and evil are just as widely separated, and just as much personified as they are, for example, in Marlowe's *Doctor Faustus*, in which a good angel and a bad angel personify the conflicting impulses within that unhappy scholar's mind.

As the child develops, he gradually comes to realise that the same person may be bad at one time, good at another; but he never entirely loses his wish for a perfect, divine, all-forgiving and all-understanding mother. Nor, unfortunately, does he lose his capacity for making other people into devilish, subhuman creatures who are bent on nothing but evil. If men did not retain this capacity, the mediaeval persecution of witches would never have taken place; nor would the slaughter of six million Jews in concentration camps. Traces of the wish to make life into a simple matter of black and white, good and evil, can be found in mediaeval morality plays, and later in the early Westerns, before sophistication had, by the imputation of mixed motives, made both villains and heroes less exciting.

Every human being carries with him into adult life an inner world of the imagination derived from his earliest years which, for the most part, lies dormant or 'unconscious', but which is revived under the influence of stress or emotion. The denizens of this inner world are not real human beings, with all their complexities and contradictions, but mythological figures personifying typical human needs and experience, like the images of the 'good' and 'bad' mother referred to above. These figures are always 'larger than life', and felt to be of superhuman significance. When we are deeply moved or profoundly distressed we revert to making certain human beings into mythological figures according to our own subjective needs. Thus, in 1940, when England stood alone, menaced by the might of Nazi Germany, the British people needed a leader who could take on the role of hero and saviour. They found one in Winston Churchill, who, from that day forward, was idolized as no English leader had been since the death of the Duke of Wellington. Churchill was certainly a remarkable man but, like other human beings, he was a complex mixture. He was, for example, both aggressive and magnanimous; both brave and foolhardy; far-sighted, yet lacking in judgment. But in 1940, such considerations were beside the point. England was in danger; England needed a hero. As I wrote elsewhere: 'In that dark time, what England needed was not a shrewd, equable, balanced leader. She needed a prophet, a heroic visionary, a man who could dream dreams of victory when all seemed lost. Winston Churchill was such a man; and his inspirational quality owed its dynamic force to the romantic world of phantasy in which he had his true being.'

The small child, faced with a large world which he can neither understand not master, tends to make supermen out of those adults who promise security and protection. In similar fashion, adults, threatened by disaster, will turn to, depend upon, and idolize any leader who promises deliverance from the threat. This psychological phenomenon is as inevitable as it is irrational. It is based upon the mechanism we know as 'projection'; that is, the attribution to someone in the external world of characteristics which only in part belong to him, and which mostly take origin from the inner world of the subject. Idols represent our needs and wishes; so we make them into what we want, irrespective of the complexities of their real nature.

I wrote above that the human infant came into the world in an unusually helpless state. He remains 'immature' for far longer, relative to his total life-span, than most other creatures. By the time he has passed through infancy, childhood, and adolescence, to attain a theoretical maturity, nearly a third of his life has already gone. During all this time he will be learning from his elders; first from parents, later from teachers and others who pass on to him skills which they have and he has not. For many, many years the world appears to consist chiefly of 'grown-ups' who 'know better' or who at any rate know more. Some of these grown-ups will become idols, depending upon the child's particular bent or interests. Children tend to idolise those who appear to display qualities or aptitudes to which they aspire, but which they do not themselves yet possess. Small boys make heroes out of footballers; or, if they are academically inclined, may idolise teachers who represent an intellectual ideal. How often does a boy choose his adult career because he has hero-worshipped a teacher who inspired him? We do not know; but it is certainly not uncommon. Moreover, there is a strong tendency to endow the person who is admired for one desirable quality with all the others one can think of, whether or not they deserve such idealisation. The point I am emphasising is that we idolise people who represent what we would like to become or what we need, not what we are or feel ourselves to be. The idol portrays an unrealised, perhaps an unrealisable, potential. 'Ah, but a man's reach should exceed his grasp, Or what's an *idol* for?' is a justifiable paraphrase; for, just as heaven represents a perfection never attainable on earth, so the idol is seen as impossibly clever, or beautiful, or masterful, or seductive; possessing, that is, whatever qualities the idolater needs or aspires to at the time.

As children grow up, the objects of their idolatry change. We do not worship those whom we can outstrip or those with whom we are intimate, but only those who still seem far above us. The parent who once appeared omniscient is seen to be as fallible and as limited as other human beings; the teacher an expositor, not original genius; the sportsman as skilful rather than heroic. During most of the so-called latency period, the child idolises older members of the same sex as itself, since its principal task is the establishment of itself as male or female, on equal terms with its own age-group. Boys have to learn to be masculine, and girls to be feminine; and one way in which this is done is by emulation of older members of the same sex. Some of these are made into idols. We worship our own sex before we turn to worshipping the other; and this is a necessary part of growing-up. The adolescent or pre-adolescent 'crush' is one instance of idolisation, based upon the young person's desire to become ideally male or ideally female; and often the persons chosen as idol may be very different indeed from the images projected upon them. Teenagers, because of their lack of experience, have vivid, but wildly unrealistic, day dreams of what it is like to be sexually successful. Adolescent girls, for example, dream of being irresistible houris, leaving broken hearts behind them wherever they go. In her diary, the Russian princess Maria Bashkirtseff wrote down phantasies which are not only typical of adolescence, but which reveal quite clearly one basis upon which the idolisation of stage and screen stars rests: 'To see thousands of persons, when you appear upon the stage, await with beating heart the moment when you begin to sing; to know, as you look at them, that a single note of your voice will bring them all to your feet; to look at them with a haughty glance – that is my desire.'

A male equivalent is Ian Fleming's hero, James Bond. Bond is ruthless, brave, sophisticated, and irresistible to women, whom he mostly discards when they have enjoyed sex together. He is essentially a cardboard figure; an adolescent phantasy unlike any real human being, but a phantasy entertained by vast numbers of the male sex, as the sales of the books bear witness. Ian Fleming's stories appeal much more to men than to women, since it is male phantasy which Fleming is portraying. Indeed, women often dismiss the books as exemplifying the childish side of being male, which of course they do. But women who do this often fail to reveal their own addiction to 'romantic' novels, which are the feminine equivalent of the same phenomenon.

As boys and girls grow up they normally achieve a secure sense of their own masculinity and femininity, and therefore come to feel themselves to be on more or less equal terms with their peers. They thus have less need of idols of the same sex with whom to identify themselves. However, no-one outgrows this stage of development completely; and, in particular, homosexuals of either sex are unable to do so. Homosexuals are generally people who are both lacking in confidence in their own sexual identity, and also have fears of the opposite sex. They therefore continue to idolise members of their own sex to an even greater extent than we all do. The man who has never been sure of his own manliness tends to worship an exaggerated ideal of masculinity, as the 'butch' pinups of homosexual males attest. The woman who remains uncertain of her own femininity will tend to persist in her adoration of the feminine in other women. Heterosexual people can easily detect remnants of the same sort of feelings in themselves; for which of us ever attains complete sexual confidence, or does not have some lingering feeling that X or Y is more masculine or more feminine than we ourselves are? People who become matinée idols usually fulfil a double role, for they appeal, in varying degree, to both sexes. A male idol not only sets his female worshippers swooning with desire, but also personifies a masculine ideal for a number of male admirers, whether or not these latter are predominantly homo- or heterosexual. In the same way, a glamorous actress may be set up as a model of femininity for her female admirers to emulate, as well as making masculine hearts beat faster.

I wrote earlier that the people we idolise represent needs as well as aspirations. Since sexual fulfilment, at any rate in youth, is one of the most pressing

human needs, it is scarcely surprising that human beings tend to make idols
out of those who personify ideal hopes of sexual fulfilment. Moreover, it is
those human beings who most lack sexual fulfilment in reality who become
most deeply involved in idolisation. Adolescents, who have not yet established
a stable sexual life; adults who have tried and failed to do so; those who have
never had a chance of sexual fulfilment, and other categories of the frustrated
and disappointed constitute the majority of the most passionate 'fans'. But this
is not the whole story. There are no human beings who ever find that all their
desires are fulfilled in reality; and this, to my mind, is part of the human
condition. There is something intrinsically frustrating about human childhood,
perhaps connected with its longevity, which results in human beings taking
with them into adult life an inner world of the imagination which is never, and
can never, be totally satisfied by what the real world has to offer. Because of
this, human beings are restless creatures, always seeking, never wholly finding,
satisfaction. In my view, man's creativity, his culture, his religion, his science,
and his art are all dynamically motivated by the fact that he can never find
complete fulfilment by the direct satisfaction of his instincts. Man's special
adaptation to the world has its roots in the imagination; and imagination itself
has its origin in the frustrations and dissatisfactions of the real.

The images we build up within our minds of the opposite sex are derived
from many sources, not least of which is the necessarily frustrating experience
of early childhood. As we grow and develop, these images are modified by all
kinds of influences; by our experience of different people; by our reading; by
the images of man and woman presented to us by the media of communication.
But there remains within us all a mythological sub-stratum of mind which
creates figures of the imagination who do not necessarily closely correspond to
real persons. I wrote above of how it happens that the image of the hero-
saviour is activated when people are in situations of danger, and of how they
will attach this image to whoever will take on the role for them. A similar
process occurs whenever we fall in love. The person in love does not see his
beloved objectively, any more than the person who is frightened sees his hero-
saviour objectively. What the lover sees is a real person; but a person transformed, made magical by the image which he is projecting upon the beloved,
an image which takes origin from within himself, and which represents his
own idealised need.

It is a commonplace observation that being 'in love' does not last; although
being in love is the usual most precursor of learning to love another person as
he or she is in reality. However happy two people may be together, there will
always be some part of each which is unfulfilled by the other; some scope,
therefore, for the romantic imagination to exercise its myth-creating activity.
When people make idols of stars of stage and screen, they are finding
repositories for myth; and in this way the stars are fulfilling a valuable
function.

But what is it like to be a myth, and what effect does idolisation have upon those who experience it? It is, of course, enormously gratifying to be applauded and admired by hundreds of people. Even to be constantly recognized in the street by persons one has never met, an experience shared by all those who have appeared at all frequently on television, enhances self-esteem to some extent. Some of the greatest actors and actresses have been people who are basically unsure of themselves, and who find it difficult to believe that anyone really likes or loves them. For such people, public approval is particularly important; and every success is an injection of self-esteem. Indeed, this often seems to be the reason for taking up the profession of acting, which is notoriously overcrowded, underpaid, and extremely hard work, especially in the early part of an actor's career. Moreover, those who are unsure of themselves in ordinary social life can, on the stage, gain the approval they so much want without actually having to make a close relationship with anyone. If an actress is successful she can feel herself to be adored by her public, but she is protected from actual real involvement by the intervening footlights.

It is a sad fact, that, in our civilisation, many children grow up with very little feeling of ever having been accepted and valued by their parents as persons in their own right. One response to the depression thus engendered is to try desperately to play various roles, hoping that one or other assumed identity will gain the approval which has been felt to be lacking. I believe that many of the most accomplished actors and actresses, perhaps especially those who are expert mimics, are people who have never attained a sure sense of their own identity, and who become experts at playing roles because they have always done so since early childhood. Such people, paradoxically, often say that they feel more themselves when acting a role upon the stage than they do when trying to be their 'real' selves in social life. Indeed, they do not know what the real self is actually like, since they have been unable to make the kind of intimate relationship on equal terms with another person which would provide them with this information.

For such people (and I am not saying that *all* actors and actresses are like this) idolisation is both extremely rewarding and extremely dangerous. The public is notoriously fickle, and if the whole of a person's self-esteem depends upon the applause of the multitude, he or she is intensely vulnerable to transient failure or to a change in public sentiment. It is not difficult to think of actresses who were superficially happy so long as they were successful, but who clearly had no deep or stable relationship to fall back on when times were bad, and who thus turned to alcohol, to drugs, or to psychiatry, and often to all three at once.

Moreover, idolisation tends to confirm a person in role-playing rather than helping him or her to find a stable identity of their own, or to make any deep relationship with another. Actors and actresses are notorious for the instability of their personal lives, although there are notable exceptions. One reason for this is the strong tendency to identify with the roles that are thrust upon them. The very words 'prima donna' now imply far more than their literal meaning. Some actresses who have become idols retain humility and humanity when off the stage; but others become intolerably arrogant and inconsiderate. If one is constantly idolised it is extremely difficult not to go along with the public's conception, and to come to believe that one is a very remarkable and important person, superior to the general run of human beings, entitled to privilege and excused from normal obligations to others.

Psychiatrists are familiar with a very similar phenomenon in practice of their own profession. A psychiatrist is constantly treated by his patients not only as a 'father-figure' but as a kind of guru, possessed of all the wisdom of the ages. If he identifies with this role, he is finished as a human being, and will not last long as a good psychiatrist either. Really to help another person requires both patience and humility; and so does making a genuine, as opposed to a 'stage,' relationship.

Actors and actresses who become idols must be able to discard the roles which are thrust upon them by the public if they are not to be damaged by idolization. The best protection is, of course, a happy marriage; for no-one other than a loving marital partner is able to bring an inflated spouse down to earth with both firmness and kindness combined. The difficulty which so many film stars appear to have in making such a marriage is often, I think, because they are identifying with an ideal role, demanding another such as a partner, and are thus recurrently doomed to disappointment, not only with the partner, but with themselves also. Idols provide the public with much valuable stimulus to the imagination; but to be an idol is a fate which, though widely envied, is actually no light matter.

About the Contributors

The editor
ANTHONY CURTIS is the author of *The Pattern of Maugham*, a centenary portrait of the novelist. He is a well-known figure in the London literary and publishing world, and is the literary editor of the *Financial Times*, having previously been literary editor of the *Sunday Telegraph* for eight years and before that deputy editor of the *Times Literary Supplement*. He has recently had two plays performed on Afternoon Theatre on BBC radio 4.

The contributors
GEORGE AXELROD has written and directed many highly successful plays and films. His *The Seven Year Itch* gave a new expression to the language and he was the author of *Will Success Spoil Rock Hudson?* He worked closely with Marilyn Monroe and has latterly published a novel.

CECIL BEATON originally made his name as a photographer but he is today equally well-known as a diarist and writer, and as a designer of ballets, operas, plays and other theatrical productions among them the legendary *My Fair Lady*.

IVOR BROWN began his career as drama critic in Manchester in 1919, and continued it on *The Observer* till 1954. He was also editor of *The Observer* during the war. He is an authority on Shakespeare and on words about both of which he has published many books.

VIVIAN ELLIS has many successful West End musicals and hit songs to his credit. His long association with A. P. Herbert and Sir Charles Cochran spanned twenty-five years and culminated in *Bless the Bride*. He also writes light-hearted books about the stock market and other grave topics, and is Vice-President of the Performing Rights Society.

ROLAND GANT is the literary director of a London publishing house and author, with Nadia Legrand, his wife, of *Mésentente Cordiale*, a quizzical look at Anglo-French relations. Before the war he worked as a blues singer in Parisian and American nightspots and has written a novel with a jazz background, *World in a Jug*.

RONALD HAYMAN has written ten books about playrights, a book about techniques of acting and the biography of John Gielgud. He has worked as a theatre director and contributes regularly to the Arts page of *The Times*.

PHILIP HOPE-WALLACE has been delighting readers of *The Guardian* with his witty and perceptive reviews of theatre and opera since 1946, and has made many hundreds of broadcasts about aspects of the arts and records.

MICHEÁL MAC LIAMMÓIR, the distinguished Irish actor and co-founder of the Gate theatre, Dublin, with Hilton Edwards, starred in a film of *Othello* with Orson Welles about which he published a journal, *Put Money in My Purse*. He has written several plays and appeared in a one-man show about Wilde, *The Importance of Being Oscar*.

RAYMOND MANDER and JOE MITCHENSON are the authors of some fifteen books of theatre history of which the most recent was on the art of Pantomime, and they have been connected with hundreds more through providing illustrations and detailed information from their famous Theatre Collection started over thirty years ago.

DAPHNE DU MAURIER, the celebrated novelist, is also a biographer of Branwell Brontë, and her own distinguished father and family. She lives and works in Cornwall.

SHERIDAN MORLEY is the son of actor Robert Morley and the grandson of Gladys Cooper. He is the author of a biography of Noël Coward, edits an international theatre annual. He works on BBC television's Late-Night Line-up as an interviewer, and is now deputy features editor of *The Times*.

DILYS POWELL has been chief film critic of *The Sunday Times* since 1939, and is equally well-known as a broadcaster and as the author of several books on Greece.

GEORGE OPPENHEIMER is a New York drama critic for *Newsday* and covers the Broadway theatre for the *Financial Times*. He has also written for films and for the stage. His best known play is *Here Today* which starred Ruth Gordon.

DAVID ROBINSON, film critic of the *Financial Times* for many years, now has that post on *The Times*. He is the author of a history of the cinema and of film comedy and a regular contributor to *Sight and Sound*.

GEORGE ROWELL teaches at Bristol University's Drama Department. His books include a standard history of the Victorian Theatre and several editions of Victorian plays. He has also written plays and collaborated on musicals with Julian Slade.

ANTHONY STORR has held a variety of appointments as a psychiatrist in hospitals and clinics. He has published several books one of the most recent being the *Dynamics of Creation*. He is a regular contributor to *The Sunday Times*.

O. Z. WHITEHEAD is a well-known American stage and film actor who appeared in the famous first edition of *New Faces*. In 1960 he played Sir Andrew Aguecheek opposite Katharine Hepburn's Viola in *Twelfth Night* in Stratford, Connecticut. Since 1963 he has lived in Dublin, working both as an actor and for the Community of the Bahai Faith.

SANDY WILSON created that legendary show *The Boy Friend* and other nostalgic musicals including *The Buccaneer*, *Valmouth* (from Firbank's novel) and most recently *His Monkey Wife* (from John Collier's book). He has also appeared in a one-man show of his own songs, and writes both stories and reviews.

Index

Ace of Clubs, 95
Achard, Marcel, 68, 136
Ackland, Rodney, 104, 171
Actors' Equity (Britain), 183
Actors' Equity (USA), 118
Actors' Fidelity League (FIDO: USA), 118
Actors' Orphanage (Britain), 46, 47
Adams, Maude, 119
Adam's Rib, 160
Adelphi Theatre (London), 55, 61
The Admirable Crichton, 44
The Adventures of Robin Hood, 161
After All, 171
After October, 104
After the Girl, 51
Agate, James, 73, 77, 79, 83-4, 172
Ah, Wilderness!, 118
Aherne, Brian, 119
L'Aigle a Deux Têtes, 138
Ainley, Henry, 2, 33-4, 36
Albery, Sir Bronson, 21
Albery, Donald, 175
Alexander, Sir George, 2, 23, 25-30, 31, 33, 36, 37
Alfie, 182
Alhambra Theatre (London), 78
Alias Jimmy Valentine, 115
All About Eve, 160
All God's Chillun, 103
Allen, Kelcey, 112
Allgood, Sara, 103
Ambrose, Bert, 74
Ambrose Applejohn's Adventure, 102
American theatre (Broadway), 54, 56, 57, 64, 65, 73, 77-8, 80, 92, 107, 163, 166; the great days of Broadway, 108-21; Lilian Gish, 122-31; *see also* Hollywood
Amiel, Denys, 136
Amphitryon 38, 136
Anderson, Maxwell, 117
Anderson, Percy, 5
André Charlot's London Revue, 77, 120
Andrews, Robert, 86, 87
Anna Karenina, 148, 155
Anouilh, Jean, 135, 178, 179
Antonioni, 166
Applause, 163, 187
April, Elsie, 60
The Arab, 148
Arabian Love, 148

d'Arcy, Margaretta, 183
Arden, John, 183
Ardrey, Robert, 177
Arletty, 133-4, 135-6
Arliss, George, 115
The Armies of the Night, 166
Arms and the Man, 116
Arnaud, René, 135
Arnaud, Yvonne, 66, 105, 179
Arts Theatre (London), 174-5
As You Were, 66
Ashcroft, Peggy, 88
Ashmore, Peter, 175
Ashton, Frederick, 73
Astaire, Fred, 160
Atelier Music-Hall, 136
L'Atelier Theatre, Paris, 135
Athénée Theatre, Paris, 136-7
Atkins, Zoe, 110, 128
Atkinson, Brooks, 109
Attlee, Lord, 61
Aubrey Smith, Sir C., 97
Augier, Emile, 22
Aumont, Jean-Pierre, 137
Auprès de Ma Blonde, 68
Autumn Crocus, 105
Axelrod, George, 141, 163-7
Ayer, A. J., 175
Aynesworth, Allen, 53
Ayres, Lew, 112

Bacall, Lauren, 163, 187
Bagnold, Enid, 53
Bakst, Leon, 54
Bancroft family, 21, 22
Bancroft, George, 40
Bancroft, Sir Squire, 23, 30, 37
Bankhead, Tallulah, 120
Banky, Vilma, 151
Bara, Theda, 151
Bardelys the Magnificent, 148
Barnes, Winifred, 50
Barrault, Jean-Louis, 135, 136
The Barretts of Wimpole Street, 121
Barrie, Elaine, 113, 114
Barrie, J. M., 41, 44, 55, 102, 103, 107
Barrymore, Ethel, 107, 109, 110-11, 113, 114, 118, 119, 128
Barrymore, John, 107, 110, 111, 112-14, 119
Barrymore, Lionel, 107, 110, 111-12, 113, 114, 119

Barrymore, Maurice, 110
Barthelmass, Richard, 130
Bashkirtseff, Princess Maria, 192
Bates, Alan, 184
Bates, Blanche, 119
The Battle of Shrivings, 180, 181, 186
Battling Butler, 78
Baty, Gaston, 134, 135, 136
The Bauble Shop, 23
Bauer, Harry, 138
Bayes, Norah, 54
BBC, 66, 67, 70
Beaton, Cecil, 2, 3–19, 32, 49, 50–7, 63, 156
Beatty, Admiral, 52
Beaumont, Muriel, *see* Maurier, Muriel du
The Beaux' Stratagem, 171
Becque, Henry, 105, 177
Beerbohm, Max, 32, 82
Beerbohm Tree, Sir Herbert, 33, 37, 46
Behrman, S. N., 51, 117, 119
Belasco, David, 118–19, 149
Bell, Marie, 138
La Belle et la Bête, 178
The Bells, 88
Belmondo, Jean-Paul, 162, 165
Belmore, Bertha, 80
Ben Hur, 148
Benelli, Sem, 112
Bennett, Alan, 180
Bennett, Arnold, 34
Bergman, Ingmar, 166
Bergman, Ingrid, 156, 160, 187
Berliner Ensemble, 184–5, 186
Bernard, Tristan, 136
Bernhardt, Sarah, 51, 60, 109, 132
Bernstein, Henry, 138
Berry, Jules, 138
Berry, W. H., 4, 8
The Betrothal, 53
Betty, 50, 51
Big Ben, 61, 67
Big Business, 80
The Big Drum, 26
The Big Parade, 148, 149
A Bill of Divorcement, 121
Billy Liar, 183
Biography, 119
The Bird of Paradise, 115
The Birth of a Nation, 124
Bitter-Sweet, 54, 65, 93, 103
Black, George (Senior), 71
Blackbirds of 1934, 76
The Black Pirate, 144
Blackstone Theatre (Chicago), 123, 127

Blakely, Colin, 184
Blanchar, Pierre, 138
Blanchard, E. L., 62
Bless the Bride, 60, 61, 64, 67
Blithe Spirit, 170, 172
Blonde Bombshell, 158
Blonde Venus, 157
Blood and Sand, 146
The Blue Angel, 157
'The Blue Boy Blues', 51
The Blue Train, 12, 63
Bobby, Get Your Gun!, 80
Bogaërt, Lucienne, 134, 137
Bogart, Humphrey, 160, 161, 162
Boland, Mary, 115
Boote, Rosie, 63
Bost, Pierre, 137
Boucher, Victor, 134
Bouffes-Parisiens (Paris music-hall), 139
Boulevard theatre, *see* French theatre
Bouquet, Romain, 137
Bourdet, Edouard, 134, 138
Bow, Clara, 152, 158
Boyer, Charles, 138, 155, 156, 160, 161
Braithwaite, Dame Lilian, 37, 105
Brando, Marlon, 166
Brasseur, Pierre, 138
Bray, Yvonne de, 138
Brecht, Berthold, 179, 184–5
Brett, Maurice, 11
Bric-a-Brac, 52
Bridgman, Cunningham, 62
Brief Encounter, 95
Brisson, Carl, 69
Bristol Hippodrome, 64, 65
Britannicus, 137
Broadway, *see* American theatre
Broadway Jones, 118
Broken Blossoms, 130–1
Brook, Peter, 175, 186
Brooke, Rupert, 54
The Brothers Karamazov, 135
Brown, Clarence, 147
Brown, Ivor, 2, 31–8, 80, 81, 82, 92, 172
Brown, John Mason, 116, 120
Buchanan, Jack, 59, 68, 69–70, 71, 73, 76–9, 83, 84, 92
Buchner, Georg, 135
Buckmaster, Herbert, 51
Bullough, Sir George, 10
Bullough, Ian, 10, 11, 12, 15, 17
Bullough, Mrs Ian, *see* Elsie, Lily
Burell, John, 176
Burke, Billie, 116, 119
Burton, Richard, 181–2
By the Way, 71

Cabaret, 171
The Cabaret Girl, 81
Café de Paris, 96
Cagney, James, 118, 119, 133, 160
Caine, Hall, 35
Calderón de la Barca, 135
Camelot, 182
Camille, 146, 155, 156
Campbell, Mrs Patrick, 26, 44, 46, 53, 87
Camus, Albert, 178
Candida, 88, 123
Cantor, Eddie, 118
Capra, Frank, 158, 159
Captain Blood, 161
Captain Brassbound's Conversion, 187
Captain Jinks of the Horse Marines, 110
Capucines Theatre (Paris), 133
Careless Rapture, 82
Carina, 62
Cartel des Quatre, 135, 136
Carter, Desmond, 62
Carter, Mrs Leslie, 110, 119
Casablanca, 160
The Case of Rebellious Susan, 22, 23
Casino de Paris, 55, 139
Casino des Tourelles, Paris, 139
Cassidy, Claudia, 128
Casson, Lewis, 105
Caste, 22
Catherine, 64
Cavalcade, 93–4, 95, 104
Cecil, Hugh, 11
Chaplin, Charlie, 149, 151, 154
The Charge of the Light Brigade, 161, 181
Charig, Phil, 69, 78
Charlie Girl, 69
Charlot, André ('Guv'), 49, 59, 60, 61, 64, 73, 91
Charlot, Mrs André ('Flip'), 60
Chauve-Souris company, 60
Cheirel, 133
Chekhov, Anton, 105, 122
Chekhov, Michael, 123
Chevalier, Maurice, 133, 139, 160
Les Chevaliers de la Table Ronde, 138
Chichester Festival Theatre (Britain), 171
A Chinese Honeymoon, 4
'Chirp, Chirp', 78
The Christian, 35
Chu Chin Chow, 35, 102
Churchill, Winston, 7, 110, 111, 190
The Cigarette Maker's Romance, 36
Cinderella, 149
cinema, 141–67; *see also* Hollywood
The Cingalee, 4
The Circle, 110

Circonstances Atténuantes, 134
Clair, René, 158
Clair de Lune, 113
Claire, Ina, 51, 119
La Claque, 68
Clarence, 115
Clarkson, Joan, 62
Claudel, Paul, 135
Clements, Sir John, 37, 171
Close, Ivy, 51
Clowns in Clover, 72
Clunes, Alex, 174–5
Clyde, June, 78
Cocéa, Alice, 137
Cochran, Sir Charles B., 4, 49, 55, 59–62, 64, 65, 66–8, 69, 71, 73, 74, 78, 93, 95
Cochran, Lady, 59, 67
Cocteau, Jean, 55, 132, 134, 136, 138, 178
Cohan, George M., 54, 115, 117–18
Colbert, Claudette, 119, 160
Colette, 135
Coliseum Theatre, London, 76
Collier, Constance, 112
Collins, José, 54, 64–5
Collins, Lottie, 64
Colman, Ronald, 149, 156
Colombe, 179
Comédie des Champs-Elysées, Paris, 136
Comédie Française, Paris, 134, 137
Les Compagnons de la Chimère, 136
Compton, Fay, 87–8, 105, 172
Conan Doyle, Arthur, 33
Confessions of an Actor, 113
Connolly, Cyril, 96, 97, 175
The Conquering Power (Eugène Grandet), 146
The Constant Couple, 174
The Constant Wife, 172
Conversation Piece, 68, 93
Cooke, Alistair, 144
Cooper, Lady Diana, 8
Cooper, Gary, 156, 160
Cooper, Gladys, 47, 51–3
Copeau, Jacques, 132, 134–5
The Copperhead, 112
Coquette, 121, 150
The Corn is Green, 104, 111
Cornell, Katharine, 120, 121
Cortes, Ricardo, 148
The Cossacks, 148, 149
Costello, Dolores, 113–14
Cotton, Elsie (Lily Elsie's mother), 10
Cotton, William Thomas (Lily Elsie's father), 10

The Count of Luxembourg, 9, 17
Courtenay, Tom, 184
Courtneidge, Dame Cicely, 66, 70-2
Courtneidge, Robert, 59, 70
Courtney, Margaret, 114
Coward, Sir Noël, 7, 49, 54, 56, 65, 66, 75, 80, 83, 89-98, 115, 117, 119-20, 170, 171, 172
Cowardly Custard, 120
Cowl, Jane, 119
Coyne, Joseph, 4, 5, 6-7, 8, 9, 14
Craig, Gordon, 134
Crawford, Joan, 151, 152, 160
Crest, Ben, 102
Crest of the Wave, 83
Crisp, Donald, 130
Criterion Theatre, London, 21, 23, 27, 30, 35
The Critic, 174
Cromwell, John, 123, 124
Crouse, Russel, 119, 123, 125, 126
Cukor, George, 156
Curtis, Anthony, 163-7, 170-9
Curzon, Frank, 41
Cussell, Hon. Charles, 10
Cynara, 103

Daily Express, 90
Daily Mail, 79-80, 81
Daily Telegraph, 62
Daly's Theatre, London, 5, 8, 14, 32, 50, 52, 54, 63, 64, 65, 69, 90
La Dame aux Camèlias, 22
The Damned, 157
Dance, George, 4
'Dance, Dance, Dance Little Lady', 96
The Dancing Years, 80, 84
Dane, Clemence, 121
La Danseuse Eperdue, 133
Dare, Jack, 36
Dare, Phyllis, 36, 47, 52
Dare, Zena, 11, 16, 36, 52
Darlington, W. A., 176
Darrell, Maudi, 10
Darrieux, Danielle, 161
Dauphin, Claude, 137, 139
David Garrick, 22
Davies, Marion, 119, 152
Davis, Bette, 156, 160, 161
Davis, Bette Ann, 175
Day, Clarence, 123-4
Day, Mrs Clarence, 125, 126
Day, Edith, 54, 73
Day, Frances, 60, 73
The Day After the Fair, 187
Dead of Night, 177

Dean, James, 162
Dear Brutus, 44-5, 46, 103
Dear Octopus, 102
Decker, John, 114
Déclassée, 110, 128
La Défense, 133-4
Delubac, Jacqueline, 133
Delysia, Alice, 55, 60, 66-7
Le Demi-Monde see *The Fringe of Society*
Denville Home for retired actors and actresses, 47
Desert Inn, Las Vegas, 96
Desert Island Discs (BBC), 66
Design for Living, 117
Deslys, Gaby, 55-6, 139
Destry Rides Again, 157
Deval, Jacques, 137
The Devil is a Woman, 157
The Devil's Disciple, 32
Devine, George, 179
Diaghilev ballet, 55, 60
Dick Whittington, 88
Dickens, Charles, 166
Dickson, Dorothy, 81, 82-3, 84
Dietrich, Marlene, 1, 96, 156-8, 160
Diplomacy, 21
Dishonoured, 157
The Distaff Side, 172
Dobson, Austin, 32
Doctor Faustus, 182, 189
Doctor Kildare, 112
The Doctor's Dilemma, 116, 121
The Dollar Princess, 8-9, 51, 63
A Doll's House, 135, 137
Dolores, 119
Don Q, 144
Doro, Mario, 119
Dorziat, Gabrielle, 138
Douglas, Melvyn, 119
Down to Earth, 144
Dramatis Personae, 116
Dranem, 133, 139
Draper, Ruth, 79
'Dreams that Don't Grow Old', 63
Dressler, Marie, 118
Drew, Georgianna, 110
Drew, John (Junior), 110, 112
Drew, John (Senior), 110
Drew, Louisa (*née* Lane), 110, 111
Dreyfus, Max, 78
Drury Lane Theatre, London, 54, 65, 81, 82, 83-4, 94
Dulcy, 116
Dullin, Charles, 134, 135-6
Dullin, Jean, 134

Dumas, Alexandre (the younger), 22
Dunne, Irene, 160, 161
Durbin, Deanna, 160
Durgnat, Raymond, 155
Dürrenmatt, Friedrich, 117
Duse, Eleonora, 60

Eadie, Dennis, 53
The Eagle, 147
L'Echange, 135
L'Ecole des Veuves, 134
Eddy, Nelson, 159, 160
Edward VII, King, 109
Edward VIII, King, 68
Edward My Son, 171
Edwardes, George ('The Guv'nor'), 4-5,
    7, 8-9, 17, 58, 59
Edwards, Hilton, 87
'Egypt, My Cleopatra', 4
Eldorado (Paris music-hall), 139
Eldridge, Florence, 119
Eliot, T. S., 49, 102, 173, 178
Elizabeth, Princess (now Queen Eliza-
    beth II), 61
Elizabeth the Queen, 117
Elliott, Maxine, 109
Ellis, Mary, 81-2, 84
Ellis, Vivian, 49, 58-74, 79
Elsie, Lily ('Little Elsie'), 2, 3-19, 32,
    49, 50, 51, 52, 53, 56, 63, 73
Elsom, Isobel, 51
Embezzled Heaven, 111
Emerson, John, 143
'The Empire Depends on You', 71
Empire Theatre, New York, 122, 123,
    124, 125, 128
An Enemy of the People, 135
Les Enfants du Paradis, 136, 138
English Stage Company, 184
d'Erlanger, Baronness Emile, 63
L'Eternel Retour, 178
Evans, Dame Edith, 37, 105, 172, 173
An Evening with Mark Twain, 166
The Explorer, 32
The Eyes of Youth, 145

Fainsilber, Samson, 137
Fairbanks, Douglas (Senior), 119, 141,
    143-5, 148, 149, 150, 156, 161
Fall, Leo, 8
Fallen Angels, 92, 93
Family Reunion, 102
'Fancy Our Meeting', 78
Fanfare, 63
Farjeon, Herbert, 102
Farrar, Geraldine, 109

The Father, 104
Une Femme Libre, 137
Fenwick, Irene, 112
Fernandel, 133, 134
Feuillére, Edwige, 138
Field, Lila, 91
Fields, Lew, 120
Findlater, Richard, 177
Finlay, Frank, 184
Finney, Albert, 183, 184
The First Gentleman, 171
The First Mrs Fraser, 34
First World War, 35, 46, 51, 52, 54, 98,
    102, 118, 126, 135, 139, 142, 143, 145,
    151
Fitzgerald, Scott, 151
The Flag Lieutenant, 34
The Flame of New Orleans, 158
Die Fledermaus, 64
Fleming, Ian, 192
The Flying Trapeze, 78
Flynn, Errol, 156, 160-1
Les Folies Bergère, 67
Folies Bergère (Paris music-hall), 133,
    139
Folly To Be Wise, 71
Fonda, Henry, 160
Fontanne, Lynn *see* Lunt, Alfred and
    Lynn
For Me And My Gal, 161
For Services Rendered, 102-3
For the Love of Mike, 80
Forbes-Robertson, Sir Johnston, 2, 35,
    172
Ford, John, 123, 129
Fordred, Doris, 103
A Foreign Affair, 158
Forget-Me-Not, 37
Forster, E. M., 53
The Fortune Hunter, 112
Forty-Five Minutes from Broadway, 117-
    18
Forty Years On, 180, 181, 186
Foulsham and Banfield (photographers),
    7
The Four Horsemen of the Apocalypse,
    145-6, 147
Fowler, Gene, 113, 114
Francillon, 22
Ffrançon-Davies, Gwen, 105, 173
French theatre and cinema, 162, 178;
    influence on English 19th-century
    theatre, 20-1; Cochran's Parisian dis-
    coveries, 66-8; *monstres sacrés*, 107,
    132-9
Fresnay, Pierre, 68, 137

Fric-Frac, 134
The Fringe of Society, 22
Frohman, Charles, 107, 119
Front Page, 121
Fry, Christopher, 175, 178
Fun of the Fayre, 73
Furber, Douglas, 78

Gabin, Jean, 133
Gable, Clark, 119, 154, 156, 159–60, 161
Gaiety Girls, 62–6
Gaiety Theatre, London, 9, 21, 51, 52, 58, 62, 64, 65, 68
Galsworthy, John, 103, 112
Gant, Roland, 107, 132–9
Gantillon (French playwright), 136
Garbo, Greta, 1, 141, 148, 152, 154–6, 157–8, 159, 161, 172
Garfield, John, 119
Garland, Judy, 161–2
Garrick Theatre, New York, 134
Garrod, H. W., 176
The Gaucho, 144
The Gay Lord Quex, 176
George V, King, 9, 114
George and Margaret, 102, 174
George M., 118
George M. Cohan, Prince of the American Theatre, 118
Geraldo (band leader), 67
German, Edward, 37
Gershwin, George, 78
Gershwin, Ira, 78
Get-Rich-Quick Wallingford, 118
Gide, André, 134, 135
Gielgud, Sir John, 37, 45, 103, 104, 122, 169, 172–4, 175, 176, 178, 180–1, 182, 186
Gigi, 138, 139
Gilbert, John, 148–9, 154
Giraudoux, Jean, 136, 177
The Girl From Utah, 51
Gish, Dorothy, 125, 126–7, 128, 129
Gish, Lillian, 107, 122–31, 150, 156
Glamorous Night, 81–2
Glass, Bonnie, 145
The Glass Menagerie, 115
Globe Theatre, London, 175
Glyn, Elinor, 152
Glyn, Gertrude, 10, 13
God and My Father, 123–4
Godard, Jean-Luc, 162
Goddard, Paulette, 119
Golden Earrings, 157
The Goldfish, 91
Gone With the Wind, 159

A Good Little Devil, 149
Good Night, Sweet Prince, 113
Goodner, Carol, 103
Gordon, Ruth, 126
Gore Brown, R., 103
Gorki, Maxim, 135
Gower, Sir William, 37
Grable, Betty, 161
The Grand Giggle, 47
Grand Hotel, 155
Grant, Gary, 157, 160
Granville Barker, Harvey, 33, 34
The Grapes of Wrath, 123, 129
Graves, George, 4
Graves, Peter, 83
Gravey, Fernand, 137
The Great Adventure, 34
The Great Name, 91
The Great Waltz, 93
The Green Bay Tree, 104
The Green Hat, 121, 148
Greene, George, 122
Greene, Graham, 137
Grey, Joel, 118
Griffith, D. W., 91, 130, 143, 149, 150
Griffith, Richard, 109
Grumpy, 34
Grunsby, Sydney, 45
The Guardsman, 116
Guétary, Georges, 67
Guinness, Sir Alec, 37, 175, 177, 178, 181, 182
Guitry, Lucien, 60, 67, 132, 133
Guitry, Sasha, 60, 67, 132–3, 137; *see also* Printemps, Yvonne
Gunther, Mizzi, 5
Guthrie, Tyrone, 178

The Habit of Happiness, 143
Hackett, James K., 115
Haggard, Rider, 55
Hahn, Renaldo, 68
Haigh, Kenneth, 184
Hale, Binnie, 64, 66, 78, 79
Hallam, Basil, 55
Hall, Willis, 183
Hamilton, Patrick, 177
Hamlet, 88, 101, 110, 113, 114, 122–3, 172–3, 174, 177, 181, 182, 183–4
Hammond, Kay, 170–1
Handke, Peter, 186
'Hansel and Gretel', 9
Happiness, 115
Happy Birthday, 121
The Happy Hypocrite, 82
Hardy, Thomas, 187

Hare, Sir John, 37, 45, 46
Harlow, Jean, 158–9
The Harp of Life, 115
Harris, Jed, 122
Harris, Katherine Corri, 113
Harris, Sam, 118
Hart, Lorenz, 118
Hart, Moss, 118, 171
Harvey, Martin, 36
Harwood, H. M., 103
Hawtrey, Charles, 2, 34–5, 53, 91, 102
Hay Fever, 92, 97
Hayes, Helen, 115, 120–1
Hayman, Ronald, 169, 177, 180–8
Haymarket Theatre, London, 34, 172
He Comes Up Smiling, 143
Hearts of the World, 91
Hecht, Ben, 121
Helburn, Theresa, 116
Held, Anna, 119
Helen, 65
Hellman, Lillian, 120
Hello Rag-time!, 54
Hello Tango!, 54
Hell's Angels, 158
Henderson, Jane, 176
Henry IV, 177
Henry V, 83–4, 176
Henry VIII, 101
Henson, Leslie, 58
Hepburn, Audrey, 160
Hepburn, Katharine, 111, 119, 160
Herbert, Sir Alan P., 60, 61, 62
Herrand, Marcel, 135–6
'Hiccup Time in Burgundy', 77
Hicks, Sir Seymour, 10, 49
Hide and Seek, 71
Hillman, Eddie, 73
His House in Order, 26, 27, 28–30, 31
His Majesty the American, 143
His (Her) Majesty's Theatre, London, 35, 37, 60, 68
Hitchcock, Alfred, 158
Hobson's Choice, 174
Hodgson, Winifred Graham, 10
Hoey, Iris, 51
Hollingshead, John, 21
Hollywood, 51, 54, 60, 81, 97, 110, 112, 115, 119, 137, 138, 139, 171; idols of silent movies, 142–52; and of talkies, 153–62; Axelrod's views, 163–7; *see also* American theatre
Holm, Ian, 184
Home, 181, 186
Home Chat, 93, 95
Hoover, President Herbert, 110

Hope-Wallace, Philip, 49, 99–105
Hopkins, Arthur, 109, 111, 119
Hopkins, Miriam, 119
Horizon, 175
Horne, Lady Allen, 50
Hotel Imperial, 151
The House of Regrets, 175
The House that Jack Built, 71
Howard, Cecily (now Mrs Webster), 7, 8
Howard, Leslie, 113
Howard-Tripp, June, *see* June
Howes, Bobby, 63, 70, 79–80
The Hucksters, 159
Hughes, Howard, 158
Hugo, Victor, 22
Huis Clos, 175
Hulbert, Jack, 70–2
Hulbert, Pamela, 71
Hull, Miss E. M., 146
Hunter, Glenn, 115
Huston, John, 159

I am a Camera, 171
I Killed the Count, 174
Ibañez, Vicente Blasco, 145, 146
Ibsen, Henrick, 135
I'd Rather Be Right, 118
An Ideal Husband, 26
Idiots' Delight, 116
'If You Could Care For Me', 66
'If You Were the Only Girl in the World', 63
'I'll Follow My Secret Heart', 68
'I'm a One-Man Girl Who's Looking For a One-Girl Man', 79
Imperial Theatre, London, 32
The Importance of Being Earnest, 25, 26, 27, 173
In Again, Out Again, 144
In Which We Serve, 91, 94, 95
Ingram, Rex, 145, 148
Innes-Ker, Robert, Lord, 65
Innocent and Annabel, 88
An Inspector Calls, 177
Intermezzo, 136
The Intimate Strangers, 116
Inverclyde, Lord, 73
Irene, 73
The Iron Mask, 144
Irving, Sir Henry, 21, 22, 25, 30, 37, 45, 172, 183
Isaacs, Willie, 10
Isherwood, Christopher, 171
The Island of the Mighty, 183
It Happened One Night, 159

Jackson, Sir Barry, 37
James, Julia, 52, 63
Jamis, Elsie, 55
Jamois, Marguerite, 136
Jannings, Emile, 157
'A Japanese Sandman', 63
Jerome, Jerome K., 35
The Jest, 112, 113
Jesus Christ Superstar, 167
Jezebel, 160
Johnston, Justine, 119
Jones, Henry Arthur, 2, 22–5, 26, 30
Le Jouer, 20
Jours Heureux, 138
Jouvet, Louis, 134, 135, 136–7
Judgment at Nuremberg, 158
June (Howard-Tripp), 72–4, 78
Juno and the Paycock, 103
'Just a Little Love, a Little Kiss', 64
Justice, 112–13

Kalff, Marie, 135
Kaufman, George S., 115, 118, 171
Kean, 138
Keaton, Buster, 154, 156
Keene, Doris, 35
Kelly, Gene, 161
Kelly, Grace, 160
Kennedy, President John F., 167
Kern, Jerome, 78, 81
Kerr, Deborah, 187
Kick In, 112
Kiki, 119
The King and I, 65
King Lear, 174, 176
King's Rhapsody, 84
Kingsway Theatre, London, 34
A Kiss for Cinderella, 103
Kit-Kat Club, 72
The Knickerbocker Buckaroo, 143
Knobloch, 52
Kolb-Bernard, Capitaine René, 67
Ladies in Retirement, 104
The Lady Dandies see *Les Merveilleuses*
Lady in the Dark, 56
Lady Madcap, 4
Lady of the Camellias, 110
Lady Windermere's Fan, 26
The Lady's Not For Burning, 175
Lambert, Gavin, 178
Lane, Louisa, *see* Drew, Louisa
Lang, Fritz, 157
Langley, Noël, 171
La Rue, Danny, 183
The Last of Mrs Cheyney, 47, 53
The Last Waltz, 64

Lauder, Harry, 4
Laughton, Charles, 19
Laurell, Kay, 119
Laurette, 114
Lavallière, Eve, 132
Lawrence, Gertrude, 49, 56–7, 59, 77, 91, 92, 119, 120, 178
Lawton, Frank, 66
Laye, Dame Evelyn, 54, 65–6, 69
Lean, David, 95
Lederer, Francis, 119
Ledoux, Fernand, 138
Lee, Vanessa (Lady Graves), 68
Lehár, Franz, 4, 5–6, 7, 9, 19
Lehmann, Beatrix, 175
Lemon, Jack, 165
Lenormand, Henri-René, 135, 136
Levey, Ethel, 54–5
Lewis, C. S., 176
Lewis, Lloyd, 128
The Liars, 23, 24
Life Magazine, 124, 147
Life With Father, 119, 123–30 *passim*
The Likes of Her, 103
'Lilli Marlene', 157
Lillie, Beatrice, 56, 59, 75, 77, 92, 120
Lindley, Mrs Charles, 123
Lindsay, Howard, 119, 123, 125, 126
Little Annie Rooney, 149
A Little Bit of Fluff, 35
'Little Boy Blues', 72
The Little Cherub, 4
The Little Foxes, 120, 160
Little Lord Fauntleroy, 149
The Little Michas, 4
The Little Millionaire, 118
Lloyd, Harold, 153
Lloyd, Marie, 72
Lloyd George, David, 9, 52
'Lloydie', 86
Lombard, Carole, 160
London Assurance, 22
London Calling, 56, 91
London Hippodrome, 54, 68, 73, 76, 78, 79
London Pavilion, 73
Lonsdale, Freddie, 47, 51, 53
Look Back in Anger, 93, 179, 184
Loos, Anita, 143
Loraine, Robert, 104
Loraine, Violet (Lady Joicey), 63
Loty, 133
Love Affair, 161
'Love Can Find A Way', 64
Love for Love, 173
Love on the Dole, 103

The Love Parade, 139
Loy, Myrna, 158, 160
Loyalties, 103
Lubitsch, Ernst, 151
Lucile (dress designer), 5, 8, 9, 10
Lulu Belle, 119
Lunt, Alfred and Lynn (née Fontanne), 91, 107, 115–17, 135
Lunt, Hattie, 116
Lyceum Theatre, London, 21, 30, 37
Lynn, Olga, 14
Lyses, Charlotte, 132

'Ma Belle Marguerite', 67
'Ma Pomme', 139
MacArthur, Charles, 121
Macbeth, 21, 101, 112, 173, 177
MacCarthy, Desmond, 7
McClintock, Guthrie, 121
MacDonald, Jeanette, 139, 159, 160
McEvoy, Ambrose, 51
La Machine à Ecrire, 138
McKenna's Flirtation, 4
Mackenzie, Compton, 88
Mac Liammóir, Mana, 85
Mac Liammóir, Micheál, 49, 85–8, 91
McMaster, Anew, 85
Macqueen-Pope, Walter, 63
'Mad Dogs', 96
Madame Pompadour, 65
Maeterlinck, Maurice, 53
The Magistrate, 174
The Maid of the Mountains, 54, 64
Mailer, Norman, 166
Major Pendennis, 110
Mamoulian, Rouben, 157
'The Man I Love', 78
The Man Who Came to Dinner, 171
The Man Who Invented Women, 119
Manners, J. Hartley, 114, 115
Mansfield, Richard, 2
Manson, Héléna, 135
Marais, Jean, 138, 178
Marat-Sade, 186
March, Frederick, 119
Marchat, Jean, 136
Marco Millions, 117
Marconi, Lana, 133
Marie Walewska, 155, 161
Marina, Duchess of Kent, 61
Marion, Frances, 147
Marius, 137
The Mark of Zorro, 144
Marked Woman, 160
Marlowe, Julia, 119
Marshall, Herbert, 119

Marshalov, Boris, 124
Martin, Rita, 11
Mary, Queen (wife of George V), 9, 114
Mary Rose, 103, 105
Masks and Faces, 22
Massine, Léonide, 105
Mata Hari, 155
Mathews, Charles James, 22
Mathis, June, 145
Matthau, Walter, 165
Matthews, Jessie, 59, 72
Maude, Cyril, 34
Maugham, Somerset, 32, 51, 53, 102, 107, 110, 172, 175
Maurier, Daphne du, 29, 37, 39–48, 178
Maurier, Sir Gerald du, 2, 32, 39–48, 49, 53, 90, 91, 92, 95, 111, 112
Maurier, George du, 46
Maurier, Guy du, 46
Maurier, Muriel du (*née* Beaumont: Gerald's wife), 44, 46, 48
Max, Edouard de, 137
Maya, 136
Mayer, Arthur, 109
Mayerling, 161
Mayne, Clarice, 72
Meet Me in St Louis, 162
Memories, 111
Mencken, H. L., 126, 128
Mercenary Mary, 72, 73
The Merry Widow, 4, 5–8, 9, 10, 13, 14, 17, 32, 63, 64, 69, 148
Les Merveilleuses (or *The Lady Dandies*), 4, 5
The Message From Mars, 35
Meteor, 117
Metro-Goldwyn-Mayer, 112, 113, 114, 146
Michaelis, Robert, 14
Mid-Channel, 26
Miles, Bernard, 174
Millar, Gertie, 9, 52, 63
de Mille, Cecil B., 150
Miller, Arthur, 166
Miller, Gilbert, 41
Minnelli, Vincente, 161
The Misfits, 159
Miss Elizabeth's Prisoner, 32
Mistinguett, 133, 139
Mitchell, Yvonne, 176
A Modern Musketeer, 144
The Mollusc, 174
The Mollycoddle, 144
Molnar, Ferenc, 116
Molyneux, Edward, 53
Mon Gosse de Père, 133

Monroe, Marilyn, 162, 164, 167
Monsieur Beaucaire, 33, 147
Monsieur Verdoux, 51
Les Monstres Sacrés, 132
Montel, 133
Montgomery, Field-Marshal, 61
Montherlant, Henri de, 178
Moore, Colleen, 152
Moore, Mary, 26
Morehouse, Ward, 118
Moréna, Marguerite, 138
Moreno, Antonio, 148
Morgan, Frank, 119
Morgan, J. Pierpont, 109
Morlay, Gaby, 138
Morley, Robert, 171, 175
Morley, Sheridan, 49, 89–98
Morocco, 157
Morris, Chester, 119
Moss, Binkie, 15
Les Mouches, 136
Mounet-Sully, 132
Mr Cinders, 69, 79
Mr Fix-It, 143
Mr Whittington, 76, 77
Mrs Dane's Defence, 23, 24–5, 30
'Mrs Worthington', 96
The Mummy and the Hummingbird, 112
Murray, Mae, 145
Music in the Air, 81
Mutiny on the Bounty, 159
My Dear Children, 114
My Lady's Dress, 52

Naldi, Nita, 151
Nares, Owen, 12, 35–6, 47, 91, 103
Nathan, George Jean, 108
The National Anthem, 115
National Theatre, London, 97, 186
Naughton, Bill, 182
Nazimova, Alla, 109, 146, 151
Neagle, Dame Anna, 68, 69, 77
Neame, Elwin, 51
Negri, Pola, 141, 147, 151, 154
Nesbitt, Cathleen, 54
Neville, John, 182–3
The New Aladdin, 4–5
New Amsterdam Theatre, 64
New Moon, 65
New Theatre, London, 43, 174, 176, 177
New Theatre, Oxford, 60, 178
New York Times, 77–8
New Yorker, 124
Nichols, Beverley, 96, 97
Night Must Fall, 104
Ninotchka, 156

Normand, Mabel, 150
Nouvelle Revue française, 134
Novarro, Ramon, 148
Novello, Ivor, 12, 49, 80–4, 85–7, 89, 90–1, 92, 93, 95, 96, 97, 105, 178
Now Voyager, 160
Nymph Errant, 82

O, Mistress Mine, 68
Objective Burma, 161
Oedipus, 186
Offending the Audience, 186
Oh, Coward, 120
Oh Evening Star, 128
Oh, Oh, Delphine!, 51
Olcott, Chauncey, 115
Old Acquaintance, 172
Old Dutch, 120
The Old Jew, 45
The Old Maid, 160
Old Vic, London, 101, 174, 176, 177, 182
Olivier, Sir Laurence, 1, 37, 45, 97, 101, 169, 176–7, 181, 182
On Approval, 56
On With the Dance, 49, 66, 92, 93
The Only Way, 36, 101
O'Neill, Eugene, 81, 103, 105, 117, 118, 135, 136
Opera Comique Theatre, London, 62
Oppenheimer, George, 107, 108–12
Operette, 93
Orme, Denise, 63
Orphée, 178
Osborne, John, 93, 97–8, 184
Othello, 88, 174
O'Toole, Peter, 183, 184
Our Dancing Daughters, 152
Our Miss Gibbs, 63
Our Mrs MacChesney, 110
Our Nell, 64
Out There, 115
Outward Bound, 103, 115
'Over My Shoulder', 72
'Over There', 118
Oxford University Dramatic Society, 178, 182; *see also* New Theatre, Oxford
Ozeray, Madeleine, 137

Pacific 1860, 93, 95
Le Page, 133
Pagnol, Marcel, 137
Palace Theatre, London, 12, 52, 61, 64
Palace Theatre, New York, 109–10
Pamela, 12
Paolo and Francesca, 33

Paramount Studios, 146
Les Parents Terribles, 138
'Parisian Pierrot, Society's Hero', 56
La Parisienne, 105
Park, Bertram, 11
Parker, Dorothy, 109
'The Party's Over Now', 96
The Passing of the Third Floor Back, 35
Pat and Mike, 160
Pathé Studios, 150
Pavlova, 73
Pavlow, Muriel, 172
Peace in Our Time, 95
Pearce, Vera, 77, 79–80
The Pearl Girl, 51, 88
Pearson, Hesketh, 26
Peer Gynt, 178–9
Peg O' My Heart, 114–15
Perchance to Dream, 87
Perier, François, 138
Perrey, Mireille, 80
Peter Ibbetson, 112
Peter Pan, 102
Petrass, Sari, 50
The Petrified Forest, 160
Petticoat Lane (BBC), 67
Philip, Prince, 61
Philipe, Gérard, 138–9
Phillips, Stephen, 33
Phi-Phi, 137
Phoenix Theatre, London, 171
The Physician, 23
Piccadilly Incident, 69
Piccadilly Theatre, London, 173
Pickford, Mary, 130, 141, 144, 145, 149–50, 156
picture postcards (of matinée idols), 36, 51, 52, 53, 63
Pilcer, Harry, 55
The Pilgrim, 154
Pinero, Arthur, 2, 26, 28–9, 30, 31, 36, 53, 175
Pink Dominoes, 21, 23
Pirates of Penzance, 63
Pitoëff, Georges, 134, 135, 137
Pitoëff, Ludmilla, 135, 137
Pitoëff, Sacha, 135
Pitoëff, Svetlana, 135
la Plante, Laura, 153
Playfair, Sir Nigel, 37
Playhouse Theatre, London, 53
Playhouse Theatre, Nottingham, 182
Playhouse Theatre, Oxford, 175–6, 178–9
Plays Pleasant, 34
Pleasence, Donald, 175

Polaire, 139
Pollak, Robert, 128
Pollyanna, 149
A Poor Little Rich Girl, 149
Popescu, Elvire, 137
'Poppy', 66
Porter, Cole, 56, 82, 92, 96
Post-Mortem, 95
Powell, Dilys, 141, 153–62, 172, 177
Powell, William, 158
The Power and the Glory, 137
Present Indicative, 96
Present Laughter, 95
Price, Nancy, 76
Priestley, J. B., 171
Prince Edward Theatre, London, 63
Prince of Wales Theatre, London, 21, 58, 63, 70
Prince's Theatre, London, 105
The Princess and the Butterfly, 26, 27–8, 30
Printemps, Yvonne, 62, 67–8, 91, 132–3
The Prisoner of Zenda, 88, 148
Private Lives, 93, 119, 171
The Private Lives of Elizabeth and Essex, 161
Puget, Claude-André, 138
Puppets, 64
Pushkin, Alexandr, 147
Pygmalion, 26, 116

Quadrille, 96
Quai des Brumes, 138
The Quaker Girl, 51, 119
Queen Christina, 148, 149, 155, 156
Queen's Theatre, Manchester, 5

Racine, Jean, 137
Raimu, 133
Rambova, Natacha, 147
Randolph, Elsie, 76, 77, 78–9
Rasputin, 114
Rattigan, Terence, 172
Ray, Gabrielle, 9, 17, 52, 63
Reaching for the Moon, 143, 144
Rebecca, 29
Rebecca of Sunnybrook Farm, 149
The Recruiting Officer, 174
Red Dust, 159
Redemption (The Living Corpse), 112
Redgrave, Sir Michael, 37, 177, 181
Redgrave, Vanessa, 183
Regnard, Jean-François, 20
Reichenberg, Suzanne, 132
Réjane, 105, 132
Relative Values, 96

Renoir, Jean, 137
Renoir, Pierre, 137
Reunion in Vienna, 116, 117
La Revue des Nouveautés, 134
Richard II, 182
Richard III, 112, 176
Richard of Bordeaux, 104
Richardson, Sir Ralph, 37, 102–3, 176, 177, 178
Richardson, Tony, 178–9
Ring Round the Moon, 179
Rip, 133, 134
Robert's Wife, 36
Robertson, T. W., 22
Robeson, Paul, 103
Robin Hood, 144
Robinson, David, 141, 142–52, 154
Robson, Flora, 102–3
Rodgers, Richard, 118
Rogers, Ginger, 160
Roland, Gilbert, 148
Romains, Jules, 136
Romeo and Juliet, 113, 182
Roosevelt, Eleanor, 110
Roosevelt, President F. D., 118
The Roots of Heaven, 161
Rose Marie, 159
Rosy Rapture, 55
Rouleau, Raymond, 136
Round, Violet, 14
Roussin, André, 68, 137
Rowell, George, 2, 20–30
Royal Court Theatre, London, 33, 90, 179, 184
Royalty Theatre, London, 90
Rudolph Steiner Hall, London, 178
Running Riot, 58
Rutherford, Margaret, 170
Rylands, George, 172

Sagan, Leontine, 82
St Clair, Mal, 151
St James' Theatre, London, 23, 25, 26, 27, 28, 29, 30, 31, 33, 41, 47, 48, 53, 68
Saint Joan, 103, 121, 135
St John, Florence, 62
St John Ervine, 34, 36, 77
St John Hankin, 173
Saints' Day, 175
Salacrou, Armand, 137
Sally, 81, 82
Salou, Louis, 138
Samson Agonistes, 178
Sarment, Jean, 134, 136
Sartre, Jean-Paul, 136, 138, 175, 178
Sawyer, Joan, 145

Le Scandale de Deauville, 133
The Scarlet Empress, 157
Schlesinger, John, 178
Schlumberger, ——, 134
School for Scandal, 21, 22
Scofield, Paul, 178, 179, 181, 182
The Scoundrel, 91
The Sea Beast, 113–14
The Sea-Hawk, 161
The Second Mrs Tanqueray, 26–7, 30, 53, 104, 110, 176
Second World War, 14, 60, 65, 66–7, 69, 80, 84, 91, 95, 96, 97, 111, 135, 136, 137, 139, 145, 158, 170, 171–6, 190
See See, 5
Seiter, William A., 153
Sennett, Mack, 150
September Tide, 178
Serlin, Oscar, 123, 124, 125, 126, 128–9
Seven Keys to Baldpate, 118
Seven Sinners, 158
The Seven Year Itch, 163, 166
Severol, Geneviève, 133
Le Sexe Faible, 138
Shaffer, Peter, 180
Shakespeare, William, 25, 33, 101, 102, 104, 105, 112, 120, 135, 166, 172–3, 174, 176, 177, 178, 183–4
Shanghai Express, 157
'Shanty Town', 82
Shaw, George Bernard, 23, 26, 27, 32, 33–4, 37, 91, 100, 103, 113, 116, 117, 121, 135, 174, 187
She, 55
She Stoops to Conquer, 22
Shearer, Norma, 113, 156
The Sheik, 146, 147, 148
'The Sheik of Araby', 146
Sheppey, 176
Sherwood, Robert E., 116, 121
'She's My Lovely', 70, 80
The Shop Girl, 65
Si que je serais roi, 133
Siegfried, 136
Sigh No More, 95
Sills, Milton, 119
The Silver Box, 103
Simon, Michel, 134, 135, 137
Sinatra, Frank, 167
Sire le Mot (His Majesty the Word), 136
Sirocco, 90–1, 93
Skinner, Cornelia Otis, 119, 123
Smith, 110
Smith, Cecil, 128
Smith, Dodie, 102, 171
Smith, Maggie, 88

'Solomon', 82
'Someday I'll Find You', 95
Son of the Sheik, 147
Son of Zorro, 144
Sons O'Guns, 80
Sothern, E. H., 119
Spencer, Marian, 172
Spender, Stephen, 173
The Spoilers, 158
'Spread a Little Happiness', 79
Stage magazine, 116
Stage Fright, 158
Stagestruck, 115
Stand Up and Sing, 68–9, 77
Stanwyck, Barbara, 119
Starr, Frances, 119
Steinbeck, John, 123
Stephens, Robert, 184
Stern, G. B. ('Peter'), 93
Sternberg, Joseph von, 157
Stevens, Ashton, 128
Stevenson, Adlai, 110
Stewart, James, 160
Stickney, Dorothy, 119, 123, 125, 130
Still Dancing, 66
Stiller, ——, 151
Stoll Theatre, London, 67
Stone, Lewis, 115
Storr, Dr Anthony, 169, 188–95
Straight, Beatrice, 123
Strange, Michael (John Barrymore's wife), 113
Strange Interlude, 81, 117
Stratford Theatre (Royal Shakespeare Company), 174, 178, 183, 184
Strauss, Oscar, 9, 64
Streamline, 61
Strindberg, August, 104
Stroheim, Erich Von, 148
Studholme, Marie, 36
Suite in Three Keys, 95
Sunday Times, 90
Sunny, 78
Sunset Boulevard, 143, 151
Susan Lenox: Her Fall and Rise, 154
Swanson, Gloria, 141, 150–1, 154
'Sweet So And So', 78
Swinley, Ion, 101
Synge, John Millington, 135

The Taming of the Shrew, 8, 145, 150
Tarkington, Booth, 115, 116, 147
Tashman, Lilyan, 119
The Tavern, 118
Taylor, Charles A., 114
Taylor, Elizabeth, 162

Taylor, Laurette, 94, 114–15
Taylor, Nellie, 51
Teacher's Pet, 159
Tearle, Sir Godfrey, 37, 49, 183
Tellegen, Lou, 105
The Tempest, 88
Tempest, Dame Marie, 1, 5, 32, 34, 62–3, 97, 105
Tennent, H. M., 174, 187
Terris, Ellaline, 10
Terry, Dame Ellen, 37
Tessier, Valentine, 134, 137
Thackeray, William Makepeace, 20, 110
Thanks for the Buggy Ride, 153
That's a Good Girl, 77, 78
Theater Magazine, 108
Théâtre de la Michodière, Paris, 68, 134
Théâtre des Variétés, Paris, 137
Théâtre du Vieux Colombier, 134, 135, 136
Théâtre Français, 138
Theatre Guild (USA), 116, 117, 121
Théâtre Montparnasse, 136
Theatre Royal, London, 90
Theatre World, 77, 79, 80
Theatrical Garden Party, 47
'There Once Were Two Prince's Children Who Loved . . .', 6
There Shall Be No Night, 116, 117
There's Always Juliet, 172
'There's Always Tomorrow', 69
Thérèse Raquin, 76
The Thief of Bagdad, 144
This Happy Breed, 95
Thomas, Augustus, 112
Thomas, Olive, 119
Thorndike, Dame Sybil, 37, 88, 101, 103
The Three Musketeers, 144
The Three Sisters, 103, 105
The Thunderbolt, 26
Thunder Rock, 177
Tiger at the Gate, 177
Tilley, Vesta, 4
The Times, 70, 78, 80, 83, 84
titles (conferred on actors), 36–7
To a Lonely Boy, 111
Toddles, 34
'Together Again', 70
Tolkien, J. R. R., 176
Tolstoy, Leo, 112, 135
Tone, Franchot, 119
Toni, 78
Tonight's the Night, 88
Tovaritch, 137
Tracy, Spencer, 119, 158, 160
Travers, Ben, 68

Trelawney of the Wells, 36
Trewin, J. C., 171
Trilby, 46
Truman, President Harry S., 110
The Truth Game, 12
Tucker, Sophie, 72
Twain, Mark, 166
Twelfth Night, 102
Twenty Questions (BBC), 67
Two-Faced Woman, 156
Tyler, George C., 115
Tynan, Kenneth, 95, 174, 178, 179, 184

Ulman, Charles H., 143
Ulric, Lenore, 119
Uncharted Seas, 146
Uncle Harry, 177
Uncle Vanya, 122
Under Your Hat, 71
United Artists Corporation, 147, 149
Up in Mabel's Room, 35
Ustinov, Peter, 175, 178

Valaida, 76
Valentino, Alberto, 148
Valentino, Rudolph, 1, 141, 143, 145–8,
    151, 156, 159, 165
Valk, Frederick, 174
Vanbrugh, Dame Irene, 37
Van den Berg, Joseph, 64
Van Druten, ——, 171–2
Vane, Sutton, 103
Vanity Fair, 20
Vaudeville Theatre, London, 64, 73
'Veni, Vidi, Swing It, Baby', 80
Le Venin, 138
Ventura, Marie, 137
Veterans, 180–1, 186
Viceroy Sarah, 76
Victoria Regina, 121
Vidor, King, 148
Vilar, Jean, 136
'Vilia, oh Vilia, the Witch of the Woods',
    6, 8
The Visit, 117
Les Visiteurs du Soir, 136
Vitold, Michel, 136
'*V'la les croquants*', 139
Volpone, 135, 136
The Vortex, 89, 90, 92, 93, 104
Le Vrai Procès de Jeanne d'Arc, 135

Waiting for Godot, 175
Wake Up and Dream, 78
Walbrook, Anton, 66
Waller, Lewis, 1, 32–3, 36

Wallis, Bertram, 9
The Waltz Dream, 9
Waram, Percy, 124, 127, 128
Ward, Dame Genevieve, 37
The Ware Case, 40
Warfield, David, 119
Warner, David, 184
Warner, H. B., 114
Washington Square Players, 121
The Waste Land, 49
The Watched Pot, 174
Waterhouse, Keith, 183
The Way of the World, 105
Wayne, John, 158, 159, 161
We Barrymores, 112
Webb, Clifton, 73, 120
Webb, Lizbeth (Lady Campbell), 67
Webb, Mabel, 120
Wedding in Paris, 66
Weill, Kurt, 56
Welch, Elisabeth, 82, 84
Welchman, Harry, 105
Welles, Orson, 88, 160
Wellman, ——, 158
Whatever Happened to Baby Jane, 160
'When a Woman Smiles', 68
When the Clouds Roll By, 144
'Where Have All the Flowers Gone', 157
White, Claude Graham, 54
White, Pearl, 150
Whitehead, O. Z., 107, 122–31, 150
Whiting, John, 96, 175
'Whose Baby Are You?', 73
Wilcox, Herbert, 69
Wilde, Oscar, 26, 135
Wilder, Billy, 158, 164
Wilkinson, Elsie, 15
Will Shakespeare, 121
Williams, Emlyn, 104, 111, 166
Williams, Tennessee, 115, 166
Williamson, Harold, 8
Williamson, Nicol, 183, 184
Wilson, Sandy, 49, 75–84
Wimperis, Arthur, 66
Windhurst, Bretaigne, 124, 125, 126, 127
Winn, Anona, 67
Winn, Godfrey, 96, 97
Winterset, 178
The Wizard of Oz, 161
Wodehouse, P. G., 33–4, 74
Wolfit, Sir Donald, 174
A Woman of Affairs, 148
Woman of the World, 151
Woman of the Year, 160
Women Have Been Kind, 109
Wood, Charles, 180, 181

The Wooing of Eve, 115
Woolf, Julia, 62
Woollcott, Alexander, 111, 171
Wyndham, Sir Charles, 2, 21–5, 26, 27, 28, 30
Wyndham's Theatre, London, 21, 23, 37, 41–2, 43, 48
Wynn, Ed, 118

Yankee Doodle Dandy, 117, 118
The Yankee Prince, 118
Yes, Madam?, 79
Yevonde, 11

Yonnel, Jean, 137
You Never Can Tell, 33–4, 91
Young, Clara Kimball, 145
The Young Idea, 91
Young Woodley, 171

Ziegfield, Florenz, Ziegfield Follies, 61, 64, 109, 119
'Zigeuner', 95
Zola, Emile, 76
Zolotov, Maurice, 115, 116
Zukor, Adolph, 149